COLONIAL ODYSSEYS

COLONIAL ODYSSEYS

*Empire and Epic
in the Modernist Novel*

DAVID ADAMS

Cornell University Press

ITHACA AND LONDON

Publication of this book was made possible, in part, by a grant from
The Ohio State University.

First published 2003 by Cornell University Press
First printing, Cornell Paperbacks, 2003

Printed in the United States of America

Library of Congress Cataloging-in-Publication Data

Adams, David.
  Colonial odysseys : empire and epic in the modernist novel / David
Adams.
      p. cm.
Includes bibliographical references (p.   ) and index.
      ISBN 0-8014-4161-7 (alk. paper) — ISBN 0-8014-8886-9 (pbk. : alk.
paper)
    1. English fiction—20th century—History and criticism.   2.
Imperialism in literature.   2. Forster, E. M. (Edward Morgan),
1879–1970. Passage to India.   4. Conrad, Joseph, 1857–1924. Heart of
darkness.   5. Epic literature, English—History and criticism   6.
Woolf, Virginia, 1882–1941. Voyage out.   7. Modernism
(Literature)—Great Britain.   8. Colonies in literature.   I. Title.
  PR888.I54A33 2003
  823'9109358—dc21   2003012660

Cloth printing   10 9 8 7 6 5 4 3 2 1

Paperback printing   10 9 8 7 6 5 4 3 2 1

FOR
JANET WALLACE ADAMS
and
IN MEMORY OF
JOHN EDWARD ADAMS
(1923–1993)

Contents

Acknowledgments

While writing this book I have benefited from the varied audience and broad expertise provided by a large, multicampus English department. Many Ohio State colleagues have read sections of the manuscript, including Kelly Anspaugh, Murray Beja, Jared Gardner, Leigh Gilmore, Sebastian Knowles, Valerie Lee, Linda Mizejewski, and Bill Sullivan; over time, Mark Conroy, John Hellmann, and Jim Phelan have each read most of the manuscript. They often struggled through first drafts; their requests for clarification and suggestions for amplification have helped shape the text throughout.

In Lima, Deb Burks and Beth Sutton-Ramspeck have provided welcome support, as have the revolving faculty services staff. Librarians in Columbus and Lima and at the New York Public Library have repeatedly demonstrated a gracious resourcefulness. Colleagues at Jagiellonian University in Cracow, where I spent a Fulbright year in 1997–98, offered spirited responses to my fledgling interpretations of "Karain," *Nostromo*, and *Ulysses*.

Bernie Kendler not only suggested useful refinements to the title, but his gently ironic email—a medium not generally friendly to dry humor—has lightened the review process. He also recruited two superb readers for the manuscript who have shed their anonymity: Paul Armstrong and Stathis Gourgouris. Their enthusiasm did not prevent them from offering astute suggestions to revise and extend the argument. Teresa Jesionowski and Herman Rapaport have edited the manuscript with tact and insight.

The writing of this book has coincided with my time at Ohio State, but many of the ideas germinated in the preceding years while I was teaching at Reed College, Wake Forest University, Cornell University, and the City

University of New York. The colleagues and friends who have provided support and inspiration are too plentiful to enumerate in full. They include Lloyd Davis and Julia Duffy, Burt Kimmelman, Paula Giuliano, Mitchell Levenberg, Gerhard Joseph, Peter Behrenberg, Lea Ritter-Santini, Bob Wallace, Bruce Krajewski, Stacey Vallas and Reinier Warschauer, Jennifer Dellner, Géraldine Deries, Sarah Boxer and Harry Cooper. Kingsley Weatherhead provided valuable early lessons on writing about the modernists.

Teaching the texts analyzed in this book has had an animating effect; shifting periodically to classroom discourse has helped broaden my perspective. For their interest and insights, I am indebted to my students in Lima, Bellefontaine, and Columbus, and to their predecessors in Portland, Winston-Salem, Ithaca (especially the hospitable Telluriders), and New York.

Allen Mandelbaum introduced me to the work of Hans Blumenberg as well as of countless others. With energetic benevolence, Allen guided me through a doctoral dissertation and a decade of intellectual development that culminated in the conception for this book. His influence on my work, in other words, extends well beyond what is suggested by the frequent references to him in the pages that follow. His phone calls continue to provide glimpses of previously unimagined intellectual terrain—and thus weeks' worth of material for musing and reading.

Janet Adams and Marta Sajewicz have both provided indispensable assistance with child care when major deadlines loomed, and both presented me with unsolicited public-library research that found its way into the study (Jan on Conradian sea lore and Marta on the history of the word *sekularyzacja*). West-coast relatives (Steve, Karen, Kyle, Elise, Nancy, Blair, Jordan, Taylor, Casey) have provided moral support, and John's silence has left its mark throughout this work.

Monika Major has responded to Writer's Neurosis with a helpful blend of sympathy, irony, indifference, and patience—her involvement has been vital. Emil, born mid-manuscript, has brought a chaotic sanity to the revision of "tata book."

"To be myself," notes Bernard in Virginia Woolf's *The Waves*, "I need the illumination of other people's eyes, and therefore cannot be entirely sure what is my self." But if this book is in a sense the product of fifty pairs of eyes, its remaining blind spots and eccentricities are mine alone.

* * *

Generous research support from The Ohio State University at Lima has made it possible to complete the manuscript in a timely fashion. I first presented some of my discussions and adaptations of Hans Blumenberg's philosophy in lectures sponsored by New York University, the Werner Reimers Stiftung in Bad Homburg, and the University of Tulsa. "Remorse and Power," on Conrad's "Karain," appeared in *Modern Fiction Studies*, published by Johns Hopkins University Press, and a Polish translation of an early version of my Cyclops interpretation appeared in *Wokół Jamesa Joyce'a*, published by Universitas Press.

D.A.

Columbus, Ohio

COLONIAL ODYSSEYS

Introduction

For the boy playing with his globe and stamps,
the world is equal to his appetite—
how grand the world in the blaze of lamps,
how petty in tomorrow's small dry light!
                    —ROBERT LOWELL, "The Voyage," after Charles Baudelaire,
                                                                    "Le Voyage"

Modernist British fiction includes a group of colonial odysseys, stories in which characters journey from the familiar world of the West to an alien colonial world. Joseph Conrad's *Heart of Darkness* is the most famous work of this sort, and much of his other fiction fits the pattern as well. The title of Virginia Woolf's *The Voyage Out* announces her use of the odyssey theme, and her subsequent work elaborates on the concerns central to this first novel. E. M. Forster's best novel, *A Passage to India*, belongs to this subgenre, as do Evelyn Waugh's *A Handful of Dust*, *Black Mischief*, and *Scoop*. These works initially seem to defy many of our received notions about modernist aesthetics and literary history, for they take the novel on an outward voyage rather than an inward turn. Collectively they serve as a reminder of the extent of the British empire as characters travel to South America, Africa, and the East (though some of Conrad's work attributes its imperial imaginings to European powers other than Great Britain). They promise fictional explorations of the relationship between Britain and her colonies at a time when the British empire was at—and just past—its height, for the emergence of such stories as part of high culture follows closely upon Britain's final period of significant imperial expansion. Edward Said argues that the British novel's profound engagement with non-Western cultures has been "usually suppressed for the most part"; his method of reading contrapuntally demonstrates that

"Western cultural forms can be taken out of the autonomous enclosures in which they have been protected, and placed instead in the dynamic global environment created by imperialism" (*Culture and Imperialism* 51). What is striking about these colonial-odyssey novels, however, is that at first glance they appear not to suppress or repress the imperial context; they seem rather to anticipate the contrapuntal contextualization of post-colonial criticism by incorporating some of the most remote outposts of empire into their representations of British life. Their protagonists negotiate the passage, literally and figuratively, from England to England's Others.

This initial characterization of modernist colonial odysseys is only half of the story, however, and thus is misleading by itself. Such narratives are often distracted from the geopolitical phenomena they seem to represent, because they take their cue from an ancient tradition of exploring the depths of the self by imagining it on exotic or fantastic travels. While none of the novels under consideration here invokes Homer as systematically as Joyce's *Ulysses* does nor as intensively as some modernist poems do, each nevertheless establishes a relation to *The Odyssey* and the epic tradition on multiple levels, ranging from local allusions and echoes to plot structure and other elements of genre. The relation thus established is usually ironic, always distant. For example, none of these novels depicts a triumphal homecoming (which is also the first clue that they do not participate in the adventure-tradition celebration of empire); the emphasis, as Woolf's title indicates, is on the voyage *out*. The characters who succeed in returning to their earthly point of departure are few in number and peripheral, and they land in a London as unredeemed and unredeemable as any of the colonies they visit. Whether it is the dark, grimy fog of Conrad's London or the social depravity of Waugh's, this geographical home is simply not the *telos* of these novels. Though there is nostalgia to be found in the stories, as I hope to demonstrate, they do not manifest the sort of *nostos* that animates *The Odyssey*. Their ambivalence about "home" nevertheless takes the odyssey myth as a constant point of reference, and thus the authors' reception of the epic tradition threatens to expose the apparent engagement with foreign cultures as yet another self-reference, another rumination on Western forms, fears, and fantasies.

One of the aims of this book is to explore the relation between the two contexts named in the phrase *colonial odyssey*. The administration of empire and the reception of the odyssey myth are not of course mutually exclusive concerns for these writers, but in modernist literature the two no longer reinforce each other unambiguously. Elleke Boehmer's claim that the genre of travel tales provides "one of the defining stories of imperial expansion" (201) applies most convincingly to the popular adventure tradition from which the modernists are departing. The modernist travel tales, distantly echoing *The Odyssey*, explore also the unease produced by imperial rule. They serve as defining stories of anxiety about imperial disintegration, transforming the odyssey into an increasingly morbid reflection on national identity and the meaning of "home." Thus, Britain's experience governing one-fourth of the world's land and population confirms the continued efficacy of the odyssey myth only by dramatically distorting it, lopping off the all-important homecoming, for example, or reducing the story, as in *Heart of Darkness*, to its *katabasis* (descent-to-Hades) episode. Conversely, viewing Britain's imperial activity through the lens of the odyssey myth imposes a certain blindness in relation to the colonized Other even as it ensures access to the West's robust tradition of self-critique, so that, for example, Forster can get India wrong, or Conrad the Congo, even as they expose the excesses of the imperial subject. To follow this tortured interaction between empire and epic, one must look beneath the surface, among the underlying needs and anxieties to which the stories are responding.

Turning to this stratum of needs and anxieties makes clear that British responses to imperialism and modernist responses to ancient Greece provide alternative paths into the tangle of phenomena known as modernity.[1] British imperialism is a decidedly modern phenomenon, whether one views it from an economic perspective (as the "highest" stage of capitalism) or from a cultural one (shaped by Enlightenment ideology). And the novel is a decidedly modern genre, whether one views it in relation to its class origins or, following Lukács, as the epic of a godforsaken age. Thus one can most fully understand these colonial odysseys, with their uneasy blend of political setting and literary form, as complex responses to the discontents of the modern age. While acknowledging the multiple causes and forms of these discontents, I view them as deriving primarily from the survival of theological questions in an age when the answers to these questions were no longer viable. Modern thought has struggled to cope with forms of curiosity that Christian theology implanted, encouraged,

---

1. The terms *modernity* and *modernism* remain confusing—especially in adjectival form. Many analyses of modernism as a response to modernity tend to minimize the temporal differences of the two phenomena, identifying modernity with the forces of modernization strictly contemporary with the cultural phenomena under consideration. (Said and Jameson, whom I discuss in chapter 2, provide examples of this synchronicity in some of their discussions of modernism.) To avoid confusion (especially in the use of adjectives), I draw a sharp distinction throughout this book between *modernity* (adj. *modern*) and *modernism* (adj. *modernist*). Modernity (or the modern age), understood in opposition to antiquity and the Middle Ages, dates to the sixteenth century (if not much earlier), and therefore literary modernism, referring to high culture between approximately 1890 and 1940, can be seen as one in a series of responses to the challenges of modernity.

and claimed to satisfy—curiosity about, for example, the absolute and the individual's relation to it. The result is a uniquely modern incommensurability of question and answer, a disjunction between curiosity and knowledge, a gulf dividing desire from its fulfillment. The authors under consideration here illustrate this incommensurability, forgoing faith in the Christian answers while still struggling with inherited questions about the absolute.

The methodological decision to privilege this understanding of modern discontent is justified by the preoccupations of the novels themselves. Despite their settings and structure, the explicit concerns of the narratives are often less political or literary than metaphysical: in each of the novels a central character dies as a result of the journey, inviting reflection on the negation of existence. Conrad's Kurtz and Lord Jim, Woolf's Rachel Vinrace, Forster's Mrs. Moore, and Waugh's Tony Last and Prudence all die after reaching the most distant point from England on their journeys.[2] More often than not, the deaths lack clear physical causes, reflecting instead a melancholy drive toward death. Through such characters the modernists explore the individual's troubled relationship to the absolute, making use of odyssey motifs to project their anxieties onto British imperial experience. Freud's concept of the uncanny (*Unheimliche*, "unhomey") as something familiar or homelike that has been repressed describes the dynamic of these novels, where the authors' imaginative encounters with distant, uncanny colonies produce familiar, insular presentations of life as an odyssey, with death as the home port. This home offers no fulfillment or refuge (as Freud's concept indicates)—the adventurers find no redemption in death. In the absence of theology, on which an earlier age depended to give meaning to death, literature is often called upon to fill what Salman Rushdie (echoing Pascal and St. Augustine) names "a god-shaped hole." These novels try but fail to answer that call. The effort shapes their structure, and the failure accounts for their Thanatos.

The attempt to answer theological questions with secular ideas, to fill the god-shaped hole with human constructs, is what Hans Blumenberg calls "reoccupation." Blumenberg has shown how this process reshapes and often overextends cultural constructs: human reason strives for ab-

2. We are not told of Tony Last's death but are left to assume that he will spend his remaining days trapped in the jungle with the works of Dickens. Among the novels mentioned above, only Waugh's *Scoop* lacks doomed wanderers, unless they are to be found in the novel's passing reference to the earliest European visitors to Ishmaelia, who "were eaten, every one of them; some raw, others stewed and seasoned—according to local usage and the calendar (for the better sort of Ishmaelites have been Christian for many centuries and will not publicly eat human flesh, uncooked, in Lent, without special and costly dispensation from their bishop)" (105–6).

solute knowledge, utopian visions try to rival paradise, the human subject imitates the absent God. This pattern explains some of the overreaching of modern thought: for example, when it assumes responsibility for redeeming the dead—indeed, for redeeming all of human history.[3] The demand by Conrad and others that art be redemptive expresses this sense of responsibility, and their use of odyssey motifs expresses their despair in laboring under such a burden. The hero's descent into hell to encounter deceased predecessors, a standard scene throughout the history of the epic, becomes for the modernists an opportunity to acknowledge the unsatisfied need to redeem the dead.[4] The resulting melancholy helps explain the protagonists' deaths, for Thanatos, as Freud shows, is connected to a guilt-laden identification with the dead.

The overreaching of Western thought triggered by reoccupation also manifests itself as arrogance and oppressiveness when it comes into contact with other cultures. This particular aspect of reoccupation reached its zenith and its limit in the New Imperialism, when European powers, Britain in particular, had in their own view "filled up" the globe: a geographical totality took the place of the totality based on transcendental sources in Christian thought. When Woolf's Rachel Vinrace asks in *The Voyage Out*, "What is the meaning of it all?" she does not turn to a transcendental authority for an answer; rather, like other colonial-odyssey protagonists in this period, she travels across the globe as a way of traversing all time and space in search of an answer that she never finds. This attempted substitution of empire for theology transfers the focus of the redemptive impulse from the dead to colonial subjects. Viewed from the epistemological and moral framework shaped by reoccupation, the colo-

3. The applications of Blumenberg's concept that I am proposing are not ones that he would have welcomed. He steadfastly resisted commenting on the moral and political implications of intellectual history, and readers not admiring such reticence have tended to attack his philosophy at its foundation. The present volume attempts to address these moral and political aspects of literature from a position sympathetic to his theory of the modern age. In Germany he has been widely recognized, especially since his death in 1996, as one of the twentieth century's most important philosophers. Major works of his appearing to date in English, representing only a small portion of the material available in German, are *The Legitimacy of the Modern Age*, *Work on Myth*, and *The Genesis of the Copernican World*. English translations of shorter works are listed in Behrenberg and Adams, "Bibliographie Hans Blumenberg."

4. These scenes have an affinity with what Harold Bloom calls the "uncanny effect" of *apophrades*, or the return of the dead (16). Throughout this book I discuss the pressure in the modern age to use human memory as a secular form of redemption, pressure that creates a sense of belatedness in relation to the dead. This is clearly a different account of belatedness than one finds in Bloom's *Anxiety of Influence*, which focuses on literary influence, yet the theories and the interpretations they produce exhibit certain parallels and affinities. For useful readings of the British modernists informed by a Bloomian notion of belatedness, see Meisel.

nial subject becomes an embodiment of loss, a plea for redemption—and thus sometimes receives the blame for the malaise of the modern age. The modernists remain locked within this framework, but they recognize that it is in crisis, unable to fulfill its own ambitious aims.

The modernist colonial odysseys, in short, are unable to dispense with questions about the totality of the world and of history, yet they are able to expose the deficiency of available answers. This ambivalence about reoccupation shapes the way they reinforce and critique imperial culture, and it shapes their use and abuse of the odyssey tradition. Their insularity, tied to an often clumsy projection of Western cultural forms and fears onto overseas sites, appears not simply as a means of extending power over non-Westerners, but as part of an urgent attempt to cope with the profound cultural crisis of modernity. Thus a reader's expectation that these works will comment usefully on Europe's relations with particular colonies is generally disappointed, even if the uncanny content of these novels offers access to some of the deepest anxieties motivating imperial conquest.

* * *

Waugh's *A Handful of Dust* (1934) provides an extreme and therefore useful example of this insular representation of the globe. Tony Last, victim of a decaying, predatory social world and his own naïveté, fails miserably to build a comfortable domestic life with Brenda at his country house, Hetton. In order to escape, he joins an expedition to South America in search of a City. (The South American episode was inspired by Waugh's own journey to British Guiana and Brazil in 1932–33.) Waugh emphasizes the City's elusive, mythical character by having Dr. Messenger, the expedition leader, explain that "every tribe has a different word for it" and that "none of them [the natives] had ever visited the City, of course" (220). Tony's clearest images of the City come during his fever-inspired delirium:

> The gates were open before him and trumpets were sounding along the walls, saluting his arrival; from bastion to bastion the message ran to the four points of the compass; petals of almond and apple blossom were in the air; they carpeted the way, as, after a summer storm, they lay in the orchards at Hetton. Gilded cupolas and spires of alabaster shone in the sunlight. (283)

The City is part El Dorado, part projection of Tony's neo-Gothic ideals (and thus "a transfigured Hetton" [222]), part City of God. From the depth of delirium, Tony also delivers one of the novel's central messages: "there is no City" (288). The message is confirmed when he finds himself the captive of illiterate Mr. Todd "at the extreme end of one of the longest threads in the web of commerce that spreads from Manáos into the remote fastness of the forest" (285). Tony is apparently destined to spend the rest of his life reading the works of Dickens repeatedly to Mr. Todd.

The central critical challenge presented by the novel is how to relate the social satire set in England to Tony's South American journey. One of Waugh's friends, the novelist Henry Yorke (Henry Green), acknowledged his own aversion to exotic settings, while criticizing the Amazon episode for being "so fantastic that it throws the rest out of proportion" (qtd. in Sykes 142). In *Exiles and Émigrés*, Terry Eagleton similarly observes a conflict between the realistic and symbolic uses of Tony's journey, an observation that can be applied in varying degrees to all of the modernist colonial odysseys. Eagleton explains that

> Waugh wants to use foreign experience in two ways: as an escape from relative unreality to relative reality; and as an extended symbol of contemporary fever, chaos and futility. Yet these modes obviously conflict: and in the end the symbolic meaning predominates, to suggest that there is, after all, no escape to a reality beyond Society. The American exploration reveals the hollowness of English culture as 'metaphysically' rather than socially determined. (56)

In this passage and throughout his discussion of the novel, Eagleton captures many of the essential features of the colonial-odyssey subgenre: a fading of the literal meaning of the colonial odyssey before its metaphysical meaning; a desire to discover a totality missing at home by traversing the globe; a recognition that the missing totality cannot be realized through colonial experience, which merely confirms the lack discovered at home. Waugh's social satire and social conservatism shape his handling of these themes and make him an especially appropriate target for Eagleton's Marxist analysis. Waugh presents Tony's victimization as a class-specific problem before extending it across the sea; the novel projects the hollowness of upper-class life initially onto England as a whole, ultimately onto the Amazon and all human existence.

There remains some room, however, for reconceptions of the totality that the novel represents as absent. For Eagleton that totality is English society or culture. Drawing on Perry Anderson's analysis, in "Components of a National Culture," of an absence at the center of twentieth-century English culture that was filled mostly by émigrés, Eagleton notes "the inability of indigenous English writing, caught within its partial and one-sided attachments, to 'totalise' the significant movements of its own culture" (15). Though Waugh indeed represents the meaninglessness of

individual experience as a social problem, the novel also provides hints of
other ways to conceive of this lack of meaning, ways to supplement and
complicate Eagleton's conception of the social totality. Some of these hints
come in the novel's theological references, including the mythical City that
Tony seeks. Eagleton suggests that "the recourse to myth" was one modernist strategy to compensate for the lack of a "total understanding" of society (he is speaking primarily of Eliot); the "internally coherent and autonomous realm of mythology" allowed "a displacement of attention
outside the confines of English . . . society" (222–23). Tony's City plays this
function for him—but not of course for Waugh, who makes it an object of
irony. *A Handful of Dust* certainly represents English hollowness as universal, as Eagleton observes, but it also undermines the illusory compensa-
tions for this hollowness promised by certain religious and imperial
myths. It suggests that such hollowness can have metaphysical as well as
social determinants.

Early in the novel we encounter the elderly vicar in Tony's village
church who delivers sermons composed years earlier, during a lifetime of
service in India. "He had done nothing to adapt them to the changed conditions of his ministry and they mostly concluded with some reference to
homes and dear ones far away" (39). For example:

> Though miles of barren continent and leagues of ocean divide us [from
> our dear ones at home], we are never so near to them as on these Sunday
> mornings, united with them across dune and mountain in our loyalty to
> our sovereign and thanksgiving for her welfare; one with them as proud
> subjects of her sceptre and crown. (39)

The hilarious absurdity makes a mockery of the sermon's religious and
imperial dreams of totality: the world is not "united" by Tony's brand of
Sunday-morning religion, nor by celebration of an empire ruled by Victoria. A parody of sentimental, patriotic faith, Waugh's sermon serves as a
preview of the lesson of Tony's Amazon adventure, the lesson that the empire provides a tempting but inadequate means of reoccupying the void
opened up by the retreat of Christianity in the modern age.

Blumenberg provides an unusual account of the relation between the
novel's English and South American episodes by focusing on another crucial theological reference near the end of the novel.[5] Mr. Todd, showing

---

5. One surprise Peter Behrenberg and I encountered while compiling a bibliography of
Blumenberg's work was that in the 1950s he published a series of essays on Anglo-
American modernists—Eliot, Hemingway, Faulkner, and Waugh (as well as one on
Kafka)—in a Catholic periodical, *Hochland*.

Tony the grave of his predecessor, asks him whether he believes in God. Tony answers, "I suppose so. I've never really thought about it much," to which Mr. Todd responds: "I have thought about it a *great* deal and I still do not know . . . Dickens did" (291). Perhaps, Blumenberg suggests, this is the key to Tony's fate: one who is entirely indifferent to the question of God's existence becomes the captive of one for whom this question possesses a burning urgency. "What bitter irony, which undermines and overturns the whole novel at the end!" ("Eschatologische Ironie" 243). Blumenberg calls this an "eschatological irony," a "structural principle" running through Waugh's work as a kind of secular judgment day. In the case of *A Handful of Dust*, Eagleton's critique of the Amazon adventure remains more persuasive than Blumenberg's inventive explanation, simply because the irony of Tony's enslavement by Mr. Todd is not so much more bitter than the irony evident earlier in the novel. Blumenberg's interpretation nevertheless suggests another absence that makes itself felt throughout the novel, an absence of community conceived in theological terms. If we set aside his attempt to locate the irony primarily near the end of the novel, then his analysis suggests a useful way to identify this theological dimension: "the significance that irony possesses in Waugh rests on the conviction that the indifference of modern humanity to its fundamental questions can be broken only by the most gruesome shock of having its reality dismantled" (243).

In short, the novel offers a critique of the malaise of secular culture, implicating also the remnants of Christian and imperial myth. But it remains so preoccupied with this malaise that it shows little inclination or capacity to turn outward even as it depicts a voyage out; it demonstrates little openness to what is new or Other, concentrating all its attention instead on domestic discontent. Thus *A Handful of Dust* usefully illustrates the colonial-odyssey tension between literal and metaphorical exploration, between global totality and metaphysical absence, between imperial strength and moral fatigue. But if the other modernists writing colonial odysseys exhibit the same tension, they are not as determinedly antimodern as Waugh, not as inclined to resort to an "eschatological" irony in response to the modern age. However preoccupied they may be with inherited questions about the absolute, they remain committed to thoroughly modern means of addressing and manipulating these questions; however ambivalent they may be about the experience of modernity, they retain a fundamental commitment to the age in which humans go it alone, without the prop of an extrahistorical being. In the end, these other modernists—Conrad and Woolf in particular—offer more profound critiques of modernity than Waugh, precisely because they do so from deeper within, drawing on the understanding derived from a commitment to the age's fundamental assumptions and methods of thought.

* * *

This book consists of four chapters. The first focuses on the odyssey tradition, the second on the imperial context of modernism, and the third and fourth on Conrad and Woolf, respectively.

The first chapter positions the modernists in relation to two literary traditions diametrically opposed to each other in their uses of ancient Greek epic. Popular Victorian adventure stories, the immediate literary precursors to modernist colonial odysseys, exhibit a fervent Hellenism; they employ the odyssey myth both to escape from the problems of modernity and to celebrate the empire. Modernist colonial odysseys, in contrast, move away from Hellenism and attach themselves to a tradition of centrifugal odysseys represented by Dante and Tennyson, who emphasize Ulysses' restlessness and deny him a homecoming. Forster exemplifies this transition well: after spending much of his career under the influence of Cambridge Hellenism, he eventually acknowledged its limitations while confronting the problems of modernity more directly in his only colonial odyssey, *A Passage to India*.

The second chapter discusses Said's secular criticism, Joyce's *Ulysses*, Lukács's *Theory of the Novel*, and Jameson's "Modernism and Imperialism" in order to demonstrate that the mimetic focus of the modernist novel encompasses nationalism and imperialism but also reaches beyond them to theological problems that help shape the novel, nationalism, and imperialism alike. Blumenberg's description of the way modern culture struggles to reoccupy the god-shaped hole opens the way to explore further the concern with redemption, power, and death in modernist colonial odysseys. This exploration eventually leaves behind the consideration of political contexts altogether in order to speculate on the metaphysical implications of the morbidity found in modernist colonial odysseys.

No author demonstrates the phenomenon of reoccupation better than Conrad, the subject of the third chapter. Its effects appear in his frustrated desire to make art redemptive ("Karain," the preface to *The Nigger of the "Narcissus," Lord Jim*, and *Heart of Darkness*), in the melancholy preoccupation with Hades and the unredeemed dead ("Karain," *Lord Jim*, and *Heart of Darkness*), in the problematic attempt to legitimate political power in the absence of absolute authority (*Nostromo*), and in the ambivalence about British imperialism evident throughout his work. Conrad's pervasive pessimism derives from his sense that the need to reoccupy the god-shaped void is both inescapable and impossible to satisfy.

In Woolf, who is the focus of the fourth chapter, we find not only unhappy examples of the attempt to fill the god-shaped hole, but a concerted effort to leave it empty. While Forster turned to the colonial-odyssey pattern only slowly and late in his career, Woolf followed the opposite trajectory: after her first novel, *The Voyage Out*, she never again returned to the form. Instead, metaphors with which she explores the range of human experience—"globe," "sea voyage," and "tunneling," for example—undergo a fundamental shift, assuming a narrower geographical scope while retaining metaphysical weight. This rhetorical shift enables her to resist reoccupation and thus to explore redemption, power, and death in less comprehensive terms. By struggling to restrain human thought from filling a god-shaped hole, she dispenses with the need to traverse the empire and history in search of comprehensive knowledge, and she can begin simultaneously to moderate the Thanatos of the colonial-odyssey novels.

The double focus of the study, on odysseys and colonies, makes possible a synthesis of two critical traditions: the concern, dating to the modernists themselves, with modernism's use of classical models, and the more recent postcolonial and Marxist interest in modernism as a cultural buttress for (and occasionally critique of) imperialism.[6] The indispensable insights generated by these political approaches have transformed our understanding of modernism, but they have done so by viewing it as part of a synchronic economic or cultural system ("imperialism") without the longer historical or diachronic perspective offered by other approaches. The colonial-odyssey novels invite an integration of critical methods; the integration results in a skeptical assessment of the modernists' relation to Greece and in a new understanding of the historical intellectual influences on imperialist culture. This balancing of multiple perspectives becomes possible when we recognize in modernism the pervasive effects of the modern age's attempts to fill the void left behind by an omnipotent God.

6. While I aim in the first two chapters of this book to show the interaction among diverse elements of modernism, I make no attempt to offer a comprehensive overview of either modernism or critical approaches to modernism. Useful overviews and distinctive approaches can be found in Beja ("James Joyce and the Taxonomy of Modernism"), M. Bell, Benjamin, Calinescu, Chefdor et al. (eds.), DeKoven (*Rich and Strange*), Eagleton, Eysteinsson, Jameson, Kaplan and Simpson (eds.), Kenner, Levenson, Longenbach, Lukács, Meisel, Menand, North, Pecora, Perl, Perloff, Rabaté, Robbins ("Modernism in History"), and Witemeyer (ed.).

Figure 1. The title page of Francis Bacon's *Novum Organum* (1620), part of his projected *Instauratio magna*. The engraving, by Simon Pass, shows Odysseus beyond the Pillars of Hercules. By permission of the Folger Shakespeare Library.

1

Beyond the Pillars of Hercules

The self-consciousness of the modern age found in the image of the Pillars of Hercules and their order, *Nec plus ultra* [No further], which Dante's Ulysses still understood (and disregarded) as meaning "Man may not venture further here," the symbol of its new beginning and of its claim directed against what had been valid until then. On the title page of Bacon's *Instauratio magna* [*Great Renewal*] of 1620, Odysseus's ship was to appear behind the Pillars of Hercules, interpreted by this self-confident motto: *Multi pertransibunt et augebitur scientia* [Many will pass through and knowledge will be increased].

> —HANS BLUMENBERG, *The Legitimacy of the Modern Age*

A second Odyssey, long again,
equal, it may be, to the first. But without
Homer, alas, without hexameters.

. . . .

Gradually, while the shores of Ithaca
vanished in the way before him
and he set all sails west,
to Iberia, to the Pillars of Hercules,—
far from every Achaian sea,—
he felt he was alive again, that
he had cast aside the heavy bonds
of known, of household things.
And his adventuring heart
exulted in a cold and vacant love.

> —CONSTANTINE P. CAVAFY, "A Second Odyssey"

Two brief passages, from Conrad's "Youth" and Woolf's *Jacob's Room*, set the tone for the use of ancient epic in modernist colonial fiction. The passages treat the tradition ironically, producing a humor that initially masks their gravity. They provide our first points of reference for assessing the relation of British modernism to the odyssey tradition.

In "Youth," Marlow tells the story of his first voyage to the East, in an old ship loaded with coal, the *Judea*. Just short of Bangkok the cargo explodes and the helmsman goes overboard. The farce of Conrad's scene stands out in sharper relief, assuming its full significance, when contrasted with the *locus classicus* for overboard helmsmen, the end of book 5 of Virgil's *Aeneid*, where Neptune announces his intention of taking the life of Aeneas' Palinurus with the comment that "one life shall be enough instead of many" (1077). Palinurus is steering Aeneas' fleet through a calm night when he is seduced by sleep and the god catapults him overboard. Allen Mandelbaum has identified this as one of the most sublime passages in the *Aeneid*, with Virgil turning to parataxis and using a minimum of simile in representing death.[1] The entire passage (5.1103–52) deserves a careful reading, but here I reproduce only the final lines:

> Father Aeneas felt his ship drift, aimless,
> its pilot lost; he took the helm himself
> and steered his galley through the midnight waters,
> while sighing often, stunned by the disaster
> fallen upon his friend: "O Palinurus,
> too trustful of the tranquil sky and sea,
> you will lie naked on an unknown shore."

This last line, which, Mandelbaum concludes, "summons all the wisdom that is possible under a Stoic dispensation," finds the starkest of contrasts in Conrad's wistfully ironic reflection on youth (even though Conrad also often strives for a Stoic wisdom). The captain of the *Judea* assumes the helm only briefly after the explosion before the helmsman is rescued:

> Someone had the sense to look over, and there was the helmsman, who had impulsively jumped overboard, anxious to come back. He yelled and swam lustily like a merman, keeping up with the ship. We threw him a rope, and presently he stood amongst us streaming with water and very crestfallen. (26)

Virgil's sublime has become Conrad's farce.

1. Mandelbaum has described the Palinurus episode as Virgil's best paratactic passage. The occasion was a lecture titled "Gates of Horn, Gates of Ivory."

My second example, a passage from Woolf's *Jacob's Room*, refers explicitly to the epic tradition. Fanny Elmer, one of the women infatuated with Jacob, struggles to preserve her memory of the man that she, like the narrator and reader, will never know well.

> To reinforce her vision [of Jacob] she had taken to visiting the British Museum, where, keeping her eyes downcast until she was alongside of the battered Ulysses, she opened them and got a fresh shock of Jacob's presence, enough to last her half a day. But this was wearing thin. (170)

The thinness of effect serves as a comment not only on the elusiveness of Jacob, but on the efficacy of the "battered" odyssey tradition. In place of the august adventurer, now reduced to "eyeless," lifeless stone, we have the ineffectual if touching mourning rituals of a solitary woman.

Our understanding of the irony often involved in the modernists' appropriation of classical models has expanded steadily in recent decades. Modernist uses of Greece are manifold, however, and the irony in these passages by Conrad and Woolf is difficult to reconcile with some common assumptions about modernist literature. For one thing, postcolonial criticism has taught us to watch for the ways in which imperial culture employs its domestic forms and traditions to claim knowledge and thus power over non-Western peoples, and an ironic distancing of the most ancient of Western stories would seem to work against such uses of culture. For another, a common view of modernism, deriving from the modernists themselves, is that it embraces ancient myth and classical form as antidotes to Romantic excess and modern disorientation. Such critical perspectives are not prepared to account for the appearance in modernist fiction of a cowardly merman helmsman or a battered Ulysses unable to stir a woman's passion. Yet much recent criticism has focused on modernist irony, opening the way to consider the skepticism of the colonial odysseys about any continuity between ancient Greece and modern Britain. In this chapter, I begin to demonstrate and explain the turn away from Greece and the odyssey tradition in modernist colonial fiction.

This explanation consists of three stages: the first two provide background and context, drawing on a diverse range of sources to illustrate post-Romantic Hellenism and the evolution of the odyssey tradition, while the third focuses on the case of Forster. I begin with a discussion of late-Victorian popular adventure stories, which manifest an enthusiasm for empire and a vigorous Hellenism—they manifest none of the irony we have just witnessed in Conrad and Woolf. I then contrast the ideals of Hellenism to the transformation of Greek figures in the epic tradition. The contrasting uses of Greece in these two contexts set the stage for considering the dilution of Hellenism in modernist colonial fiction, particularly in the work of Forster. Forster provides the most revealing example of the relation between Hellenism and colonial adventure, precisely because his career follows a trajectory from one to the other. Whereas Conrad and Woolf began their writing careers committed to the colonial-odyssey paradigm and its ambivalence about Hellenism, Forster is a revealing transition figure—his enthusiasm for Hellenism slackened only late in his novel-writing career, which culminated in *A Passage to India*, his only colonial odyssey. Discussion of this novel provides an opportunity to begin articulating the challenges of modernity that are evaded in Hellenism but reflected in modernist fiction.

The Adventure Tradition and Ancient Greece

The popular adventure stories that flourished from the closing decades of the nineteenth century to World War I offer an important prelude and foil to modernist colonial odysseys. In their structure and subject matter they share a superficial similarity with the modernist works, but they are more zealous both in their support of empire and in their Hellenism. Their Hellenism is so thoroughly sublimated that often we do not associate them with this tradition; they are fantasies in which Hellenism is not so much an ideal as an already realized virtue. In 1888 George Saintsbury expressed a view widespread at the time when he wrote in "The Present State of the English Novel" that late-Victorian romance was not medieval but Greek in its inspiration, returning "to the earliest form of writing, to the pure romance of adventure" (125).[2] The relation of this popular adventure tradition to imperialism has already received substantial critical attention; here I wish, by means of two notable examples, to highlight its use of ancient Greece.[3]

The obtrusive misogyny and racism of the first example, H. Rider Haggard's *She* (1886), are supported by extreme claims about the legacy of

2. I quote from the expanded version of the essay first published in 1892. Saintsbury welcomes the rise of romance as a response to the exhausted possibilities of Victorian realism: "Romance is of its nature eternal and preliminary to the novel. The novel is of its nature transitory and is parasitic on the romance. If some of the examples of novels themselves partake of eternity, it is only because the practitioners have been cunning enough to borrow much from the romance" (127).

3. Examples of criticism on the popular adventure story relevant to the present study include the work by Brantlinger (chap. 8), Cheyfitz (chap. 1), N. Daly, Howkins, Katz, McClintock (chap. 6), Torgovnick (chap. 2), and White. Torgovnick's useful discussion of Tarzan and primitivism comes shortly after her analysis of the Cyclops episode in Homer, but she does not discuss Burroughs' relation to Greece.

Greece. Although the alluring She in the heart of Africa poses a sexual and racial threat to Leo, his multilayered Greekness enables this Briton to overcome the threat. In fact, Haggard insists on his English protagonist's ties to ancient Greece with an obsessive redundancy. First Haggard establishes a direct textual continuity through the inscribed potsherd, which carries absolute authority within the story. Serving as a kind of treasure map and sacred text, it comes from Greece. In the early pages of the story we find the potsherd's Greek text reproduced, along with medieval Latin, Old English, and modern English translations. Haggard began by composing the English version and hired scholars to translate it into the other languages. He also fabricated and inscribed an actual potsherd, a photograph of which he included among the plates in the first edition. It is this Greek shard that guides Leo on his adventure to the heart of Africa.

Among the writings on the potsherd is a family lineage that helps establish the second link between Greece and Britain, a racial link that is mentioned often in relation to Leo. He has the appearance of a Greek, he proves in fact to be of ancient Greek descent, and he is presented as a possible reincarnation of Kallikrates, though he is also always English. So important is this filiation that Haggard's narrator explicitly excludes modern Greece as the inheritor of the ancient tradition. England is more Greek than Greece, for the torch of civilization, as the sequence of potsherd translations and Leo's genealogy indicate, has passed from the Mediterranean to the British Isles. Not content to draw on the legacy of Greece by linking itself to the literary tradition, *She* is a colonial odyssey invoking the authority of the Greeks by fabricating its own direct material and spiritual ties. Haggard plants his claims for the authority of his own text and for the racial, cultural, and sexual superiority of British men firmly in the soil of ancient Greece.

For the second example I draw on a curious critical work from 1981, *Tarzan and Tradition: Classical Myth in Popular Literature* by Erling Holtsmark:

> I come to this study as a professional classicist, and I bring to it methods similar to those I apply to classical literature. This procedure lends itself to the study of Burroughs' novels precisely because they are conceived and to a large extent executed in a manner that speaks of a classical background and classical influences. (xiii)

A comment on the appropriateness of Tarzan as an example is in order: yes, Edgar Rice Burroughs was thoroughly American, but the Tarzan stories nevertheless offer another example of the intensive use of ancient Greece in the developed world's popular representations of empire, and

Burroughs wrote them under the influence of a strong identification with British imperial activity. The first story in the series, *Tarzan of the Apes* (1912), begins with the noble English parents-to-be of the jungle man on a journey to Africa when a mutiny on their ship leads to their abandonment on the West African coast, where Tarzan is born and they die. Official Queen's business takes John Clayton, Lord Greystoke, on this journey with his new wife: he "was commissioned to make a peculiarly delicate investigation of conditions in a British West Coast African Colony" (2), and thus the narrator has culled many of the details of the story from the "official records of the British Colonial Office" (1).

Holtsmark finds numerous Homeric techniques and themes in the Tarzan stories, including formulaic repetition, ring composition, chiasmus, *mythos*, the heroic ideal—even a *katabasis* in the second of the tales, *The Return of Tarzan*. Formulaic repetition and ring composition may have facilitated oral transmission of the ancient epic, but Holtsmark cannot explain Burroughs' need for them, and his praise of Burroughs for rivaling not only Homer's sense of adventure but also his "commentary on man and his condition" remains unconvincing (6). Nevertheless, Holtsmark's work helps demonstrate once again the importance of a perceived vital link to ancient Greece in popular celebrations of the British empire. In contrast to the modernists' colonial odysseys, where even England itself can prove uncanny, the Tarzan stories depict an Englishman strangely at home in an African colony. What becomes repressed or forgotten for a time is a noble Englishness that rises to the surface even in the jungle, where it emerges as an innate virtue, "the natural outcropping of many generations of fine breeding, an hereditary instinct of graciousness which a lifetime of uncouth and savage training and environment could not eradicate" (Burroughs 217).

In the process of attaching themselves to the image of Greece as the birthplace of civilization, these popular authors inherit from the Greeks a sense of superiority in relation to other, "barbarian" peoples. In itself this inheritance is not surprising, though it produces a contradiction when turned against the Greeks, making them a symbol of primitivism as well as civilization. The epic parallels and racial allusions suggest that Tarzan always already fulfills the heroic ideal, and yet his "return" from Africa shows him passing from savagery to enlightenment and retracing the process of evolution described by Darwin. He is an embodiment of the dictum that ontogeny recapitulates phylogeny, and both ends of the process—the primitive as well as the civilized—are associated with the Greeks. In *She*, Haggard similarly turns an African journey into time travel and ends up with a seemingly contradictory attitude toward the Greeks. The affiliation with Greece confirms England as the standard-bearer of civilization, and yet Leo verifies this affiliation only by traveling to the heart of Africa and, in a sense, back to an ancient incarnation of himself.

Andrew Lang, classicist and anthropologist, found that Haggard's fiction conformed nicely to his own theory that primitive African societies provided close analogues to the barbarous people that had produced Homer's works. Lang, a translator of Homer, perceived *King Solomon's Mines* to be the product of a modern Homer capable of reinvigorating English prose, and thus he befriended Haggard. (Robert Louis Stevenson received similar praise from Lang, who called *Treasure Island* a romance surpassed only by *The Odyssey* and *Tom Sawyer*.) Haggard made substantial revisions to *She* between its serial and book publication in response to Lang's suggestions, and then the two collaborated on a romance about Helen of Troy, *The World's Desire* (1891). But these two were by no means alone in equating ancient Greece with contemporary Africa: Francis W. Newman (to cite one other striking example) earned the scorn of Matthew Arnold by describing Homer as a "noble barbarian," a "savage with the lively eye" whose verse must have sounded "like an elegant and simple melody from an African of the Gold Coast" (qtd. in Arnold, *Translating Homer* 187). The analogy became common enough that Woolf could have one of her characters echo it in *The Voyage Out*: "When I think of the Greeks I think of them as naked black men," Miss Allan comments, "which is quite incorrect, I'm sure" (114). Woolf's playful depiction of the popular-romance view of Greece blends the ideal of civilization with noble savagery.[4]

In these last examples, where dismissal of primitive savagery has given way to praise of noble barbarism, images of Greece (and Africa) serve not

---

4. The oxymoron of Greek barbarism also gained support from anthropology, for example in Claude Lévi-Strauss's comparison of Native American mythical figures to Odysseus. But anthropology and archaeology transformed classical studies and the view of ancient Greece in the late-nineteenth and early-twentieth centuries. Lang's efforts in anthropology are generally recognized as the work of an amateur, but he stands at the beginning of this development, which is represented more notably by Sir James Frazer, who began publishing *The Golden Bough* in 1890. For reasons of economy, I have focused my attention on the various literary predecessors to the modernist odysseys, but the striking contrast I sketch between modernism and late-Victorian romance is explained in part by the shift in the perceptions of primitivism and Greece brought on by developments in anthropology and archaeology. On this shift, see Bell, "Metaphysics" 20–21 and Kenner 41–53. For an analysis emphasizing the continuity of classical studies before and after the influence of anthropology, see Turner 115–34. (Turner's entire work, *The Greek Heritage in Victorian Britain*, provides a useful account of nineteenth-century Hellenism.) A later rejection of the analogy between Africa and Greece comes from Wyndham Lewis, who seizes on a phrase from DuBois's *Dark Princess* to suggest that primitivism, no longer noble, is a threat to the racial and cultural integrity of Europe: "The Congo . . . is flooding the Acropolis." See *Pale Face* 29–43, 85, 273 and DuBois 20.

only as evidence of British superiority but also as an implicit critique of modernity. Lang wrote a poem, "The Odyssey," in which he describes "the surge and thunder of the Odyssey" as a welcome relief from "modern speech." His hope that romance writers would reinvigorate English prose is itself a dream of renaissance as antidote to disenchantment. In "A Note on Modernism," Edward Said associates this implicit critique with the romance of empire: "The central theme [of the realist novel] by the late nineteenth century was disenchantment. . . . Into this narrative of loss and disablement is gradually interjected an alternative" which includes "the novel of frank exoticism and confident empire" (*Culture and Imperialism* 187). In other words, popular romance embraces imperialism not as an aspect of modern civilization but as an antidote to it. We have seen that in these adventure stories (and the related pseudo-scholarship) Greece evokes the same exoticism and confidence as empire; the classical and colonial worlds are both viewed through the lenses of romance and the noble-savage theme. So the British alliance with Greek civilization and admiration of Greek primitivism, contradictory though they may seem, both serve to encourage and legitimize Britain's imperial endeavors. This encouragement and legitimization are acts of denial not merely in relation to the colonies but in relation to Western culture, for the wishful thinking that produces the world of romance represses a dissatisfaction with modernity. The imagined presence of Greece constitutes a claim to have banished disenchantment.

Modernist Nostalgia

The Hellenism of the popular adventure stories presents in extreme form a nostalgia that has been one of the defining elements of the modern age from its beginning. Greece has long served as a steadying if sometimes distant ideal for a weary Christian culture. Indeed, the history of modernity may be seen as a sequence of returns or revivals, with each period attempting to mitigate or escape the unsettling aspects of modern experience more successfully than its predecessors. Individual authors and movements within each period can be sorted according to their perceptions of ancient Greece and its legacy: its present vitality, inaccessibility, or obsolescence; the modes of its transmission; the value of its influence and the desirability of a renaissance; most fundamentally, what it represents, what it *is*.

If the Renaissance initiated a classicism that diluted the influence of Christianity, it was Romanticism that turned Hellenism most decisively against the modern age, in particular against the Enlightenment (which had been championed sometimes at the expense of the ancients). "But still the heart doth need a language, still / Doth the old instinct bring back the old names" (qtd. in Bush 54). This well-known passage from Coleridge's translation of Schiller's *Die Piccolomini* complains of needs not satisfied by modern rationality and commerce, a complaint echoed, for example, in the early work of E. M. Forster, with its persistent critique of bourgeois life and undeveloped hearts. From Romanticism onward, Hellenism consisted of a thorough mix, though in varying degrees and configurations, of anti-modern and anti-Christian impulses. Matthew Arnold strengthened both impulses in Victorian, Edwardian, and modernist culture: he exhibited a Romantic rejection of "this strange disease of modern life" with "its palsied hearts" ("Scholar Gypsy" lines 203, 205), and he provided a stimulus for secular humanism by portraying Greece in a way that suggested the possibility of a dignified life outside of religion. Characteristic of late-modern Hellenism, including its modernist manifestations, is this turn away from the otherworldly focus of Christianity in the desire to recover a sense of the adequacy of human forms. In other words, Hellenism became an attempt to return from transcendence to immanence.

Whatever variations one finds in uses of ancient Greece, the underlying dissatisfaction with post-Christian modernity is something shared by authors of a wide variety of literary talents and political persuasions. Arnold wrote in 1869 that "everywhere we see the beginnings of confusion, and we want a clue to some sound order and authority" (*Culture and Anarchy* 96), and over half a century later, when the confusion had expanded beyond its beginnings, T. S. Eliot imagined the modernists, Joyce in particular, had found such a clue in Greece: "In manipulating a continuous parallel between contemporaneity and antiquity," Joyce finds "a way of controlling, of ordering, of giving a shape and a significance to the immense panorama of futility and anarchy which is contemporary history" ("*Ulysses*, Order and Myth" 270). Acknowledging (like Arnold) the "anarchy" more openly than did the romance writers, Eliot is cautious about presenting the "mythical method" (271) as a means of renaissance. The idea of "a continuous parallel" remains ambiguous, if not skeptical, about continuity: not the tradition but the parallel is continuous, and the resulting "order" seems imposed rather than organic. His characterization of *Ulysses* is largely unconvincing—the parallels are in fact multiple and discontinuous, and their function is not always to bring order—but the essay's invocation of Greece is a familiar response to disenchantment. For Eliot as well as for the romance writers, a discontent with modernity is bound to a nostalgia for Greece, a desire to return to the home of civilization or to recover a feeling that civilization provides a suitable home.[5]

No modernist is more skeptical than Virginia Woolf on the question of Britain's proximity to Greece, and yet at times she too participates in this nostalgia. Although she reminds us that "between this foreign people and ourselves there is not only difference of race and tongue but a tremendous breach of tradition" (*Common Reader* 23), her interest in Greece as an ideal is evident, for example, when she discusses the state of mind in which one must read Plato in an attempt to mend the breach:

> Truth, it seems, is various; Truth is to be pursued with all our faculties. Are we to rule out the amusements, the tendernesses, the frivolities of friendship because we love truth? Will truth be quicker found because we stop our ears to music and drink no wine, and sleep instead of talking through the long winter's night? It is not to the cloistered disciplinarian mortifying himself in solitude that we are to turn, but to the well-sunned nature, the man who practises the art of living to the best advantage, so that nothing is stunted but some things are permanently more valuable than others. (*Common Reader* 33)

This passage attributes the breach to Christianity more than to modern disenchantment. Woolf's contrasting of Christian moral severity with Greek variety echoes Arnold's distinction between Hebraism and Hellenism, with the difference that Arnold's opposition is more explicitly based on race and has in this respect an affinity with the romance writers (though Woolf's climatological references imply a racial as well as a religious basis for her distinction).[6] When Arnold diagnoses the need for order and authority in *Culture and Anarchy*, he too looks to the Greeks for help. The Renascence, as he describes it, had not yet gone far enough in England, where Puritanism impeded its progress. In believing that the human spirit's alternations of Hebraic moral stringency and Hellenic intellectual flexibility had favored the former in England, he offers as a corrective an image of ancient Greece that is first and foremost Homeric. More specifically, it is Odyssean: no Greek figure, historical or mythical, is more defined by intellectual flexibility than wily Odysseus, whose very

5. If Eliot associated Homer with order, he could also draw on the odyssey tradition to represent modern anarchy, "the horror of the illimitable scream / Of a whole world about us" (*Waste Land* 58–59). The manuscript version of *The Waste Land* contains a passage based on Dante's Ulysses canto and Tennyson's "Ulysses": "The sea with many voices / Moaned all about us" (56–57) echoes lines from Tennyson that I discuss below. Eliot deleted the entire passage on the advice of Pound.

6. On Arnold's use of race, see Baldick 36, 218–19.

name designates him "a man of many turns," or "polytropic."[7] No Greek figure better exemplifies Woolf's contention that truth is various.

Odysseus' wiliness emerges not only within the Homeric epics, but in his subsequent wanderings through literary history. If modernity's uses of Greece are many, no figure participates in this variety more readily than Odysseus. That his reception appears to range more widely than that of many other mythical figures is perhaps to be expected: the craftiness of his character lies open to the craft of successive generations of readers and poets. Any attempt to narrate the development of this character through the nearly three millennia of his recorded history must be prepared to contend with such vicissitudes, and W. B. Stanford, treating Ulysses as a "theme," offers an ambitious example of such a narration. First published in the 1950s, *The Ulysses Theme* breathes the spirit of its time: it employs the history-of-ideas methodology imported from Germany, with thorough scholarship grounding a grand sweep through the Western tradition. Stanford views the history of Ulysses as the product of an ongoing compromise between "mere repetition" and excessive innovation by audience-sensitive authors wishing neither to bore nor to offend.

Two of Stanford's observations about the patterns of this reception are particularly relevant as background for the colonial-odyssey narratives. The first concerns Ulysses' relation to modernity, and more fundamentally to the interaction of civilization and barbarism. Stanford's epilogue offers a concluding insight about the ongoing victory of Enlightenment values: "in the tradition as a whole the authors who believe in the ultimate triumph of reason over passion in Ulysses' heart command the weightier authority" (246).[8] The second observation emerges when he uses terms Joyce also used to identify a radical antinomy in the tradition between centripetal and centrifugal forces, between Ulysses as a home seeker and Ulysses as a home deserter. The centripetal and centrifugal forces are traceable not only in the character but also in his various authors as they make choices about returning to or departing from the models provided by predecessors. Stanford's two observations can be related to each other in multiple, complex ways. Sometimes the centripetal force preserves tradition and order, whereas the centrifugal movement leads to anarchy and

7. For a useful analysis of Odysseus' *polytropia*, see Bergren.

8. Following this assertion, Stanford acknowledges, somewhat apologetically, his tendency to interpret Ulysses allegorically, but such a tendency, dating to the Greeks themselves, requires no apology. Indeed, from this historical distance every reading of Odysseus is inescapably allegorical. For the Greeks' allegorizations, see especially book 10 of the *Republic*, where Plato (or his Socrates) describes Homer's narratives as three removes from reality. For an account of the subsequent Neoplatonic allegorization of Homer, which sacrificed most levels of meaning other than the allegorical, see Lamberton. See also Blumenberg, *Work on Myth* 77 and *Höhlenausgänge* 235–42.

chaos (to borrow the terms that Arnold and Eliot share). However, another kind of order—the Enlightenment "triumph of reason"—may be associated with the centrifugal movement of the modern Odysseus who travels beyond the Pillars of Hercules (which the classical world perceived as the limit set for humankind) to acquire new knowledge with impunity (see figure 1).

Paradoxically both the centripetal and the centrifugal forces find expression in nineteenth and twentieth-century Hellenism. The dream of renewal embodied in Hellenism reveals the circularity of the notion of renaissance: for those wishing to escape the discontents of the present, Ulysses serves simultaneously as a figure of liberating progress and an object of nostalgia. The notion of renaissance finds a radically optimistic embodiment, as we have seen, in the romance of adventure stories. Indeed, by projecting a world in which renaissance has always already succeeded, they repress the need for it, rendering the concept meaningless. This extreme finds its antithesis in the pessimistic paradoxes of the Frankfurt school, for which culture proves itself savage over and over again—proves itself indeed the mere organization and intensification of barbarism—and thus the notion of a renaissance remains out of the question. Max Horkheimer and Theodor Adorno understand Enlightenment as a process of individuation that alienates the self from its own past and from nature, so that the existence of the self depends on self-sacrifice. They perceive that Homer's Odysseus is already such a figure of Enlightenment: in the interest of self-preservation he must repeatedly practice self-renunciation, as when he binds hinds himself to the mast to avoid succumbing to the sirens' entrancing song of "all things that come to pass on fruitful earth," including the story of Odysseus' own past griefs and heroism (Homer 250). His homecoming is possible only when he severs himself from his own past and mythic prehistory, and thus "the quintessential paradox of the epic resides in the fact that the notion of homeland is opposed to myth" (78). If the romance writers imagine an enchanting world without need of renaissance, Horkheimer and Adorno recognize that Odysseus' "triumph of reason" is as indispensable as it is costly. For the romance writers, the return is always already accomplished; for the Frankfurt school, return means the death of the self, and thus Odysseus is not at home in the world even when he returns home to Ithaca.

The colonial-odyssey fiction of the modernists often comes close to this Frankfurt School pessimism; offering little hope of renaissance, such fiction also offers no other escape from the dialectic of Enlightenment. Nostalgia, the mind's solitary, sentimental *nostos*, may survive, but these novels clearly stand in the tradition of the centrifugal odyssey, asserting that things fall apart, the center cannot hold. The consequences of home desertion are ominous: the voyage out leads usually to death, sometimes to a hell that never dies. Rather than using adventure as a means to invest the colonies with the fullness of romance, the modernist British odysseys employ a parallel maneuver with opposite results: they project onto colonies the discontents of modernity.

The darkness of the vision finds expression in these novels not only structurally, through the mortal defeat of the centrifugally propelled protagonists, and intertextually, through ironic echoes of the epic tradition, but also in the fact that they do not make more extensive, constructive use of this tradition. That they do not appears to be a deliberate repudiation— and thus a constitutive element of their meaning—when we remember to what extent the resources of the odyssey tradition, of Greek literature in particular, were available to the authors. Forster and Woolf were of the first generation to come of age following Arnold's intervention on behalf of Hellenism, and the influence of 1890s Cambridge Hellenism penetrates deep into Forster's fiction and Woolf's early writing. Waugh, a competent if unhappy public-school and Oxford student of the next generation, had suitable grounding in the classics, though the intervening years and wars (as well as individual temperament) had blunted the influence of Hellenism. We know less about Conrad's studies, but we know that before leaving the *gymnasium* in Poland he advanced far enough to learn ancient history, "tolerably good" Latin, and "a certain amount" of Greek, possibly enough to read *The Iliad* (Najder, *Chronicle* 31–38); certainly his work makes evident his familiarity with Homer and the epic tradition. These authors all knew well that the odyssey tradition offered a wealth of material germane to their concern with the fate of the imperial subject venturing to encounter the Other, and yet it fell to one of the colonials, Joyce, to exploit this tradition most fully.

Their caution can be attributed to two overlapping factors, to be explored through the remainder of this chapter and the next. The first is that their view of Greece was shaped to a large extent by the Hellenism that immediately preceded them. The Odysseus they knew was not Horkheimer and Adorno's conflicted figure but the adventurer who, as Goldsworthy Lowes Dickinson wrote in 1896, "by his religion has been made at home in the world" (4). For a variety of reasons, the modernists increasingly recognized that the goal of returning from Christian transcendence to Greek immanence, however appealing, could not be achieved by returning to the Greeks. And this leads to the second factor: increasingly they recognized that the challenges of modernity (including administering the empire) defied the inherited Hellenist ideals of immanence and adequate form. The discontents of modernity needed to be confronted and worked through, not simply evaded by invoking Greece.

The colonial-odyssey novels can usefully be read in relation to the odyssey tradition not only in spite of, but because of the authors' ironic and reticent use of that tradition. Indeed, it is often difficult not to have the odyssey background in mind while reading these novels, given the self-referential nature of the Western literary tradition. It is also necessary to have this background in mind for the task of separating the various overlapping contexts that the works bring into play—literary tradition, empire, and the discontents of modernity. Finally, this literary background can provide interpretive questions and critical concepts for approaching the colonial odysseys. For these reasons I would like to take a detour through the tradition to highlight issues confronted in odyssey adaptations long before the advent of British imperialism and even longer before the launch of the modernists' morbid imaginative journeys.

Centripetal and Centrifugal Wandering (Homer, Virgil, Dante, Tennyson)

The centripetal, home-seeking strain has been dominant in Ulysses' history—the recorded tradition begins on this note, of course, with Homer's Odysseus fighting his way back to Ithaca and Penelope. Stanford traces the subsequent fate of Ulysses' namesakes in the literary tradition, but the true successors to Homer's Odysseus are arguably the differently named epic heroes who replace him, like Aeneas and Dante. Both introduce innovations that reshape the tradition and are critical for the modernist colonial odysseys in particular, even though the latter are not in the home-seeking strain. Aeneas detaches home from its geographical anchor when he carries the household gods with him into exile from Troy and, winning Lavinia, redefines home in a way that satisfies the demands—while recognizing the costs—of empire. Dante, separated from his beloved Florence and deceased Beatrice, turns exile into a precondition for expanding his love, his home, from earthly to celestial circles; his voyage takes him to the "eternal dwelling" of the heavenly hosts, to the threshold of the Eternal Light, which he finds "dwelling" within itself (*Paradiso* 31: 12; 33: 124–25). A centrifugal force is evident in this succession of epic heroes as the conception of home assumes imperial and then theological overtones, but the centripetal force remains stronger. These heroes preserve the notion of home, in however altered a form; their journeys offer reassuring evidence about the order of the world and the significance of human life even as the perception of this significant order undergoes fundamental changes.

The centrifugal tradition is most evident not in the succession of epic heroes, in Aeneas and Dante, but in Ulysses' namesakes. If the centrifugal strain departs from the tradition's primary concern with *nostos*, it too is nevertheless a well-established, time-honored variation. In demonizing Ulysses—or having his Aeneas and Sinon do so—Virgil heightened ambivalence about the character and set up Dante to introduce the centrifugal Ulysses in spectacular fashion. The 26th canto of the *Inferno* shows Virgil and Dante passing among the fraudulent counselors in the Eighth Pouch of the Eighth Circle of Hell, where Ulysses tells his story from within the flame that conceals him:

> Neither my fondness for my son nor pity
> for my old father nor the love I owed
> Penelope, which would have gladdened her,
>   was able to defeat in me the longing
> I had to gain experience of the world
> and of the vices and the worth of men.
>
> . . . .
>
>   And I and my companions were already
> old and slow, when we approached the narrows
> where Hercules set up his boundary stones
>   that men might heed and never reach beyond.

He next repeats for Virgil and Dante the exhortation he delivered to his men, when he roused them to transgress the boundary stones of Hercules by appealing to their race-based notions of civilization:

>   Consider well the seed that gave you birth:
> you were not made to live your lives as brutes,
> but to be followers of worth and knowledge.

Dante's irony thoroughly undermines this attempt to contrast Greek seed, worth, and knowledge with brutishness, for immediately after reenacting this speech to his men, Ulysses informs Virgil and Dante of the brutal consequences of transgression:

> And we were glad, but this soon turned to sorrow,
> for out of that new land a whirlwind rose
> and hammered at our ship, against her bow.
>   Three times it turned her round with all the waters;
> and at the fourth, it lifted up the stern
> so that our prow plunged deep, as pleased an Other,
>   until the sea again closed—over us.
>
>   (*Inferno* 26: 94–99, 106–9, 118–20, 136–42)

Dante's condemnation of the desire for forbidden knowledge clearly does not indicate that he perceives all enlightenment as barbaric; he merely challenges what he views to be false enlightenment, fraudulent counsel.[9] The breach of which Woolf speaks has already opened wide, so that Ulysses (like Homer) addresses Dante only indirectly, through Virgil. The size of the breach is reflected furthermore in the violent distortion of the figure: Dante's Ulysses never returns home but sails directly to his doom—and to the Eighth Circle of Hell—from Circe.

Yet this Ulysses, even in his damnation, is an ambiguous figure. He is daemonic, exercising an attraction analogous to that of Milton's Satan. His appeal is one indication that Dante does not merely reject Ulysses' thirst for worldly knowledge but identifies guiltily with his profound curiosity. As Allen Mandelbaum suggests in his introduction to the *Paradiso*, the Ulysses of the *Inferno* "may indeed represent Dante's recoiling from the very limits that the ultimate exaltation of intellect may reach, extend, transgress" (xvi).[10] In this and in other respects Dante emerges as a remarkably modern poet. Mandelbaum's "Dante as Ancient and Modern" comments on Dante's rich, obsessive play on the words "old" and "new," an obsession to which the Ulysses canto makes a modest contribution: Ulysses emphasizes his old age and that of his men as a motive force in their exploration of the "new land" that brings them short-lived joy and the whirlwind of doom (26: 137). Thus Dante's Ulysses, an ancient figure, heralds the modern age's unbridled curiosity and restless exploration of *nova terra*. Though damned, he elicits sympathy and admiration. He finds his redemption in the engraved image on the title page of Bacon's *Novum Organum* (1620), where his transgression of the boundary stones of Hercules celebrates the triumphs of the modern age.

Another long leap forward—to the nineteenth century—shows how easily Dante's Ulysses adapts to the British empire. The debt of Tennyson's "Ulysses" to the 26th canto of the *Inferno* has long been recognized and is evident not only in the centrifugal drive of the poem (though

9. In a remarkable appropriation, Primo Levi builds a chapter around this canto in *Survival in Auschwitz*. As he attempts to reconstruct Ulysses' speech from memory for a fellow prisoner, he is moved by its relevance to their plight, an "unexpected anachronism." He shows little awareness of or interest in the irony Dante injects into Ulysses' lines opposing knowledge to brutes, for he reports that in the camp setting he heard these words as if "for the first time: like the blast of a trumpet, like the voice of God" (103).

10. Croce identifies Dante more strongly with Ulysses' curiosity: "No one was more deeply moved than Dante by the passion to know all that is knowable, and nowhere else has he given such noble expression to that noble passion as in the great figure of Ulysses." Mazzotta emphasizes the proximity of Ulysses' misguided rhetoric to the prophecy on which Dante's journey and poetic undertaking depend. See also Auden, *Enchafèd Flood* 10–11 and Blumenberg, *Legitimacy* 338–41.

Tennyson has the wanderer return home for a spell and thus better accounts for his age), but in many details of Ulysses' voyage, including the overbearing desire "to follow knowledge" and accumulate "experience."[11] The question is how the British context alters the pattern—whether a more imperial, perhaps Virgilian understanding of home emerges. Matthew Rowlinson's useful article frames the question of the poem's relation to imperialism with two observations: when Tennyson wrote it in 1833, imperialist discourse and ideology had not yet formed, and yet the poem first found favor in the service of a colonialist pedagogy, entering the Tennyson canon only after appearing in late-nineteenth- and early-twentieth-century classroom texts. This pedagogical use seems especially odd when one considers the ambiguity in the poem about Ulysses' location and the location of his home. He grumbles that he must "mete and dole / Unequal laws unto a savage race, / That hoard, and sleep, and feed, and know not me," and then he decides to leave to Telemachus the task "by slow prudence to make mild / A rugged people, and through soft degrees / Subdue them to the useful and the good." While he sounds here like a colonial official preparing to return home, he also leaves Telemachus on this isle "centred in the sphere / Of common duties" while he, Ulysses, goes in search of the receding "margin." One way to construe the ambiguity is by seeing Ulysses as one who extends the notion of home to global proportions. Rowlinson mentions the epilogue to *Idylls of the King*, "To the Queen," with its reference to "Our ocean-empire with her boundless homes / For ever-broadening England," as one among many passages from the later Tennyson where this theme is made explicit (*Poems* 1755). Although content to leave the household gods in the care of Telemachus, Ulysses does not simply want to make what he experiences a part of himself but determines, conversely, that "I am a part of all that I have met."

Paralleling the ambiguities of place are the poem's temporal paradoxes. Rowlinson claims that "the interchange of early and late is without doubt the organizing trope of this poem" (271). Late in the day and late in his life, Ulysses departs from a world that is also apparently old, for he commences a new voyage in search of a "newer world"; he hopes the late hour of his life can bring "new things." This temporal interchange is reinforced also by the poem's solar imagery, or heliotropes, with Ulysses following the sun westward to evening and death, while the sun also serves peren-

---

11. Given the brevity of the poem (*Poems of Tennyson* 561–66), I do not indicate line numbers. Alan Sinfield discusses the centripetal drive of the poem in terms of Tennyson's sense of marginalization in England, though Sinfield's analysis has a quite different emphasis than the one I propose below.

nially as center, origin, source of life. Rowlinson does not bring in Dante, but our discussion of the *Inferno* has anticipated Tennyson's early/late trope (readers of Tennyson's poem might usefully read Mandelbaum's "Dante as Ancient and Modern" in conjunction with Rowlinson's article). And even Tennyson's heliotropes are anticipated by half a millennium when Dante's Ulysses, seeking *nova terra*, describes having "turned our stern toward morning" hoping for "experience of that which lies beyond / the sun" (26: 124, 116–17). This Dantean lineage might simply serve as further support for Rowlinson's Althusserian conclusion that the moment of ideology is eternal, and yet Rowlinson does tie the temporality of Tennyson's heliotropes specifically to the subsequent rise of imperial ideology, which

> needed to articulate colonial or colonized subjects both as "new" English people—new at once in the sense of being new-minted without the antecedents of British history, and in the sense of representing a new kind of Englishness—and also, so as to preserve the prestige of the parent culture, as belated and behind-the-times provincials. (271–72)

With an eye on the way the rise of English studies is tied to a colonialist pedagogy, Rowlinson focuses here on the poem's relation to readers outside England, and thus the paradoxical temporality of the work appears as a response to and tool for the administration of empire. In this regard, his analysis is characteristic of many recent analyses of the relation between culture and imperialism.

I would like to expand or shift the focus of Rowlinson's analysis in a way that anticipates my approach to modernist colonial odysseys by pointing toward the possibility of relating the poem's temporal tropes not only to residents of the colonies but to those residing in England. Such a reading can account for the sense of fatigue and weakness in the poem without making it an anachronistic or prophetic symptom of the White Man's Burden. Most narrowly, we need only remember that Tennyson wrote this poem, like *In Memoriam*, in response to the death of Hallam and that this personal loss only accentuates a discontent with modernity that surfaced throughout Tennyson's early work. "Ulysses" suggests that the fatigue, agedness, and restlessness do not derive from the burden of administering empire, but are part of the reason for acquiring it. The belatedness is not the margin's in relation to the center as much as the center's in relation to its own haunting past. Thus, Ulysses comments that "the deep / Moans round with many voices" and turns the sea into an Inferno-like abode of the dead. As in the modernist odysseys, the journey here is directed toward death, inspiring desire and fear: Ulysses seems both to seek death and to stave it off "every hour." For the death-seeker, the "newer world" is the undiscover'd country from whose bourn no traveller returns; for him staving off death, the *nova terra* is attractive not merely as an escape from the old home, but precisely because the new things it brings, including the people newly brought under the umbrella of Britishness, might help rejuvenate the home. In the latter case, the primary question is not how to increase or consolidate a formidable political power; rather, Ulysses hopes through the exercise of new power to find an echo of "that strength which in old days / Moved earth and heaven."

This survey of the Ulysses tradition has not returned us to our point of departure in late-modern Hellenism. Tennyson's Ulysses is not Homeric in character, not particularly Greek.[12] He embodies modern discontents, not their antithesis or blessed prehistory. His home, no longer familiar and safe, has become associated with estrangement and death. The centrifugal branch of the Ulysses tradition, having already stood the Greek model on its head, freely uses Ulysses to mark the distance of the tradition's origins, to represent "newer" understandings of the subject and its tribulations. The modernist odysseys clearly belong in this tradition, while the view of Greece that the modernists inherited from their immediate, Hellenist predecessors belongs to an antithetical tradition. Thus for the modernists the turn away from the centripetal longings of Hellenism involved a return to the tradition of centrifugal odysseys. And perhaps Forster illustrates this development best, since his entire writing career is structured around it.

None of the modernists absorbed late-Victorian Hellenism more thoroughly than Forster did, thanks in large part to the years he studied at Cambridge. Hellenism permeates his early work and haunts his mature work. The ideal repeated throughout *Howards End* (1910), "to see life steadily and to see it whole," is a line adapted from Matthew Arnold's description of Sophocles, and Arnold would remain an important influence throughout Forster's life. By 1910 Forster's treatment of this ideal has become ambiguous; his Margaret Schlegel recognizes "it is impossible to see modern life steadily and see it whole, and she had chosen to see it whole. Mr. Wilcox saw steadily" (161). Forster's desire to integrate the two modes of seeing is realized to some extent in the union between Margaret and Mr. Wilcox, though the success of the integration is called into question by the devastation it unleashes. Hellenism becomes further diluted in *A Passage to India* (1924), Forster's only colonial odyssey and his best novel by far. In his encounter with India he resigns himself more fully to the impossibility of seeing modern life steadily and whole, though he often

12. Bush noted this long ago (209–10).

qualifies the recognition by substituting "India" for "modern life." This substitution exports the problems of fragmentation and fatigue, entangling them with the exercise of imperial power. The pattern is roughly analogous to the one we have encountered in Tennyson's "Ulysses." Using Forster's career as a first example, I would like to explore in greater detail this intimate connection between the fascination with Greece and the writing of a colonial odyssey.

Forster's Mediterranean Ideal Succumbs to the Dust of India

Forster required over a decade, including an extended interruption in the composition process, a second sojourn in India, and multiple drafts, to make the transition from his Edwardian novels to the complex colonial perspective of *A Passage to India*. For years, in other words, his thought remained in the grip of the Hellenism he had embraced at Cambridge in the 1890s. Modern Italy served as a direct extension of ancient Greece in his early fiction; both contribute to his anti-modern and anti-Christian "Mediterranean" ideal.[13] His earlier work strove to achieve classical unity either by severely limiting its field of vision or by forcing its material into a unity not entirely earned. In his first published story, "Albergo Empedocle" (1903), he resorts to the same stratagem Haggard had used, making a young protagonist the reincarnation of an ancient Greek. Once Harold remembers his earlier existence, he realizes that in his Greek life "I was better, I saw better, heard better, thought better" (*Albergo Empedocle* 23). Recognizing that such a revival of Greece is forced, Forster locks Harold in an asylum, suggesting that the recovery of his earlier, better self has made him unfit to survive the hypocrisies of modern life, but the narrator's sympathy and Forster's ideal remain with Harold in the asylum. In *Howards End*, the role played by Howards End and its illegitimate heir is a more mature example of Forster striving for a rapprochement with modernity without sacrificing classical unity. However skeptical he may be of Margaret Schlegel's attempts to see life steadily and whole, his focus in this

13. Many of Forster's critics have commented on his Hellenism, including Trilling (chap. 2, "Sawston and Cambridge"), Crews (the chapter "The Limitations of Mythology"), and Stone, but the most comprehensive surveys of the Hellenist influences and characteristics in his work are found in two dissertations, by Hall and Papazoglou. For the stark contrast I am outlining in this section between Hellenism and the modernist colonial odysseys, it is not necessary to delineate the various versions of Hellenism (Arnold's vs. Pater's or Dickinson's, for example), nor to trace the difference between Greece and Italy in Forster's work. Both Hall and Papazoglou discuss the vicissitudes of Hellenism during this period, and Trilling suggests simply that for Forster, "as Greece was to stand for truth, Italy was to stand for passion" (37).

novel remains on a character able to "connect," however high the price. His long-delayed final novel, by contrast, is saved aesthetically by his growing pessimism, as he now focuses on representing the fragmentation. His resignation helps make *A Passage to India* at once less forced in its idealism and more expansive in its reflection.

One place his earlier idealism emerges is in the tendency to associate British colonies with the pre-modern Mediterranean world, a tendency he shares with the romance writers, though in Forster's work it remains a more peripheral concern. In "The Eternal Moment" (1905), a story published before Forster had acquired his own Eastern experiences, the non-European world makes a brief but telling appearance. Miss Raby, the heroine,

> was not enthusiastic over the progress of civilisation, knowing by Eastern experiences that civilisation rarely puts her best foot foremost, and is apt to make the barbarians immoral and vicious before her compensating qualities arrive. And here [in a European village] there was no question of progress: the world had more to learn from the village than the village from the world. (*Eternal Moment* 203)

The village is Vorta, on the southern edge of "Teutonia," and much of its romance for Raby derives from the passionate encounter she had there in her youth with an Italian attendant, an encounter that proves to have been her "eternal moment." The identification between primitive colony and pre-modern Mediterranean world is not as seamless in this passage as it often appears to be in popular adventure stories, for Raby thinks the East can eventually benefit from "progress" in a way that the village of her Italian love cannot. But the Teutonic village, Italian lover, and Eastern colony nevertheless serve common functions as sites of romance, resisting the vicious disenchantment of the civilized world.

Raby's implicit association of an Italian with the East anticipates Cyril Fielding's habit in *A Passage to India* of regarding "an Indian as if he were an Italian." Fielding "often attempted analogies between this peninsula [India] and that other, smaller and more exquisitely shaped, that stretches into the classic waters of the Mediterranean" (64). But in this habit of thought Fielding is closer to the young Forster than to the author of *A Passage to India*. Forster's own Eastern experiences made it more difficult for him to equate contemporary India with the pre-modern West. The new perspective is captured concisely in the "Recollections" of Goldsworthy Lowes Dickinson, who as a Cambridge classicist became first a mentor and later a friend to Forster. They traveled together on the voyage out in 1912, Forster's first visit to India, and years later Forster would write a biography of his friend. Dickinson wondered skeptically: "What indeed is there or can there be in common between the tradition of Greece and that of India?" (qtd. in Forster, *Dickinson* 137).

As a result of this first Indian trip, Forster wondered the same thing and, in a series of book reviews he wrote on Indian topics after returning to England, he traced the fissure back to an earlier encounter between the two traditions, namely, to Alexander the Great's incursions into India. "The Age of Misery," a 1914 review of E. J. Rapson's *Ancient India*, begins with the following summary of Hindu thought:

> Facts are a sign of decay in the world's fabric. They are like dust crumbling out of the palace walls which Brahma, after the thousand Periods ["of about five million years"] that are his night, will rebuild. We cannot conceive of the joy and the beauty of that palace, because facts have silted in through our senses and blocked the soul. (*Albergo Empedocle* 198)

Later in the review Forster turns to the arrival of the Greeks in India and offers the following conclusion about their influence: "Greece, who has immortalized the falling dust of facts, so that it hangs in enchantment for ever, can bring no life to a land that is waiting for the dust to clear away, so that the soul may contemplate the soul" (*Albergo Empedocle* 201). This is his explanation for the historical fact that, following Alexander's invasion of India, "in a few generations the Hellenic influences died out, not through persecution, but because their day was ended. Poseidon becomes Siva on the coins, Artemis a wild Apsara, and the Greek types of Gandhara are lost in the sculptured jungles of Amaravati" ("Jehovah" 731).

As metonym for the world of facts and form, "falling dust" is an ominous choice, even when the dust is "immortalized" through "enchantment." Forster's characterization appears to tip the balance in favor of the Hindu preoccupation with soul, with fatal consequences for the West. To the extent that Britain is supposed to be extending Hellenic ideals to the colonies, the British empire is also tainted by this image of falling dust. In *A Passage to India*, Forster makes explicit the ominous implications for the English:

> The triumphant machine of civilization may suddenly hitch and be immobilized into a car of stone, and at such moments the destiny of the English seems to resemble their predecessors', who also entered the country with intent to refashion it, but were in the end worked into its pattern and covered with its dust. (234)

Though multiple "predecessors" might be referred to here, the earlier book reviews suggest Forster was thinking of the Greeks in particular, and now the dust, rather than an affirmation of worldly detail, has become a sign that the Greek ideal is neither powerful nor eternal. Greece, in its failure, is now aligned with rather than opposed to the failures of modernity. The car, which in *Howards End* represented modernization at its worst, now serves as metaphor for all of Western civilization in its attempt to bring order to the muddle of India. And yet Forster has still not collapsed the distinction between civilization and barbarism: however ironic the reference to "the triumphant machine of civilization," when it hitches nothing remains but dust for the West. This suggests that he knows he cannot turn his back on modernity.

Forster's growing pessimism never leads him to abandon his Hellenism entirely, but only to recognize it as more precariously contingent than he had imagined in the earlier novels. Thus the Mediterranean ideal resurfaces at a critical moment in *A Passage to India*, at the conclusion of its second part, "Caves," when Fielding returns from India to England following Aziz's trial. The ports of call for Fielding's ship retrace the migration of civilization to Europe, a progression similar to that represented in Haggard's *She* by the succession of translations of the shard:

Egypt was charming . . . —bright blue sky, constant wind, clean low coastline, as against the intricacies of Bombay. Crete welcomed him next with the long snowy ridge of its mountains, and then came Venice. . . . The buildings of Venice, like the mountains of Crete and the fields of Egypt, stood in the right place, whereas in poor India everything was placed wrong. He had forgotten the beauty of form among idol temples and lumpy hills; indeed, without form, how can there be beauty? Form stammered here and there in a mosque, became rigid through nervousness even, but oh these Italian churches! (313–14)

Though initially this appears to oppose the religions of India to Christendom, temple and mosque to church, this is in fact Forster's classicism seeping through as an aesthetic ideal once again. Most important about San Giorgio is not that it is a church, but that it is Italian. It reflects

the harmony between the works of man and the earth that upholds them, the civilization that has escaped muddle, the spirit in a reasonable form, with flesh and blood subsisting. . . . Though Venice was not Europe, it was part of the Mediterranean harmony. The Mediterranean is the human norm. When men leave that exquisite lake, whether through the Bosphorus or the Pillars of Hercules, they approach the monstrous and extraordinary; and the southern exit leads to the strangest experience of all. (314)

This passage is a wistful nod to his earlier fiction, often set in the Mediterranean, and it returns in particular to the values of that earlier fiction, distinguishing sharply between the "right" classical form as the only apparent alternative to "wrong" muddle, now located in India.[14] Viewed as an example of imperial culture, it is remarkable for still focusing its centripetal energy on the Mediterranean rather than modern England.

In this passage the literal and the cultural-historical notions of departure and return are nicely blended. We are reminded of classical antiquity as a home or point of departure, the norm from which subsequent epochs and empires depart, geographically and temporally, toward the "monstrous," "extraordinary," and "strange," toward the modern and the exotic. Fielding, as a kind of Odyssean traveler returning from his encounter with the monstrous, reestablishes connection with the ancient norm in traversing the Mediterranean. The journey not only recapitulates the progression of civilization from Egypt to Greece and Italy, it uses these locales to insulate England from its colony: "With Egypt the atmosphere altered. The clean sands heaped on each side of the canal, seemed to wipe off everything that was difficult and equivocal" (295).[15] Not surprisingly, the narrative does not follow Fielding all the way to London; in Forsterian terms, his *nostos* is complete by the time he reaches Venice. The final sentence of the "Caves" section, following immediately on the description of the Mediterranean's three exits, shows Fielding boarding "the train northward" accompanied by "tender romantic fancies that he thought were dead forever" (314).

Given the evocative richness of every detail in the description of his return, we might see in this departure by land and revival of romance something more than realistic detail. In sparing him the journey past the just-mentioned Pillars of Hercules, the boundary stones transgressed by Dante's doomed Ulysses, Forster seems still to dream of an England blessed with Mediterranean clarity. He is fighting to keep England in the orbit of the classical norm, to prevent the centrifugal forces of modernity from reducing the nation to chaos and dust.

Imperial Accommodations in *A Passage to India*

If Fielding's Mediterranean episode reveals the stubbornness of Forster's Hellenism, India, by remaining impervious to such influence,

14. At the age of eighty, Forster wrote "Three Countries," a talk about the influence of Italy, England, and India on his fiction. He concluded by reading this final chapter of "Caves," about Fielding's journey home, as a way of summarizing the relations among the three countries—and thus of indicating his continued attachment to the Mediterranean ideal nearly forty years after completing *A Passage to India* (see *Hill of Devi* 299).

15. These sentences actually describe Adela Quested's passage home in advance of Fielding, along the same route. In her case, too, the narrative follows her return to England only as far as the Mediterranean.

serves now to constrain the classical ideal, as I suggested above. This constraint helps account for the brevity of the Mediterranean scene and for the fact that it does not serve as the novel's final word. Forster's reflections on salvation are in fact focused elsewhere, as demonstrated by his displacement and expansion of the notion of "home."

By the time of *A Passage to India*, Forster's reflections on home have shifted from a terrestrial to a metaphysical realm, reflecting Dante's and Tennyson's influence more than Virgil's. Home is no longer a particular household, England, the Mediterranean world, or the British empire, but a metaphor for universal unity and harmony. It is not only a recurring metaphor in the novel, but an extended one—a network of ideas relating to hospitality, invitation, and accommodation helps focus and link the novel's political and religious concerns. This semantic field encompasses every major plot development: the first encounter between Aziz and Mrs. Moore, beginning in confusion over whether she is welcome in the mosque and ending with the acknowledgment that "Indians are not allowed into the Chandrapore Club even as guests" (21–22); Mr. Turton's disastrous Bridge Party, to which he invites leading Indian families as well as the English in a counterproductive attempt to bridge the distance between races and cultures; the tea party hosted by Fielding which properly initiates the social interaction among him, Aziz, Mrs. Moore, and Adela; the journey to the Marabar caves, with Aziz serving as host to the British women; and the final section of the novel, in which Mrs. Moore's children and Fielding stay in a guest house while visiting Godbole and Aziz. During this series of failed and forced social connections, each of the three major religions represented in the novel makes some claim—or some attempt—to summon a "home" transcending the muddle of this world. The three sections of the novel—"Mosque," "Caves," and "Temple"—correspond roughly to Islam, Christianity, and Hinduism (and viewed in this way the novel delivers its strongest blow to Christianity, represented now for the reader as well as for Mrs. Moore by the dispiriting caves).

In the mosque that provides the title for the novel's first section, Aziz feels at home—"Islam [is] an attitude towards life both exquisite and durable, where his body and his thoughts found their home" (16)—but there is no indication that such a home is meant to be inclusive, a point Aziz later confirms in conversation: "Nothing embraces the whole of India, nothing, nothing" (160). Some Christians, in making a more ambitious effort, succeed in being more inclusive but still fail to embrace the whole. After commenting on the Bridge Party by observing that there are circles of humanity "no earthly invitation can embrace," the narrator proceeds to speculate that

all invitations must proceed from heaven perhaps; perhaps it is futile for
men to initiate their own unity, they do but widen the gulfs between them
by the attempt. So at all events thought old Mr. Graysford and young Mr.
Sorley, the devoted missionaries. . . . In our Father's house are many man-
sions, they taught, and there alone will the incompatible multitudes of
mankind be welcomed and soothed. Not one shall be turned away by the
servants on that verandah, be he black or white. . . . And why should the
divine hospitality cease here? Consider, with all reverence, the monkeys.
May there not be a mansion for the monkeys also? (37)

On this question, Mr. Graysford and Mr. Sorley part company. Mr. Sorley
says yes to monkeys "and he has sympathetic discussions about them
with his Hindu friends." Though less sympathetic to jackals, he acknowledges that

> the mercy of God, being infinite, may well embrace all mammals. And the
> wasps? He became uneasy during the descent to wasps, and was apt to
> change the conversation. And oranges, cactuses, crystals and mud? and
> the bacteria inside Mr. Sorley? No, no, this was going too far. We must ex-
> clude someone from our gathering, or we shall be left with nothing. (38)

Having given Sorley his moment, the novel sends Mrs. Moore into the
Marabar caves and thereby destroys the refuge of Christianity: "all its divine words . . . only amounted to 'boum' " so that the universe now "offered no repose to her soul" (166).

The monkeys, jackals, and wasps are recurring images in the novel
pointing to the greater inclusiveness of the Hindu home, for Godbole has
little trouble integrating them, at least momentarily. Unflappable Godbole
looks as if he might transcend racial and cultural differences as well: "his
whole appearance suggested harmony—as if he had reconciled the products of East and West, mental as well as physical, and could never be dis-
composed" (77). The invitations he issues appear to be the most generous,
and he directs them not only to the creatures of this world but to "my
Lord." As he explains of this Lord, "absence implies presence, absence is
not non-existence, and we are therefore entitled to repeat, 'Come, come,
come, come' " (198). In contrast to both the social and the divine invitations, which are intended to make people feel at home, whether it be in
the house of a friend or the house of the lord, the imperative "Come!" directed at the deity is a lament for the lack of a suitable home—it is an expression of suffering and plea for salvation. Hinduism is depicted as the
most energetic, most determined religion in issuing these pleas of the
homeless, in trying actively to initiate a divine homecoming. And Hinduism is the religion that takes center stage in the brief third and final sec-

tion of the novel, where Forster flirts with a kind of mysticism that he represents through the activities of Godbole and the Hindu religious festival as the rains arrive in India.

It is above all this flirtation with Hinduism that marks the distance Forster has traveled from his emulation of Greece, for the Hindu ceremony is, quite deliberately, "a frustration of reason and form" (319). In "The Gods of India," another book review from 1914, he describes Hinduism in this way:

> Outside the "trayful of dolls" [which Hindu deities appear to be] are the hands that hold the tray, and occasionally tilt it and present the worshipper with emptiness. Krishna and Siva slither into the void. Nothing is more remarkable than the way in which Hinduism will suddenly dethrone its highest conceptions, nor is anything more natural, because it is athirst for the inconceivable. Whatever can be stated must be temporary. (*Albergo Empedocle* 223)

This anticipates and serves as a gloss on the Hindu festival at the end of the novel, when the English visitors and Aziz capsize along with the trayful of gods being thrown away at the climax of the procession. This is the path to truth that Godbole and Hinduism offer, and despite his flirtation Forster clearly is not satisfied. The Hindu religious festival does not suitably answer questions raised throughout the novel; in Forster's handling, the Lord does not answer Godbole's invitation to come. In remaining so thoroughly inconceivable and unseen, the Hindu revelations do not mitigate the discontents with which Forster is wrestling.

These questions and discontents find expression throughout the novel independent of the perspective of any one religion. In a sense, Forster naturalizes the discontents in India: though they derive from the West, he attributes them to the Indian sky and landscape. "The fissures in the Indian soil are infinite" (327) and thus "the scenery, though it smiled, fell like a gravestone on any human hope" (360). The prominence the setting assumes as a symbol of homelessness is evident from the novel's opening and closing passages and from its most important scene, at the Marabar caves. The opening chapter claims that "the overarching sky" in Chandrapore "settles everything," while reminding us of the colorless expanse beyond this "immense vault" (5). The famous final scene has both earth and sky, along with features of the landscape, raising a "hundred voices" to separate Aziz and Fielding, denying them a friendship: "No, not yet. . . . No, not there" (362). Meanwhile Marabar, the novel's most distinctive geographical phenomenon, is also its most severe representation of human vulnerability and unanswered needs. Each cave there "mirrors its own darkness in every direction infinitely" (138); when light is introduced into this void, its reflection instantly brings division, disunity: "The two flames approach and strive to unite, but cannot" (137). And a cave's acoustic effects are similar to its optical effects: all human desire to see life whole is disappointed, every plea for meaning and salvation triggers the answering echo "ou-boum."

Scattered among these three landmark scenes are numerous other passages in which India represents human impotence and suffering, either by providing a negative response to human longing or by embodying that longing and issuing the pleas for salvation itself, through its landscape. In one instance, it is Mrs. Moore's appeal that goes unanswered:

> [God] had been constantly in her thoughts since she entered India, though oddly enough he satisfied her less. She must needs pronounce his name frequently, as the greatest she knew, yet she had never found it less efficacious. Outside the arch there seemed always an arch, beyond the remotest echo a silence. (54)

In another instance, the landscape itself makes a similar appeal: "The countryside was too vast to admit of excellence. In vain did each item in it call out, 'Come, come.' There was not enough god to go round" (93–94). The parallel between these two passages suggests it is Mrs. Moore's God that is "not enough" to go around, that Forster's narrator imposes Europe's theological quandary onto India. Another textual trace of this projection can be found in a passage where the narrator employs a heliotrope:

> Here [in India] the retreat is from the source of life, the treacherous sun, and no poetry adorns it because disillusionment cannot be beautiful. Men yearn for poetry though they may not confess it; they desire that joy shall be graceful and sorrow august and infinity have a form, and India fails to accommodate them. (234)

The disillusioned men referred to so generally are above all Europeans. Desiring that their "infinity have a form," they seek but do not find such accommodation in imperial India. Seeking adequate form might seem to be Forster's Hellenist impulse at work, but to seek and not to find a form for infinity is an especially acute problem of modernity, of an age in which God is perceived to be absent. When Forster exports this problem to India, it is no wonder he remains unsatisfied: the novel tells us that the Hindu ceremony approaches infinity precisely by discarding forms, and his essays have acknowledged that the beauty and joy of the palace of Brahma remain inconceivable, buried by dust. The result suggests that British dreams of discovering renewed power and meaning through empire are illusory; the empire fails to accommodate them.

Forster himself maintained that the novel was concerned less with the two countries' difficult relations than "with the difficulty of living in the universe" (qtd. in Furbank 2: 308). "The book is not really about politics," he asserted; "it's about something wider than politics, about the search of the human race for a more lasting home, about the universe as embodied in the Indian earth and the Indian sky" (*Hill of Devi* 298). My discussion of homelessness and hospitality in the novel supports his assertion, yet this use of India is not without political implications, and for the most part these implications reinforce the novel's political ambiguity. By concentrating the muddle in India, the novel comes close to justifying British rule by suggesting that India needs to have order imposed on it. But by showing the futility of British hopes for a more lasting home, the novel also exposes and undermines some of the motives helping to shape imperial rule. Paradoxically, in other words, the representation of India amounts to a scapegoating of the colony at the same time that it critiques British imperial psychology.

The scapegoating may not have an ideological impetus at first if it derives, as I have suggested, from the projection of domestic discontent, but the ideological consequences of the scapegoating are unfortunate. India's trouble can seem to justify British rule, despite Forster's damning portrait of official Anglo-India. Painting India as a land—and landscape—of suffering, division, and muddle makes British rule seem necessary and at the same time excuses some of its failings, given how intractable the domain is. The depiction of India reinforces Fielding's claim that "England holds India for her good" (121). Criticism of the English is then limited to their unrealistic expectations of empire and to their lack of good manners and good will, as when Mrs. Moore reflects that one touch of "true regret from the heart" would have made her son "a different man, and the British Empire a different institution" (53). In a remarkable passage, the narrator links metaphysical homelessness directly to political invasion. The passage implies, in fact, that the unresolved malaise embodied in India constitutes a treacherous invitation for British imperial rule:

How can the mind take hold of such a country? Generations of invaders have tried, but they remain in exile. The important towns they build are only retreats, their quarrels the malaise of men who cannot find their way home. India knows of their trouble. She knows of the whole world's trouble, to its uttermost depth. She calls "Come" through her hundred mouths, through objects ridiculous and august. But come to what? She has never defined. She is not a promise, only an appeal. (150)

The invasion is by invitation and thus properly speaking no invasion at all—it is almost as if India has seduced her invaders.[16] However, the ambiguity of the novel's representation of empire is fully evident in this passage, which not only locates the malaise in India but then also points to the misguided motives of the most recent generation of conquerors. Tellingly, it is "the mind" attempting a conquest here, seeing its own trouble reflected in India; but the physical invasion promises no solution to this trouble. While projecting the weakness onto India, Forster also recognizes that imperial power cannot dispel or compensate for this weakness. Like Tennyson's "Ulysses," *A Passage to India* flirts with and rejects the dream that colonial travel offers a rejuvenating antidote to disenchantment.

Another scene in which the frustrated search for a transcendental home has striking political implications is at the Marabar caves, an exemplary scene of English weakness and vulnerability. In the Indian caves the ruling race experiences a double assault: Mrs. Moore experiences it metaphysically, Adela Quested physically. As Salman Rushdie and Brenda Silver have noted, a more appropriate metaphor for English/Indian relations would be the rape of an Indian woman by a Englishman, but Forster instead has the English accusing an Indian man of assaulting Adela. Forster's particular alignment of race and sex in the caves, placing the English in a vulnerable position, might be taken as metaphorical support for the suggestion that the imperial impulse originates in a sense of domestic inadequacy and fatigue that is projected abroad. To the extent the Marabar caves embody an intensified version of the modern English subject's troubled relation to the absolute, the shock experienced there by the English is a violent instance of the uncanny: the trouble they are fleeing overtakes them in the form of India. Jenny Sharpe provides an illuminating reading of the alleged assault on Adela by relating it to the 1857 uprisings in India, when fabricated stories of atrocities against English women and children circulated widely and provoked a strong reaction. Sharpe shows that in representing the English response to the Marabar incident, Forster is "critical of a community obsessed with the racial memory of 1857" (39). While agreeing that Forster has this degree of critical detachment from Anglo-India and the defenders of empire, I would merely add that his detachment from the psychology of imperial rule is not complete. Specifically, by leaving unresolved what happened to Adela in the cave, he does not dismiss the racial and sexual fears of the British as unequivocally as he might. More generally, he continues to project an English

16. For a different reading of the themes of invitation and invasion in the novel, see Heath.

malaise onto India even as he recognizes imperial rule is no cure for the malaise; he continues to locate the perplexity of post-theological Europe in the Indian landscape—in the Marabar caves—even as he recognizes that the invading English are arrogant fools for responding to an appeal intended for a god.

The theological problems of modernity will receive more thorough analysis in the next chapter of this book, but some of that analysis is anticipated already in *A Passage to India*, when the narrator comments on divine functions left unfulfilled by the retreat of God and on the human self-assertion involved in striving to assume or reoccupy such functions. For example, one of these divine functions in Christianity was to redeem the totality of history, and in the crucial passage describing the immediate effect of Mrs. Moore's cave visit, the narrator asserts that the devastating "boum" would have echoed even "if one had spoken with the tongues of angels and pleaded for all the unhappiness and misunderstanding in the world, past, present, and to come, for all the misery men must undergo whatever their opinion and position" (165). When angels are incapacitated by a feature of the Indian landscape, little wonder that humans are too. In a philosophical moment following the death of Mrs. Moore, the narrator comments further on human ineffectuality:

> It's only one's own dead who matter. . . . How indeed is it possible for one human being to be sorry for all the sadness that meets him on the face of the earth, for the pain that is endured not only by men, but by animals and plants, and perhaps by the stones? The soul is tired in a moment. (275)

Despite the nod to Godbole's efforts in the reference here to stones, the problem is the West's. The direct link between "one" human and "all" pain identifies the overwhelming burden arising when the human subject assumes divine responsibility for redemption. This passage attests to the weariness resulting from that burden.

With full recognition of the projection taking place in the novel, we recognize also a greater complexity in the relation between Forster's fading Hellenism and his ambiguous imperialism. When the most profound and un-Hellenic features of India actually belong to a displaced modernity, then the weakening of his Hellenism, initially seeming to stem from his encounter with India, appears to result as much from a resignation to the fact that Hellenism allows one neither to resolve nor to avoid the discontents of modernity. The novel's centrifugal force, evident especially in Mrs. Moore's demise, suggests that the discontents of Forster's India, like those of Tennyson's Ulysses, belong primarily to modern Europe. Projecting those discontents onto India and then setting up the Mediterranean as a buffer provides a circumspect way to confront them. The projection positions the discontents potentially to be redeemed through imperial conquest; the occupation of India, in other words, offers hope for the reoccupation of divine functions. "Your sentiments are those of a god," Mrs. Moore complains to her son about his attitude toward his work in India. Irritable, intuitive, destined to pay with her life for the malaise embodied in India, she recognizes one of the buried motives for possessing the empire: "Englishmen like posing as gods" (51). *A Passage to India* exposes such posing, exposes the false hope that imperial power can replace divine power. The failings of the Anglo-Indians and the intractable nature of the problem demonstrate the futility of reoccupation: no worldly force can provide a cure for the malaise Forster projects onto India.

2

"The Drive to Be at Home Everywhere"

The tradition of all the dead generations weighs like a nightmare on the brain of the living.
—KARL MARX, *The Eighteenth Brumaire of Louis Bonaparte*

All history backs our pane of glass.
—VIRGINIA WOOLF, *Jacob's Room*

The most fundamental interpretive questions about modernist colonial odysseys do not concern what meanings are present in their representations of the world, but what meanings are lacking; not what truth inspires their creation, but what void they attempt to fill; not what power they promote, but what debility they reveal. The readings of Tennyson and Forster in the previous chapter have already begun to examine developments in the centrifugal odyssey tradition as responses to the challenges and deficiencies of modernity. Now I propose to explore the source and shape of such deficiencies—and also their relation to imperial power, since the suggestion that some incapacity precedes the expansion of imperial influence runs counter to much recent criticism.

Recent criticism, like imperial culture itself, has frequently employed spatial metaphors of center and margin to characterize the dynamics of imperial domination. Mary Louise Pratt, for example, has spoken of modernity as a collaboration between centrifugal geopolitical forces expanding around the globe and centripetal cultural practices keeping Europe as the norm for a contrasting global periphery. Geographical expansion produces a seemingly limitless content for confirming the universal claims of Western interpretive techniques, which in turn help legitimate the expansion. Thus "modernity needs its Others"; indeed, it is constituted by them.[1] This formulation, in emphasizing the interdependence of England (for example) and its colonies, helps undermine assumptions about the cultural and political sovereignty of the center of empire and is thus a useful critique of English hegemony. But this perspective views modernity primarily as a locus of power, whatever unacknowledged debt this power owes to those who are its subjects. However restless and unlimited the project of modernity, modern culture, according to this analysis, functions first and foremost to center power in Europe.

Pratt's observation, that centrifugal expansion and centripetal knowledge complement each other, can help explain a certain homogeneity among the colonial-odyssey novels, despite their variety of settings. Collectively they disperse characters to diverse cultures and geographical regions—the Eastern Archipelago, India, Africa, and South America—while they all nevertheless follow a similar pattern, incorporating Europe's Others into a long-familiar story. In other words, the supposed exoticism of the novels is always already thoroughly assimilated. At the same time, however, these novels are shaped by many factors beyond Britain's thirst for self-confirming knowledge amid restless territorial expansion. The emphasis on the centripetal power of modern culture does not always acknowledge the extent to which modernity is itself the product of a dramatic decentering. Modern thought bears the marks of an historical rupture often associated with the collapse of Scholasticism, the rediscovery of antiquity, the industrial revolution, and the Copernican revolution. In relation to such displacement, modernist novels appear less as consolidations of imperial power than as attempts to record and perhaps to compensate for the disruption. Edward Said's critical method, so effective at uncovering the imperial subtext in literature ostensibly devoted to domestic topics, must be turned on its head for these novels, which employ colonial settings to mask their struggle with domestic discontents. In actually depicting centrifugal migration, the colonial-odyssey novels do not always have a strongly centering or centripetal effect; in projecting some of the modern age's most haunting problems, they do not inspire confidence in modern rationality; in exploring human mortality, they do not always help consolidate British power.

"Home" has been a recurring and varied motif in theories of modernity as well as in colonial fiction, and thus it offers a useful point of reference

1. This is my retrospective reconstruction of Pratt's comments, which were part of a lecture titled "Postcoloniality, Globality, and the Case of the Stolen Kidney."

for considering the relation of the odyssey novels to the problems of the modern age. The homes for which modernist travelers are nostalgic include, of course, the geographical home of London or England, and the historical home of ancient Greece, as we have seen. But such geographical locations or historical points of departure generally acquire the symbolic significance of imagined social, psychological, and metaphysical homes (hence the fact that the images of Greece, like memories of childhood, often have so little to do with historical reality). Pratt's model, when expressed in terms of home, can nicely exploit the versatility of the metaphor. The imperial home is centered in Europe, however specifically or generally, depending on the context, one conceives of this home: household, metropolis, nation, modernity. But the centrifugal force she describes is not, strictly speaking, a desertion of home, as Stanford characterizes the centrifugal branch in the odyssey tradition; rather it represents an expansion of home, reflecting a desire to be at home everywhere. (We have discovered some desire in Tennyson's Ulysses, more in Forster's characters, not merely to desert home but to expand it worldwide.) One distinction between colonialism and imperialism is that the former manifests this desire to be at home even far from the center, a desire to conquer and sometimes to settle. And then the question becomes, what is it, apart from geographical centrality, that defines a home?

In metaphorical usage, home is a place where the meaning of experience is fully immanent, where the totality of a world is fully accessible to the subject. The concept of totality is indispensable, I believe, for understanding the centrifugal force Pratt describes, the need for new content to confirm universal epistemological claims. With the concept of totality, and in particular by exploring the historical roots of the habit of thinking in terms of totality, one can bring sharper definition to the crises and questions triggering modernity's voracious appetite for knowledge and power. The historical genesis of the totalizing impulse is often overlooked in discussions of modernity and modernism, and in this chapter I supply this lack primarily by drawing on the work of Hans Blumenberg. Through this historical contextualization, I hope to illuminate some of the ways in which the modern age represents its loss of access to the totality of the world (in the novel, for example). I hope also to explore some of the makeshift homes with which modernity attempts to compensate for this loss, the sort of homes provided by romance, nationalism, imperialism on a global scale, and Enlightenment or Marxist teleologies. Any such home, in claiming to offer a lost plenitude, opens itself to attack from those who feel either suffocated or excluded, or who are otherwise disillusioned about the claim. The colonial-odyssey novels in particular are in the grip of a totalizing impulse, but they also reveal disillusionment about available outlets for this impulse—they explore the failure of imperialism to make a suitable home of a global totality and the persistence of a transcendental homelessness in the modern age.

This chapter explores various visions of home and representations of homelessness through discussions of Edward Said, James Joyce, Georg Lukács, Fredric Jameson, Hans Blumenberg, Friedrich Nietzsche, and Sigmund Freud. The varying critical perspectives derive from different understandings of the totality that modernist fiction strives to represent. The nation, global empire, and metaphysical transcendence are some of the "worlds" taken to be the ultimate mimetic focus of modernist fiction, worlds that promise a home, whether the home is perceived as a site of fulfillment or of repression, whether the totality is utopian and all-encompassing or makeshift and self-subsisting. My aim is to show how the former two worlds, nation and empire, take their shape from the latter, the transcendental quandaries of modern European thought. A methodological consequence of this approach is that any analysis of the novel's involvement in national and imperial culture must also eventually account for the way the genre responds to metaphysical questions.

Said's rejection of nationalism provides our point of departure. In place of nationalism he offers a valorized "exile," indicating, I believe, that he underestimates the persistence of the need for a "home" that nationalism promises to satisfy. Joyce's Leopold Bloom likewise rejects nationalism, but in his case the rejection expands to encompass all history, and he feels obliged to state an alternative ("love") in more affirmative terms. An attempt to align Bloom's rejection and affirmation with those of Joyce's novel as a whole leads to questions about the genre and its relation to homelessness and home-seeking in the modern age, questions that take us beyond analyses of national identity. A discussion of Lukács's description of the novel as the epic of "transcendental homelessness" brings into full view the theological implications of the home motif. Having passed through this series of political, cultural, and theological conceptions of home and exile, I shall attempt in the second half of this chapter to reconcile these levels of analysis and focus them in a manner useful for reading the modernist colonial odysseys. Blumenberg offers a way to critique and transform Lukács's preoccupation with "totality," and Jameson suggests a way to relate Blumenberg's anthropological view of totalizing thought to modernist authors and their empire. I hope to integrate these multiple critical perspectives in order to demonstrate the representational complexity of modernist colonial fiction. The key to integrating such diverse contexts and perspectives—such varying conceptions of home—will be

Blumenberg's description of the estrangement at the core of modern culture, a lack shaping and haunting modern knowledge and imagination.

Exile versus Nationalism in Said's Secular Criticism

No one has influenced postcolonial criticism more than Edward Said, and yet the term is not one he generally chooses to apply to his own work. This reticence may reflect an understandable uneasiness with the temporal implications of the prefix *post*: the suggestion that the world has moved into a period after colonialism requires a problematic blindness to neocolonialism, while Said by contrast has often criticized the continued virulence of Orientalist patterns of thought in contemporary discourse and called attention to the ongoing suffering of Palestinians. But the term "postcolonial" can be construed in many ways other than the narrow temporal one, and his disregard of the label might best be understood not as a rejection, but merely as a consequence of his enthusiasm for a curious alternative: "secular criticism."

Said's secular criticism clearly echoes and allies itself with the values of secular humanism, and yet his use of the term "secular" has provoked confusion and comment.[2] The term derives much of its complexity in his work from his practice of linking it to the experience of exile and his positive valuation of exile. Given the sort of literary and political issues he has routinely addressed, exile must of course be understood literally, as long-term physical absence from one's native country. He has explained in an interview that "secular interpretation" argues "above all . . . for the potential of a community that . . . is not geographically and homogeneously defined" (Wicke and Sprinker 233). This praise of exile has led some to see his secularism as devoid of theological implications: "Perhaps the most crucial meaning of *secular* in [Said's] usage, is as an opposing term not to religion but to nationalism" (Robbins, "Secularism" 26). Such equation of anti-nationalism and secularism is perhaps a natural extension of the notion that nationalism is a kind of religion, a notion that is itself a symptom of the intensified rivalry among European states during the modernist period. But if describing nationalism as a religion reveals something about the psychology of nationalism, it produces a very limited understanding

2. Much of this commentary has appeared in two essay collections devoted to Said, edited by Sprinker and by Ansell-Pearson, Parry, and Squires. See also *Social Text* 40 (1994) both for a symposium on Said and for Robbins' article, and see Mufti's response to Robbins.

of religion and secularism, the history of which predate and cannot be contained within ideologies of nationalism. While anti-nationalist impulses are clearly a central component of Said's thought, the deeper resonance of "secular criticism" emerges only when we emphasize its theological implications.

The conclusion to *The World, the Text, and the Critic*, titled "Religious Criticism" (complementing the introductory essay, "Secular Criticism"), conceives of religion broadly in dismissing what Said sees as a dominant strain in postwar literary criticism. He laments the "dramatic increase in the number of appeals to the extra-human, the vague abstraction, the divine, the esoteric and secret" in literary criticism, appeals which have the effect of "shutting off human investigation, criticism, and effort in deference to the authority of the more-than-human, the supernatural, the other-worldly" (290–91). While nationalism may be one such "authority," it becomes clear in such passages that his secularism constitutes a plea for critical premises and procedures that are entirely immanent in human history and thus are anti-theological in a way that extends beyond anti-nationalism. This realization also complicates the notion of exile, which becomes associated through secularism not only with anti-nationalism but with freedom from all "extra-human" and "other-worldly" authority. For "exile," as for the odyssey motif in modernist fiction, the literal, geographical sense of the term begins to fade as its metaphorical range expands. What is remarkable in Said's work, given his use of the terms "secular" and "religious," is that he never allows the metaphorical range of "exile" to expand very far.

When exile is allowed to denote more than the immediate cultural effects of geographical dislocation, we find in it a Romantic expression of alienation and the Judeo-Christian precedents for such expression. The commonplace euphemism for death as a "return home" captures the theological model of fall and redemption in the metaphors of home and exile (with expulsion from Eden serving as humankind's first experience of forced exile). The secular adaptation of these metaphors emerges, to name one convenient example, in the dictum of Novalis that "philosophy is actually homesickness—the drive to be at home everywhere" (422). Here the desire to be at home does not necessarily lead out of this world or this life, and the hopeful agent of restoration ("philosophy") is now in the hands of humankind. Lukács drew on Novalis in describing the novel as the genre representing transcendental homelessness, a description that hints at the gravity that the notion of exile can assume in the modern age. While this Romantic conception of the home/exile antithesis is modern in its content, in its indulgence of the desire for *nostos* or return it is fundamentally anti-modern. Even though Novalis and Lukács are decidedly secular in their recognition that homes must be found within history, they implicitly compare such worldly homes to those evoked by theological uses of the metaphor—they remain burdened, in other words, by the theological model of exile and return.[3] Such nostalgia is a strand of Romantic thought that survives in various permutations to the present day. Vincent Pecora, in *Households of the Soul*, has shown its continuous and pervasive influence, through the idea of *oikos*, or noble household, in nineteenth and twentieth-century ethnology and literary criticism, including deconstruction. And one might easily and fruitfully extend his analysis to much postcolonial criticism.

Not, however, to Said. The semantic range of his "home" and "exile" never extends so far. Nostalgia does not play a significant role in his work, not even implicitly or subversively. One of the most impressive features of his thought is its determined commitment to modernity, a commitment reflected most forcefully in his preference for exile over rootedness. In other words, he does not reject modern thought in his critique of modern imperialism. This commitment is also evident in a series of oppositions he employs to reject the traditional in favor of the modern: filiation vs. affiliation, for example, and *Gemeinschaft* vs. *Gesellschaft*, oppositions analogous to the home/exile dialectic I have been tracing. In connecting the high incidence of exile among modernist authors to the shift from filiation to affiliation in the literature of this period, he explains that

> if a filial relationship was held together by natural bonds and natural forms of authority—involving obedience, fear, love, respect, and instinctual conflict—the new affiliative relationship changes these bonds into what seem to be transpersonal forms—such as guild consciousness, consensus collegiality, professional respect, class, and the hegemony of a dominant culture. The filiative scheme belongs to the realms of nature and of "life," whereas affiliation belongs exclusively to culture and society. (*The World, the Text* 20)

He acknowledges that this development in literary culture parallels observations by sociologists and "developments in the structure of knowl-

---

3. For a discussion of other Romantic expressions of the home-seeking impulses that I discuss in this chapter, see Abrams' analysis of "natural supernaturalism," a term that indicates his concern "with the secularization of inherited theological ideas and ways of thinking." In "a time of profound cultural crisis," he explains, the Romantics set out "to reconstitute the grounds of hope and to announce the certainty, or at least the possibility, of a rebirth in which a renewed mankind will inhabit a renovated earth where he will find himself thoroughly at home. . . . Despite their displacement from a supernatural to a natural frame of reference, however, the ancient problems, terminology, and ways of thinking about human nature and history survived" (12–13).

edge," and he specifically notes Ferdinand Tönnies' distinction between *Gemeinschaft* and *Gesellschaft* (20). Tönnies also serves as a point of reference in Pecora's study, which shows how *Gemeinschaft* is influenced by the ideal of the *oikos*, or noble household. As a variation of the ancient Greek opposition between household and marketplace, Tönnies' opposition is evaluative as well as descriptive: his sympathy lies with the traditional rural community over modern urban society. Said's discussion of secular affiliation turns Tönnies' values on their head, a reversal apparent, for example, when Said describes religion as a kind of *Gemeinschaft*, "a token of submerged feelings of identity, of tribal solidarity" (Wicke and Sprinker 232).

Yet Tönnies' opposition also helps bring to light a tension in—and a fundamental challenge for—Said's approach. Said is often critical of "society" or "culture," terms one would associate with *Gesellschaft*, while he talks about desiring a "community," the standard translation of *Gemeinschaft*. In the interview cited above, he argues for a community that is not geographically and homogeneously defined, but as long as Tönnies' terms remain in the background, this argument appears to be self-canceling, for Said wishes to exclude the very characteristics that define a community—its rooted homogeneity. This bind highlights the difficulty of imagining what his alternative community would look like. In it, presumably, one would find the new kind of humanism Said desires, the result of "reconceiving human experience in non-imperialist terms" (*Culture and Imperialism* 276); however, the problem is that this goal remains a colorless abstraction, defined in negative terms if at all. In a discussion of Lukács, Adorno, and Fanon, Said praises their socially transgressive, "intransigent" uses of theory to resist "reconciliatory" gestures, "facile universalism," and "over-general totalizing." He sees in them "an intellectual, and perhaps moral, community of a remarkable kind, *affiliation* in the deepest and most interesting sense of the word" ("Travelling Theory Reconsidered" 265). But such a notion of community underestimates the strength of the human need for integration and totality. The impracticality of a community based on "intransigent practice" emerges when Said approves Fanon's suggestion that a national government ought to "dissolve itself" (264), but such radicalism is necessary because a more constructive notion of community risks becoming "reconciliatory" (253). This risk was anticipated in Said's discussion of the three phases of modernist culture: the crisis in filiation, the compensatory turn to affiliation, and finally—here is the obstacle to any nontraditional community—the reinscription of the authority associated with the past filiative order in the new system of affiliation. So the "affiliation can easily become a system of thought no less orthodox and dominant than culture itself" (*The*

World, The Text 20). The Sisyphean task is to keep one's affiliations liberated and liberating, in defiance of the profound co-opting power of culture.

Said's background and his political engagement give his work much of its moral force, making him a persuasive defender of secular modernity—and thus he provides an important point of reference for the ambivalent modernity of the modernist colonial odysseys. But the key concept and historical context of secularism are more fully articulated in the work of others who possess a more acute sense of the metaphysical quandaries associated with the crisis in filiation. For this articulation I propose turning to Lukács and Blumenberg, taking a route that leads through *Ulysses.*

Joyce's novel provides a useful test for Said's method of dismissing nationalism in favor of a less homogenous understanding of community. Unlike the colonial-odyssey novelists, Joyce occupies an ambiguous position in the empire, neither in the metropolitan center nor on the global periphery (and he is not attempting to negotiate the distance between these extremes).[4] An analogous ambiguity in the novel's protagonist, Leopold Bloom, an outsider in his home of Dublin, has tempted some critics to look to the novel for an example of the liberating, heterogeneous community imagined by Said as an alternative to nationalism and imperialism. But Bloom's own comments about national identity raise doubt about the existence of such a community, and other critics' observations about Joyce's mimetic strategies will lead us to look beyond Dublin in search of the novel's "home." The expanded perspective arrived at through this excursus on *Ulysses* and its critics will con-

---

4. Similarities in the experience of Conrad and Joyce deserve brief comment in light of the inclusion of one and exclusion of the other in this study (based on the fact that one created fictional journeys from the European center to the colonial periphery while the other did not). Both wrote in voluntary exile from nations that met with more success as cultural entities than as political ones. All the more striking, therefore, is the contrast between the works in which each goes farthest toward writing a national epic. The distance between *Ulysses* and *Nostromo* is not merely technical, significant as the differences in technique are; more fundamental is that Joyce's encyclopedic impulse aims to evoke Dublin life while Conrad's fiction is about its own failure to imagine society in its totality. The chapter of this book on Conrad includes an examination of Charles Gould's imposition of order on the Occidental Republic, which succeeds only temporarily and only under the threat of the violent destruction of his mine—and hence of the Republic—by dynamite. That Joyce is more successful in embodying the life of the nation is related in part, perhaps, to obvious differences in the exiled writers' positions. Joyce was a British colonial subject; Conrad never was. Joyce always returned home imaginatively in his work; Conrad never set his stories in Poland and instead turned routinely to exotic locales and exile experiences for his subject matter. In adopting England and the English language (a linguistic choice Joyce never made in the same way), Conrad made himself more distant from the struggles of Polish nationalism than Joyce ever became from the Irish situation. Conrad assumed the perspective of his adopted home and audience, the position of a European journeying imaginatively to colonies outside of Europe.

firm that the novel as a genre is inherently secular in its structures of representation, a fact emphasized by both Lukács and Blumenberg.

Excursus on *Ulysses,* Nationalism, and Mimesis

Joyce's exile, his cosmopolitanism, his rejection of Irish nationalism and the Catholic church, and his use of classical models and modernist techniques all contributed to his image as an apolitical author. But in recent years a growing body of political criticism of his work has undermined this image by reexamining his relation to imperialism and national identity. Not surprisingly, such criticism has also placed new emphasis on the concept of mimesis as readers attempt to see early-twentieth-century Irish and British history reflected in, for example, *Ulysses.* The renewed emphasis on mimesis, however, also reveals the limits of criticism that takes nationalism as its ultimate frame of reference, since the mimetic function of the genre leads well beyond the reach of national identity. Bloom's comments in *Ulysses* on nationalism and what is "really" life offer a point of reference for discussing the work of four Joyceans who make varying use, implicitly or explicitly, of the concept of mimesis.

One famous passage in the Cyclops episode demonstrates humorously, at the expense of Bloom, the challenge of defining what Joyce calls the spirit or soul of a nation. While talking with acquaintances in Barney Kiernan's pub, Bloom becomes short on words when asked to define "nation":

> —But do you know what a nation means? says John Wyse.
> —Yes, says Bloom.
> —What is it? says John Wyse.
> —A nation? says Bloom. A nation is the same people living in the same place.
> —By God, then, says Ned, laughing, if that's so I'm a nation for I'm living in the same place for the past five years.
> So of course everyone had a laugh at Bloom and says he, trying to muck out of it:
> —Or also living in different places.
> —That covers my case, says Joe.
> —What is your nation if I may ask, says the citizen.
> —Ireland, says Bloom. I was born here. Ireland.
> The citizen said nothing only cleared the spit out of his gullet and, gob, he spat a Red bank oyster out of him right in the corner. (323–24; 12.1419–33)[5]

5. References to *Ulysses* provide first the page numbers of the 1961 Random House edition, then the episode and line numbers from the 1986 Gabler edition.

Bloom's mocking interlocutors point to the difficulty of defining national identity through geography, and so his mucking response introduces into his formulation the notion of "difference." The meaning of a nation is the same people living in the same place or in different places. This definition links four terms—people, places, sameness, and difference—in every possible combination except one: Bloom never links "difference" and "people." The initial response of his companions perpetuates the omission, for their narrow understanding of place is merely the result of their absurd reduction of "people," Bloom's plural form, to the private world of the first-person singular pronoun, the "I" of "I'm a nation." But the exclusion of others in this nation of one calls attention implicitly to the question of differences among people in a national community; indeed, the question of whether and how a nation incorporates such differences may be the most important issue raised in this passage. The scene culminates in a conflict arising from racial difference, from the characters' consciousness of Bloom's Jewishness. Thus the one connection Bloom does not make explicit in his fumbling definition becomes, in its absence, the central issue in the conversation.

Bloom's omission can be understood partly as an unsuccessful attempt to evade the citizen's anti-Semitism. In responding to the citizen's hostile interrogation, he asserts his membership in the national community, and his solidarity with his pub acquaintances, by once again falling back on the sameness of place: "I was born here."[6] Insisting on differences among people within a nation would directly challenge the citizen's view and go against Bloom's conciliatory nature. Perhaps we also witness here the limits of Bloom's intelligence, less nimble than Stephen's, leaving him unable to articulate persuasively the "meaning" of a nation when he is confronted by the exaggerated Socratic challenges of pub companions. But Bloom's omission may also go beyond mere conciliation or inarticulateness and demonstrate a mature recognition of inherent limits to the meaning of nation in turn-of-the-century Dublin.

Readers of *Ulysses* have not always shared Bloom's momentary reticence on the question of diversity within a nation. Vincent Cheng, for example, has emphasized the coexistence of difference and national consciousness, and his criticism demonstrates some of the difficulties Bloom might have encountered had he wished to construct a rational response to the citizen (to which the citizen would have in any case remained deaf). Under the influence of Said, Pratt, and Homi Bhabha, Cheng offers a usefully detailed discussion of the relation between race and nation in the novel. This discussion leads to a celebration of *Ulysses* as a "performance"

6. Gifford describes the debates over whether any "Irish-born man" was truly Irish, or "only Gaels" (130). See also Cheng's discussion of this issue.

of Irish nationality—a performance "allowing for solidarity/likeness while accepting and respecting heterogeneous difference" (247). In attempting to strike a balance between sameness and difference, his concluding formulation understands sameness as shared difference:

> *Ulysses*, through the images revealed in its "nicely polished looking-glass" of the cultural contact zone that was Dublin in 1904, advocates an acceptance simultaneously of heterogeneity and difference, on the one hand, and, on the other hand, of a potential sameness and solidarity of shared similarities-in-difference—between Irish, Jewish, black, Oriental, Indian, English, Boer, paleface, redskin, jewgreek and greekjew—within a multivalent, inter-nationalist perspective. (248)

Cheng's desire here to show Joyce forgoing "binary polarization" and frozen "essences" is welcome, and his emphasis on diversity attempts to rectify Bloom's omission in defining what a nation is. But the difficulty he faces (like Bloom and the rest of us) is evident in this precarious conceptual balancing act, which produces a rather tenuous solidarity: what links different people to one another is their difference from one another.

Such tenuousness derives from the fact that Cheng sees in the "nicely polished looking-glass"[7] of *Ulysses* primarily a fully realized national identity; for him the mimetic function of the novel remains focused on 1904 Dublin, and the internationalism he perceives there, conceived for the most part as an accumulation of national identities, offers no constructive alternatives to ethnicity for understanding either identity or difference. The sensitivity we witnessed in Said to the ease with which liberating affiliations are reinscribed in systems of authority should serve as a warning about any attempt to secure identity based solely on the distinction between emancipatory and oppressive forms of nationalism, a distinction difficult to preserve (cf. Cheng 246). When the only similarity people share is their national differences, it becomes impossible to specify a solidarity that provides either the nation or the novel with cohesiveness. Conversely, understanding difference primarily in terms of national identities precludes the possibility of adequately assessing other forms of difference (metaphysical, temporal, linguistic). The forms of foreignness confronted and sometimes incorporated by Joyce and his characters are not merely national. "Difference," like "secular," is a term more usefully

7. The phrase comes from Joyce's letter of 23 June 1906, one of a series to publisher Grant Richards defending *Dubliners:* "It is not my fault that the odour of ashpits and old weeds and offal hangs round my stories. I seriously believe that you will retard the course of civilisation in Ireland by preventing the Irish people from having one good look at themselves in my nicely polished looking-glass" (*Letters* 1: 63–64).

understood as not only including but also extending beyond national contexts.[8]

Bloom himself seems aware that national consciousness is an insufficient framework for identity and that it in any case cannot be viewed merely as a passing "performance," as the multivalent spectacle of the day. The passage I have been discussing from the Cyclops episode is framed by Bloom's reflections on history, reflections that provide an important context for the difficulty he experiences in providing a positive definition of the nation for his pub companions. He is delivering an excited discourse on "persecution" when he observes that "all the history of the world is full of it. Perpetuating national hatred among nations" (323; 12.1417–18). Provoked by the citizen's anti-Semitic taunts when already upset by the thought of Boylan's tryst with Molly at "this very moment" (325; 12.1468, 1471), Bloom grows bolder and defiantly asserts his Jewishness. His indignant resistance then "collapses all of a sudden":

> —But it's no use, says he. Force, hatred, history, all that. That's not life for men and women, insult and hatred. And everybody knows that it's the very opposite of that that is really life.
> —What? says Alf.
> —Love, says Bloom. I mean the opposite of hatred. (325; 12.1481–85)

With such comments Bloom expands the discussion beyond Dublin and Irish history to a topic the novel foregrounds early on: "all the history of the world." Haines's deterministic (and thus self-exculpating) explanation of imperialism in the novel's first episode—"We feel in England that we have treated you rather unfairly. It seems history is to blame" (20; 1.648–49)—echoes in Stephen's mind in the second episode, the art of which Joyce designates as history (30; 2.246–47). It is here in "Nestor" that Stephen famously proclaims to his English employer: "History is a nightmare from which I am trying to awake" (34; 2.377). In these contexts the nightmare of history is clearly the nightmare of "national hatred among nations," and by insisting this is only a nightmare, not "really life," Bloom rejects not only anti-Semitism and British imperialism, but "all the history of the world"—and he arrives potentially at an affirmation that reaches farther as well.

8. Nolan, adapting an argument made by Wyndham Lewis, emphasizes the modernity of nationalism despite its claims to tradition, and thus she also indicates that national difference is a rather late form of difference: "a world in which people and places are growing more alike becomes obsessed with fetishizing their residual differences" (11). But she offers a very different interpretation than the one proposed here of the importance of Irish nationalism for understanding Bloom and the citizen. For his less sentimental view of Bloom, see 96–119.

Bloom's definition of love points to a view of human solidarity that is independent of and more inclusive than categories of national and ethnic identity; in fact human solidarity is here opposed to national solidarity and to history, raising questions about its prospects. Indeed, his vision of life as love leads him, paradoxically, into greater isolation, for his renunciation of nationalism and history divides him from many of his compatriots. The text amusingly calls attention to the irony of this isolating communalism in one of the chapter's interposed parodies: "Love loves to love love. . . . Jumbo, the elephant, loves Alice, the elephant. . . . You love a certain person. And this person loves that other person because everybody loves somebody but God loves everybody" (325–26; 12.1493–1501). In addition to making love banal, this passage calls into question the totalizing impulse of Bloom's ideal by hinting at its impracticality: even if everybody loves somebody, only a God can love everybody. Yet the irony does not completely negate Bloom's ethic of love, in part because he has already demonstrated a moving yet unsentimental awareness of the challenges such an ethic faces, as when, in the Hades episode, thinking of his deceased father, he contrasts a pull toward death, "the love that kills," to "warm beds: warm fullblooded life" (112; 6: 997–1005). His moving refusal to answer force with force later in the day shows that despite the challenges he is prepared to live up to his own ideal. By advocating universal love, he also implicitly acknowledges that in rejecting one absolute, such as nationalism and its hatreds, one cannot automatically dispense with the need for some other absolute; one cannot simply embrace indeterminacy and contingency and difference without leaving unsatisfied a persistent need for wholeness and integration. In striving to answer this need without *ressentiment*, Bloom's ethic is as noble as it is pitiable.

Ulysses as a whole finds itself caught in a bind similar to the one Bloom struggles with here. In its variety of style and plenitude of detail, the book seems to frustrate any search for unity; yet it also invites the reader to search and to hope for a coherent pattern of mimesis. The Cyclops episode contributes to this tension, for it is the first in which we find neither Bloom's voice nor an objective narrator. David Hayman notes that in this chapter Joyce has begun "imposing boldly stated literary conventions on an elaborately realistic matrix" (246), and Karen Lawrence similarly observes that here the initial style of *Ulysses*, which she calls the "narrative norm," completely disappears (*Odyssey of Style* 43, 101). One possible method of synthesis hinted at in this chapter, as in the book as a whole, is found in the use of Homer, a use Joyce foregrounded in the book's title as well as in its schemata, the totalizing structures he constructed and then temporarily withheld from readers. But if the epic background seems to promise a framework for integration and interpretation, the irony Joyce consistently directs at that background keeps the promise unfulfilled.

In the Cyclops episode, for example, the ekphrasis devoted to a crusty snot-rag hilariously parodies Homer's description of Achilles' shield in the *Iliad*.[9] The citizen produces the cloth to wipe his mouth after spitting into the corner in response to Bloom's claim to be Irish, and like the scenes on Achilles' shield, the embroidery on the snot-rag evokes the ideal life of the community. Joyce's ironic context undermines both the Greek and the Irish representations of this ideal. A short time later, when Bloom declares to the citizen not only his Irishness but his Jewishness, the narrator introduces a similarly ironic reference to the *Odyssey*. The burning stake Odysseus uses to blind Polyphemous becomes, in Bloom's hands, a danger to Bloom himself: "Gob, he near burnt his fingers with the butt of his old cigar," comments the narrator (325; 12.1469). Once again the mockery cuts in multiple directions: Bloom's pacifism calls attention to Odysseus' use of violence in an encounter with the Cyclops that supposedly demonstrates the superiority of civilization to barbarism; the consumed cigar and burnt fingers symbolically suggest both the inefficacy of Bloom's response to the citizen and his pain over Molly's infidelity; and the mockery reminds us anew of the narrator's opportunistic malice.

Two ideologically distant critics, Wolfgang Iser and Fredric Jameson, have described the effect of such irony in strikingly similar terms. Iser calls the Homeric scheme "a structured blank"; Jameson "an empty form" (*Implied Reader* 230; "*Ulysses* in History" 131). Because they recognize that the novel fails to fill in this blank by fully integrating classical allusion with Dublin detail, both critics implicitly reject Ezra Pound's suggestion that the Homeric correspondences are "a scaffold" of more concern to Joyce than to the reader (406). Iser associates the structured blank with "indeterminacy"; Jameson favors the term "contingency." Iser argues that

> according to whether one reads the novel from the Dublin viewpoint or from that of the *Odyssey*, one will get quite different 'images'. In the first case, the apparent lack of connection between the many details creates the impression of a thoroughly chaotic world; in the second, one wonders

9. Prier argues that a deep affinity between Joyce's style and Homer's ultimately moderates the parodic effect of this ekphrasis and the Cyclops episode (51, 57, and passim). Homer provides Joyce with an archaic style "powerfully centripetal" to balance the "centrifugal" nature of modern prose, according to Prier (62). The linguistic imitation of Homer's catalogue style is Joyce's answer to his "*real*" problem": "How is one to create meaning through language, to create a linguistics, without falling into sophistic meaninglessness?" (65).

what the return of Ulysses in modern trappings is supposed to signify. (199)

It remains for the implied reader, Iser contends, to bring together these two contexts. But he acknowledges that the proliferation of information makes this a formidable task. Thus his influential analysis of the novel's irony remains ambiguous about the extent to which a real reader should be expected to provide a synthesis. He claims the novel reveals "the indeterminate nature of all phenomena" (212) and at times he suggests the reader, rather than determining meaning, is to take from the novel this sense of indeterminacy: the achievement of *Ulysses* is that it avoids the "illusory coherence" provided by other novels (232). Yet he acknowledges in passing how unsettling the experience can be for the reader, who is overburdened with details and "can never hope to encompass it all" (233). The reader, he explains, "will search for a 'complete picture' of everyday life, and this is precisely what the novel withholds from him" (232). He concludes that "for many Joyce readers, 'interpretation' is a form of refuge-seeking—an effort to reclaim the ground which has been cut from under their feet" (233).[10]

If Iser wavers between a celebration of indeterminacy and half-acknowledged uneasiness with it, Jameson attacks the uneasiness head-on. The contingency or "dissociation of the existent and the meaningful" reflected in Joyce's representation of Dublin results for Jameson from the loss of traditional community (129). He perceives more acutely than Iser the risk of "an infinite proliferation of detail" contributing to a narrative process that might be "infinitely extended," and the Homeric correspondences intervene arbitrarily to control this risk (132). *Ulysses* demonstrates in the aesthetic realm a characteristic of all life under capitalism: the alienation of creative labor from the product of that labor. Thus Jameson views *Ulysses* as a symptom more than as a critique of the absence of community, but as a symptom it has its uses: it provokes a process Jameson calls "dereification" (133ff.). The challenges presented to the reader by the text,

10. In subsequent work Iser expands the terms from his analysis of Joyce and Homer into a general "literary anthropology." The theory of mimesis that is part of this anthropology moves him closer to the positions of Deane and Bersani, discussed below. Iser claims that mimesis aims at "making the absent present," at creating "images to mirror forth the unknowable" (*Prospecting* 282–83). The "structured blank," as he perceives the Homeric scheme in his earlier criticism, becomes the "structured void" of all fictional forms in his literary anthropology (283); the indeterminacy located between Homeric frame and Dublin detail is later generalized and transformed into "the interplay between the fictional and the imaginary" (279). Iser's late literary anthropology derives from a long tradition of philosophical anthropology and especially from the most significant recent representative of that tradition, Hans Blumenberg. See also Iser's *The Fictive and the Imaginary*.

in other words, are less an invitation to play, as Iser sometimes suggests, than a guard against a falsely "codified symbolic order" (132) or premature synthesis. Jameson's analysis serves as a useful reminder that the creation of community is not merely a question of cognition or exegesis, that literary questions of synthesis and disintegration always have a political dimension.[11]

Another pair of critics perceive Joyce to be going a step beyond indeterminacy and dereification: Seamus Deane and Leo Bersani do not merely approve or critique the lack of synthesis but discover in the novel a utopian element, a striving to imagine what a successful synthesis, community, or nation might look like. By drawing out this element, both critics remain acutely aware that Joyce shares Bloom's isolation in relation to the imagined community, that Joyce's isolating rejections are commensurate with his encyclopedic inclusiveness. This is the paradox of mimesis in *Ulysses*, which evokes an absent totality. Despite their common recognition of this paradox, Deane and Bersani offer two dramatically different descriptions of the novel's imagined community or absent totality. Deane focuses on Joyce's language,

> a language in which the desire for universality expresses itself, paradoxically, in the most arcane form imaginable. In breaking away from the restrictions of a local nationality and from the kinds of identity conferred upon him by tradition, Joyce achieved a language which, by the sheer number of its polyglot associations, appears to be all-inclusive and yet which, by the sheer complexity of its narrative orders, manages to be almost wilfully exclusive. ("Joyce and Nationalism" 178)

Bersani similarly observes that

> Joyce miraculously reconciles uncompromising mimesis with a solipsistic structure. Western culture is saved, indeed glorified, through literary metempsychosis: it dies in the Joycean parody and pastiche, but, once removed from historical time, it is resurrected as a timeless design. (170)

Despite their differences of emphasis and evaluation, Deane and Bersani both offer accounts of mimesis in *Ulysses* that capture the irony of the novel, which functions not merely as a nicely polished looking-glass but

11. For another analysis of Jameson's argument, see Kershner, who discusses Jameson and Joyce in relation to the Frankfurt School. For a reading of the Cyclops episode that sees more comedy than tragedy in its narrative economy, see Osteen: "the comic economy of *Ulysses* displays a continual competition between rigid design and riotous exuberance," resulting in an "anguished laughter" (274).

strives to create the reality it wishes to represent. For Deane, such irony in Joyce carries an Irish accent:

> In revealing the essentially fictive nature of political imagining, Joyce did not repudiate Irish nationalism. Instead he understood it as a potent example of rhetoric which imagined as true, structures that did not and were never to exist outside language. . . . It enabled [him] to apprehend the nature of fiction, the process whereby the imagination is brought to bear upon the reality which it creates. (183)[12]

Deane is not working here with a narrowly focused socio-historical conception of mimesis, locating the novel's national affiliations in the streets of Dublin in 1904; rather he places such affiliation in the imagination, as an object of desire. Nationalism and novel share a utopian impulse. His description, in other words, focuses less on the historical consequences of nationalism—force, hatred, all that—than on the longing for community, and thus it is not strongly opposed to Bloom's common-sense understanding of what is "really life" for men and women.

Bersani's more critical response to Joyce perceives the referent of *Ulysses* as at once more general and more individual. Not just Irish nationalism but European culture is what *Ulysses* represents, but European culture à la Joyce. At his most sympathetic, Bersani understands this solipsism as a defensive reaction, an attempt to resist fragmentation. "The anxiety that *Ulysses* massively struggles to transcend—however we choose to understand its origins—is that of disconnectedness" (177). He points to Bloom's solitude as an important instance of this disconnectedness and emphasizes not merely his "social solitude as a Jew in Ireland" and his "estrangement from Molly," but his "cosmic lack of linkage": "Bloom's aloneness is metaphysical" (176). The disjunction between lived experience and "forms of intelligibility" is ours as well as Bloom's, and it finds its literary analogue in the distance between the experience of reading *Ulysses* and the "concealed structures it signifies" (178). This latter disjunction, however, is easier to manage and perhaps, through exegesis, to mend. Herein lies the motive for Joyce's representation of European culture in the novel, the solipsism of which ensures that the only community it can participate

12. For Deane's more recent version of this argument, see the sections on Joyce in *Strange Country*, including this passage: "The position of exile, the high cultural form of emigration[,] . . . was a form of dispossession that retained—imaginatively—the claim to possession. . . . For the Dublin, the Ireland, he wrote of was, in an important sense, a nowhere, a territory not yet represented" (94–95). For another important reading of nation and language in Joyce, see van Boheemen-Saaf's discussion of the "mimesis of original loss," referring to the trauma of Irish experience reflected in the haunting absence of the native language.

in is its own exegetical community: *"Ulysses* promises a critical utopia" (175).

Bloom's experience in the pub and his rejection of hatred as a basis for community have already pointed the way to such broader views of the mimetic focus of the novel as a whole. His fumbling but moving designation of life as love plants the hope for greater harmony between structures of meaning and lived experience, between desire and history. In declaring love to be more real than history, he reminds us that mimetic literature too has an object that, however elusive and unrealized, cannot be defined simply as the present diversity of nationalities. For both Deane and Bersani, the novel strives to construct meaning by integrating the fragments of experience; it strives to create a whole where none yet exists. For both critics, the irony of the novel is that it accepts the task of embodying the idea of totality (whether of nation or of European culture) when this idea is not yet embodied in experience—and may never be. In this respect *Ulysses* is firmly anchored in the history of the novel as a genre. Much of what I am saying about their views of *Ulysses* echoes Lukács's view of mimesis in a godforsaken world: the mimetic impulse attempts to create a reality that does not yet exist.[13] Of course the work of Lukács, Deane, and Bersani exhibits striking differences arising from their varying views of this imagined reality and its prospects for realization. But all three suggest that the novel is not primarily about national conflicts, that it responds to anxieties and desires that involve the national consciousness but also extend beyond it.

Transcendental Homelessness (Lukács)

We are indebted to Lukács's *The Theory of the Novel* (1916) for three related and, for the present discussion, crucial observations about the novel as a genre. He ties the genre to the concept of *totality*: the mimetic object of the novel is the absence of a complete world, a total reality. He ties it to *secular* culture (though not generally employing this word): the absence of God in the modern age is one reason for the world's incompleteness or lack of totality. Finally, he ties it to a *utopian* impulse: in pointing toward what is missing, the novel expresses the desire to realize a new totality, to make present its missing object. The three terms combined—totality, secu-

13. V. Sherry and Scholes offer two quite different accounts of Lukács's relation to Joyce. Sherry draws on *Theory of the Novel*, Scholes on the later, anti-modernist Lukács. However, both emphasize in different ways the proximity of Joyce and Lukács and in the process they undermine traditional Marxist attacks on Joyce's aestheticism. See V. Sherry 24–27 and passim; Scholes 161–77.

larism, utopia—point to needs shaping the novel; consideration of these needs will expand the notion of "secular criticism" and will suggest alternative ways to understand the relation between culture and imperialism, ways particularly germane to the colonial odyssey novels. But critical inclination and the nature of the modernist colonial odysseys will also lead me to disavow some features of Lukács's theory. The utopian dimension that he sought in the novel does not survive in the modernist odysseys, and in severely moderating this aspect of his thought we shall also be led to adopt a very different relation to the notion of totality. But first I consider the lasting contribution of his essay.

"When the structures made by man for man are really adequate to man, they are his necessary and native home," Lukács explains (64). The novel, as "the epic of a world that has been abandoned by God," records the lack of any such home in the modern age. This transcendental homelessness, associated with the loss of immanent meaning, is the precondition of the genre, which is built around the "separation between interiority and adventure" (88). Thus we might see the popular adventure writers, who imagine a harmonious integration of imperial subject and imperial exploits, as striving to write epics rather than novels, while the modernist colonial odysseys foreground the incommensurability of interiority and adventure. Like the modernist colonial-odyssey authors, Lukács acknowledges both the historical distance of the epic ideal and the impossibility of returning to it. What Woolf describes a few years later as the "tremendous breach" in tradition, he identifies here as an "unbridgeable gulf" separating the modern age from ancient Greece (31). But the distance frees him to shape the ideal he associates with Greece. Precisely because it does not now seem the most accurate description of Homer, the suggestion that "the Greek knew only answers but no questions, only solutions (even if enigmatic ones) but no riddles, only forms but no chaos" reveals much about Lukács's utopia (31). Though Greece may be closed off from us, Lukács transfers the ideal it embodies to a desired future. The famous conclusion of his monograph speaks of "those hopes which are signs of a world to come, still so weak that it can easily be crushed by the sterile power of the merely existent" (153).

Irony is the genre's dominant mode, foregrounding its own inadequacy as a structure or "native home," its distance from both Greece and a hoped-for world to come. The irony emerges in the novel's heroes, whom Lukács characterizes as seekers striving to bridge the gap between self and world. His typology of the novel identifies the two extreme forms of this frustrated seeking. At one extreme, which he calls "abstract idealism," the interiority of the hero is "narrower" than the world and the hero obsessively pursues an ideal, remaining blind to the inadequacy or unreceptiveness of the world. The resulting contradiction between the imagined and the real appears as grotesque heroism, madness, monomania, all of which are signs that the hero's relation to the world has become "purely peripheral" (106). At the other extreme, the "romanticism of disillusionment," the hero recognizes and embraces such marginalization *a priori*. Here interiority is wider and larger than adventures offered in life, and the hero chooses passivity, passing judgment on the external world by abandoning the struggle to fulfill an "over-determined" desire (116). This discussion of types indicates that the homelessness they have in common is a kind of marginalization: modernity is the product of a traumatic decentering.

The protagonists of the colonial-odyssey novels are typically closer to the extreme of abstract idealism. Kurtz and Lord Jim both exhibit a demonic idealism; Mrs. Moore, though presented after her cave disaster as having always been a disillusioned old lady, begins her adventure on an idealistic note, hoping both to arrange a marriage and to "know" India; much of Waugh's satire in *Handful of Dust* and *Black Mischief* derives from the unbridgeable gulf between expectations and experience in the lives of Tony Last and John Boot; and even Rachel Vinrace, whose passivity does not derive from disillusionment, seems to exhibit the narrowing idealism that must reject much of the external world. But these protagonists have foils or doubles near the other extreme, or they swing to the other extreme themselves. Often the transition takes the form of a fatal awakening: Mrs. Moore loses her humane curiosity, Rachel loses some of her innocence, and Kurtz accomplishes a "moral victory" in moving from monomania to horror—then each succumbs to death. The deaths often seem willed, so deep is the disillusionment. The modernist odysseys, in short, appear structurally hybrid in Lukács's typology. They show a world that is at once too much and too little for the subject, as if to give extra emphasis to the incommensurability between interiority and adventure. At the same historical moment when Lukács hoped the novel was contributing to a new integration, these novels flaunted their own failure.

Lukács would himself come to question the usefulness of the typology, but the observation that modernist odysseys blend idealism and disillusionment captures something of these works' ambivalence about colonialism, for they represent colonialism itself as both too much and too little for the European subject. The most useful component of Lukács's analysis for understanding this ambivalence is the concept of totality. What he calls the intention toward the totality of life is precisely what Said's account of exile and Cheng's notion of internationalism do not fully recognize. "The novel is the epic of an age in which the extensive totality of life is no longer directly given, in which the immanence of meaning in life has become a problem, yet which still thinks in terms of totality" (56). This formulation is richly suggestive not only for the modernist colonial odysseys, but for imperialism and for modernity more generally.[14]

The concept of totality remained central to Lukács's work even after his turn to Marxism in *History and Class Consciousness* (1923). In fact the altered character of his utopianism after its transposition from an idealist to a materialist framework reinforced his totalizing impulse. The continuing impact of the concept on Marxist thought is evident throughout the work, for example, of Fredric Jameson, particularly in his useful theory of modernism:

> Colonialism means that a significant structural segment of the economic system as a whole is now located elsewhere, beyond the metropolis, outside of the daily life and existential experience of the home country, in colonies over the water whose own life experience and life world—very different from that of the imperial power—remain unknown and unimaginable for the subjects of the imperial power, whatever social class they may belong to. Such spatial disjunction has as its immediate consequence the inability to grasp the way the system functions as a whole. . . . Daily life and existential experience in the metropolis . . . can now no longer be grasped immanently; it no longer has its meaning, its deeper reason for being, within itself. ("Modernism" 50–51)

14. Bakhtin's historico-philosophical account of the novel offers an appealing alternative to Lukács's, but an alternative of little use for reading the modernist colonial odysseys precisely because it gives less weight to the concept of totality. Like Lukács, Bakhtin contrasts the novel to the epic to emphasize its recent birth in the modern age, and he also offers an account of its relation to exploration. He attributes its newness to "a very specific rupture in the history of European civilization: its emergence from a socially isolated and culturally deaf semipatriarchal society, and its entrance into international and interlingual contacts and relationships. A multitude of different languages, cultures and times became available to Europe, and this became a decisive factor in its life and thought" (11). The modernist colonial-odyssey novels, however, are not characterized by such openness. Certainly they are responding to the rupture Bakhtin describes, a rupture still experienced in the modernist period, but one critical challenge they present is the fact that they do not make more use of the international and interlingual contacts. We have already considered the example of *A Passage to India*, where Indian voices and cultures serve in the end to give expression to modern European uncertainties. These novels are dialogical only to the extent that they show the imperial subject in dialogue with itself—and they do indeed voice doubts and uncertainties rather than speaking with monological authority. But they do not participate in an international, intercultural, or intertemporal dialogue of the sort described here by Bakhtin. They represent the centrifugal emergence from Europe not as a liberation but as a loss. To the extent the rupture opens the way for dialogue, in other words, it is a dialogue of the sort described by Lukács, the dialogue of subjects questioning the loss of transcendence. He provides the historical and conceptual framework demonstrating that the absence of and desire for transcendence is inscribed in the very genre itself even when individual novels do not fully thematize this problem.

Jameson invokes *History and Class Consciousness* in assuming that an "intention towards totality" governs representation. Unable to represent colonialism as a whole, modernist literature cannot merely accept the incompleteness of national daily life but must "by compensation" form that daily life "into a self-subsisting totality" (58). The gesture toward infinity in this literature, in other words, is an attempt both to compensate for and to mask the absence of immanent meaning, the absence of an accessible social totality.[15]

The suggestion that geographical expansion opens up a new, global understanding of totality is extremely useful; I shall return to it later in this chapter. But two considerations raise doubts about whether immanent meaning was first lost with the advent of advanced capitalism, as Jameson implies. First, he begins the essay by suggesting that 1884—the Berlin Conference—is an "emblematic" date for the codification of imperialism and inauguration of modernism, and he thereby conflates, like Said, the historical duration of modernity and modernism. Thus his economic analysis of the gesture toward infinity in modernist literature remains fundamentally synchronic and spatial in character, relating aesthetic form to the global empire and viewing that form as an effect or symptom of the mode of production. In short, his description of high modernism in this essay falls into the base/superstructure model he often labors to avoid. A second problem with his model emerges specifically in relation to the colonial odysseys. We have already acknowledged that they tell little about the colonies, and thus we are prepared to read them as vehicles of expression for some repressed content. But it makes little sense that their unconscious content would be colonialism itself. Displacement and projection by definition sever the direct link between manifest and latent meaning; colonial themes would simply not be called upon to represent repressed anxieties about colonialism. Accordingly Jameson describes modernism as the occlusion of colonial contexts, the attempt to sunder ties between literary content and this political unconscious. Acknowledging the colonial-odyssey novels as a part of modernism, or even merely as

15. In *History and Class Consciousness*, Lukács speaks of the working class's *"Intention auf die Totalität der Gesellschaft,"* and the standard English translation renders this as an *"aspiration towards society in its totality"* (174). Jameson alters the translation and the context in suggesting that "representation, and cognitive mapping as such, is governed by an 'intention towards totality' " (58). For Jameson's later defense of the concept of totality in theoretical discourse, see the final section of *Postmodernism* (399–418). Also, for a description of the concept of totality in relation to architecture, see "Absent Totality," in which he argues that "whatever its validity as a concept, we cannot do without the permanently implicit logical possibility of such an absolute totality" (122). On the history of this concept, particularly in Marxist thought, see both J. Daly and Jay.

part of a transitional moment leading into modernism, presents a challenge for Jameson's description and requires one to trace the loss of immanently apprehensible meaning in modern life to something other than colonialism.

Something more remains to be salvaged, I think, from Lukács's early, Hegelian account of this loss, for it hints at ways to trace both the loss of immanence and the related intention toward the totality of life to a time preceding advanced capitalism, and thus it offers a way to reintroduce a diachronic element into our understanding of the desire to imagine the whole.[16] His theory of the novel, by leading back to the theological roots of the concept of totality, suggests implicitly that intellectual habits can precede the emergence of related economic structures. His fruitful formulation—that the modern age *still* thinks in terms of a totality which is *no longer* given—hints that perhaps the intention toward the totality of life is a historically conditioned holdover from an earlier age. Rather than follow the later Lukács and Jameson in a Marxist critique of the earlier Lukács that leaves this intention largely unquestioned, I would like to turn to Blumenberg's rather different appropriation of Lukács's theory of the novel.

The ideal Lukács offers as a contrast to the modern world is in fact derived from two distinct epochs. The novel results from the loss of both ancient-Greek immanence and Judeo-Christian transcendence, epic immediacy and theological totality; and Lukács's description routinely merges these two losses into one. Separating them is one of the contributions of Blumenberg's essay, "The Concept of Reality and the Possibility of the Novel," which does not make its debt to Lukács's theory fully explicit. As the title suggests, it attempts to determine what concept of reality is implicit in and a prerequisite for the existence of the novel as a genre. He begins by enumerating four concepts of reality, a typology extracted from history, so that the four concepts appear to have succeeded each other as underground preconceptions through the history of the West. With the first two concepts Blumenberg distinguishes clearly between Greek epic and Christian theology.

The first concept is the "reality of instantaneous evidence," the reality of the Greeks and of the epic in particular. The second concept, traced to the Middle Ages, is a "guaranteed reality," in which a third authority (such as God) serves as mediator in the relation between subject and object. Blu-

---

16. In the 1805 *Prelude*, Wordsworth speaks of "the Imagination of the whole" (13.65). This is analogous to "the intention towards the totality of society," though Wordsworth's phrase is stylistically more felicitous—and conceptually ambiguous. By echoing it with Lukács's concept in mind, I give it a more limited sense than it assumes in the *Prelude*. However, this use of Wordsworth's phrasing becomes impractical in chapter 4, when the discussion of Woolf requires me to distinguish between wholeness and totality.

menberg labels the third concept of reality the "actualization of a context in itself," a conception that distinguishes the modern age from its predecessors and makes possible the existence of the novel; this third concept also coincides with the transition from a representational to a productive theory of knowledge.[17] The fourth concept understands reality as "that which cannot be mastered by the self." Here the reality principle stands for what resists the wishes and projections of the self.

The third, modern concept of reality, the actualization of a context, changes the status of novelty—one might even say that it introduces a genuine concept of novelty for the first time. If knowledge had previously consisted in copying or imitating pre-existent ideas or nature, then the ontological status of new representations was always secondary, or not really "new" at all. Blumenberg says in a footnote to the essay that "the reality concept of the 'open' context legitimizes the esthetic quality of the *novitas*, the element of surprise and unfamiliarity, whereas [the earlier concept of] 'guaranteed' reality does not allow anything new or unfamiliar to become *real*" (33n6). Such an open context seems to preclude the notion of the totality of reality, but it does not preclude an intention toward or ideal of such a totality. Blumenberg's essay usefully demonstrates how novelty and openness of context can coexist with traces of earlier epochs—and in particular with the desire to imagine the whole. He writes:

> Reality as a self-constituting context is a *borderline concept* of the *ideal totality* of all selves—it is a confirmative value for the experience and interpretation of the world that take place in *intersubjectivity*. Obviously this concept of reality has a sort of "epic" structure, relating to the totality of a world that can never be completed or grasped in its entirety. (33)

The concept of *novitas* on which the novel depends indicates that the form of the intended totality is still undetermined, imperceptible, or subject to negotiation. Like Lukács, in other words, Blumenberg views the history of modern literary form as a guide to the evolution of concerns traceable to medieval theology.

Because they see the genre relating to this inaccessible object, the totality of the world, both Lukács and Blumenberg also recognize irony as the

---

17. Blumenberg presented this essay to the *Poetik und Hermeneutik* group, and in the ensuing discussion he acknowledged that phenomenology, minus Husserl's transcendental perspective, presents the third concept of reality, the actualization of a context in itself. In supplements written following the discussion, Blumenberg provides an important hint about his own methodology when he speaks of the "possibility of an historical phenomenology as eidetic description" and acknowledges that such a method is based on the same concept of reality as the novel. See the discussion of "Wirklichkeitsbegriff," 226–27 (available only in German); see also the essay itself, 12n5 (in English: 32n5).

novel's essential rhetorical mode. Lukács writes: "Irony, with intuitive double vision, can see where God is to be found in a world abandoned by God; irony sees the lost, utopian home of the idea that has become an ideal" (92). Since Blumenberg does not share Lukács's Hegelian perspective, which is to say, the idealist teleology which has often been criticized or deconstructed, Blumenberg would never describe irony in this fashion. He does, however, speak of the "irony essential to" the novel and observes that "irony seems to have become the authentic mode of reflection as far as the esthetic claims of the modern novel are concerned: the novel becomes ironic through the connections with reality that it is unable to dispense with and yet incapable of forming" (40n11 and 45). In contrast to Lukács's perception of the novel as a form pointing toward a new integration of self and world, a "new complete totality" (152), Blumenberg shows the novel evolving slowly toward (though never crossing entirely over to) the fourth concept of reality: the experience of resistance. In other words, for Blumenberg the irony cannot lead to a new synthesis. But it is not needed for this purpose, since Blumenberg, like Said, remains committed to the "legitimacy" of modern thought. Only in the context of his defense of the modern age does Blumenberg's theory of the novel assume its full significance as a successor to Lukács's, and thus it is to that defense that I now turn.

Blumenberg on "Reoccupation"

For a variety of reasons, including difficulties with translation, Blumenberg's work has been slow to cross the Atlantic. But Said's description of one of his intellectual heroes, Erich Auerbach, could apply to Blumenberg as well: he is "a *Philo[lo]g* of the old tradition" (Introduction 1). In fact Blumenberg's philological range surpasses Auerbach's, though one might easily conclude that philology is of secondary importance in Blumenberg's work, which has now established him as one of the leading continental philosophers of the twentieth century. Two general affinities link the work of Said and Blumenberg, despite all their differences of tradition, discipline, style, and ideology. As Said objects to "shutting off human investigation," Blumenberg similarly argues against premature foreclosure of historical inquiry through appeals to "eidetic preformations" or historical constants. And for both, the affirmation of modernity reaches deeper than their thorough critiques: they embrace the core features of modern thought in their disavowal of its excesses and shortcomings. It is in the service of such aims that both champion thought that is secular, a term whose philosophical and historical weight Blumenberg fully develops.

Blumenberg's views on the genesis of modern thought find their fullest expression in *The Legitimacy of the Modern Age* (1966; revised 1973–76). The primary target of this book is the secularization thesis espoused above all by Karl Löwith, with its suggestion that modern thought lacks legitimacy.[18] Löwith's thesis has had little direct impact on Anglo-American thought, and thus the initial impetus for Blumenberg's defense of modernity can seem obscure to readers outside of Germany; however, much twentieth-century thought about modernity parallels the pattern of Löwith's critique, and thus the interest of Blumenberg's defense extends far beyond the argument with Löwith. The secularization thesis claims that Christian thought and modern thought are substantially the same, that the defining elements of the latter consist of disguised versions of the former: the modern idea of progress, for example, is a secularized version of Christian eschatology, or Marx's communism is a secularization of Christian paradise. Such a model suggests that modern thought is illegitimate, and Löwith attributes modernity's blurry vision to its being a bastard mix of Christian and pagan, of faith and reason. As a diagnosis of the discontents of modernity, the secularization thesis thus directs much of the blame at modernity itself. This blame reproduces on the level of intellectual history what the etymological sense of "secularization" denotes regarding material relations: the term originally described the unilateral appropriation of church property by the state and was associated with demands for restoration or compensation.[19] The secularization thesis often makes an analogous demand, implicitly if not explicitly, for the restoration of some earlier state of affairs.

While the secularization thesis *per se* has not circulated widely in England and the United States, the pattern of its philosophy of history is familiar:

An initial, positively valued state of affairs (nature, cosmos, community, relation to transcendence, or whatever) was supplanted by the 'modern' condition. And the crisis-wracked state of the 'modern world' in the twen-

18. The thesis appears in his *Meaning in History*, a study of the theological background to eighteenth and nineteenth-century philosophies of history. On the debate between Löwith and Blumenberg, see Wallace, "Progress," and also his translator's introduction to Blumenberg's *Legitimacy*.

19. It is in fact premature to view this etymological sense of secularization as obsolete, as events in formerly communist European countries have shown. In Poland, for example, the church has requested and often obtained restoration of numerous properties that had been "secularized"—not only under communism, but in some cases as long as centuries ago. Throughout this study, in keeping with common English usage, I employ the terms "secular" and "secularism" in a nonpejorative sense (to describe the results of what Blumenberg calls "reoccupation"). With "secularization," however, I refer to Löwith's thesis about the genesis of modernity, which I follow Blumenberg in rejecting.

tieth century is then naturally interpreted as evidence of the unhealthy effects of the turning away from the original, preferable state of affairs. (Wallace, translator's introduction xii)

In a chapter on "The Rhetoric of Secularization," Blumenberg associates Freud, Weber, Heidegger, Husserl, and Adorno with this pattern of thought, detecting in them "a need for a causal formula of maximum generality to account for people's discontent with the state of the world. . . . Discontent is given retrospective self-evidence" (118). We have seen the pattern in Tönnies' concepts and in Hellenism. And not only analyses of modernity but, more specifically, theories of modernism often follow this pattern of historical analysis. To cite just one example: Jameson, in an essay subtitled "Demystifying the Ideology of Modernism," grows nostalgic while reflecting on the autonomy of art:

> We are tempted to ask, not whether literary works are autonomous, nor even how art manages to lift itself above its immediate social situation and to free itself from its social context, but rather what kind of society it can be in which works of art have become autonomous to this degree, in which the older social and cultic functions of literature have become so unfamiliar as to have made us forgetful (and this in the strong, Heideggerian sense of the term) of the power and influence that a socially living art can exercise. ("Beyond the Cave" 116–17)

Blumenberg responds to the secularization thesis (and its analogues) with an alternative model of the transition between epochs that undermines the claim of their substantive identity. In his view, the modern age does not unilaterally displace Christianity but is instead the product of human self-assertion made necessary when the ambitious rational constructs of Christianity—in the form of Scholasticism—imploded under the weight of their own internal contradictions. After this collapse, certain questions that had been answered by theology needed to be addressed using other materials, other means. If modern thought often resembles theological thought, this is not because they are substantively the same but because they perform a similar function: they answer the same questions, respond to the same needs. With historical analysis that is impressively detailed and extensive, Blumenberg shows that the idea of progress, for example, cannot be a direct adaptation or corruption of Christian eschatology but is drawn rather from various other sources and then overextended in the attempt to address the curiosity inherited from Christianity about the ultimate shape of human history.

"Reoccupation" (*Umbesetzung*) is Blumenberg's term for this process of epochal transition: positions (or questions) in the structure of human knowledge, once vacated, cannot simply be cast aside; they demand to be reoccupied by a new thought or myth. The questions are not historical constants, for this stratum of human history is itself subject to transformation, though at a much slower rate than the products of human thought and imagination.[20] His perception of transformations in this underlying stratum leads to one effect of his historiography, which is a transfer of guilt: responsibility for many of the discontents of the modern age is shifted back to Christianity itself for having inordinately expanded the range of pressing questions:

> In our history this system [of man's interpretation of the world and of himself] has been decisively determined by Christian theology, and specifically, above all, in the direction of its expansion. Theology created new 'positions' in the framework of the statements about the world and man that are possible and are expected, 'positions' that cannot simply be 'set aside' again or left unoccupied in the interest of theoretical economy. For theology there was no need for questions about the totality of the world and history, about the origin of man and the purpose of his existence, to be unanswerable. This explains the readiness with which it introduced titles into the budget of man's needs in the area of knowledge, to honor which was bound to be difficult or even impossible for any knowledge that did not appeal, as it did, to transcendent sources. (64–65)[21]

Exiled from God, humankind set about trying to make itself at home in the world and, unable to dispense with the roles God had played, the modern subject attempted to assume them. One of these roles was to guarantee the meaning of "the totality of the world and history." But such a household has proved more than humans can manage. Many of modernity's excesses can be traced to its effort to match the epistemological ambition of Christian thought, an effort "as generous as it was hopeless" (65); many of the age's discontents derive from the failure of this ef-

---

20. As Blumenberg explains, "We are not dealing with the classical constants of philosophical anthropology, still less with the 'eternal truths' of metaphysics. . . . It is enough that the reference-frame conditions have greater inertia for consciousness than do the contents associated with them, that is, that the questions are relatively constant in comparison to the answers. . . . During the phases in which the function of this frame of reference is latent—in periods, that is, that we assign to the epochs as their 'classic' formations—we must expect, above all, gains by extension and losses by shrinkage" (*Legitimacy* 466–67).

21. Christianity's introduction of new epistemological needs demonstrates that an answer can materialize for a variety of reasons and then generate the corresponding curiosity: "Questions do not always precede their answers" (*Legitimacy* 66). Lukács similarly describes the transition in ancient Greece from epic through tragedy to philosophy as a transition from answer to question.

fort, resulting in a persistent incommensurability of question and answer. Blumenberg's analysis recognizes the fundamental legitimacy of the modern age in its attempts to cope with a problematic inheritance, but he also stops well short of a celebration of the age, suggesting instead that its excesses need to be reigned in.

While the intellectual shift Blumenberg is narrating evolves gradually over centuries (we are not speaking of a sudden epistemic break that can be precisely dated and located, as Foucault would have it), he does attempt to identify a century when the scale tips and divine authority no longer outweighs the importance of worldly human endeavor. He locates the epochal threshold between Nicholas of Cusa (1401–64) and Giordano Bruno (1548–1600), between the Cardinal who viewed the world as the self-contraction of an unknowable God and the heretic who saw the means to gnosis in infinite human self-expansion. (Copernicus [1473–1543] occupies, significantly, the historical space between them.) The exhaustion of the logic of God's descent into the world opened the way for human ascent to world mastery. This analysis from *The Legitimacy of the Modern Age,* supplemented by a philosophical anthropology developed in Blumenberg's 1971 essay on rhetoric, led to a remarkable half-sentence distillation of his view of the genesis of the modern age: "Trying to think the God absolutely away from himself, as the totally Other, he ["man"] inexorably began the most difficult rhetorical act, namely, the act of comparing himself to this God" ("Anthropological Approach" 456).[22]

Pulled into the God-shaped Vacuum

A metaphor describing the subject's relation to the absolute offers a way to reflect on the implications of reoccupation: a "god-shaped vacuum" resides within the self, according to some. (The phrase, long favored in American pulpits, is generally attributed, only half accurately, to Pascal and St. Augustine.) The shape of the vacuum is taken as evidence of the existence of God, or at least serves as adequate incentive to wager on God's existence; in other words, the shape defines the Other that logically must exist to make the self complete. The desire, in short, serves as evi-

22. I have silently emended the English translation by adding capitalization. See Wallace's corresponding translator's note (458 note q). Less easy to emend satisfactorily is the sexually exclusive language in this translation: where the English reads "man . . . himself," the German has "Menschen . . . sich." The same problem applies to quotations from Lukács and others. Though it is generally easier to avoid sexist language in English than in German, the standard translations of these works often sound more sexually specific than the German originals.

dence of the desired object.[23] Salman Rushdie has commented that litera-ture is an attempt to fill a "god-shaped hole" in him, and here the lack is clearly given a different significance: it is a sign of the disappearance rather than existence of God.[24] With the hole now serving as a metaphor for loss, it also suggests the possibility of being filled in—it invites reoccu-pation. The metaphor nicely implies that whatever attempts to fill the hole—literature, for example—must expand and mold itself to the shape of God. In reoccupying the vacated site, human endeavor adapts itself to the functions once fulfilled by God.

The negative image of a vacuum or hole, implying a certain deficiency in human nature, is in accord with Blumenberg's philosophical anthropol-ogy. While Blumenberg remained remarkably consistent throughout his career, this is one component of his theory that he developed in significant ways following the publication of *The Legitimacy of the Modern Age*. What this book refers to as " 'positions' in the framework of the statements about the world and man" and as "the budget of man's needs in the area of knowledge" becomes more fully articulated in a later essay through the notion of the *Mängelwesen*, the creature of deficiency.[25] Humankind lacks sufficient instincts to determine behavior—signs in the world, in other words, lack univocal meaning for this creature—and the creature must therefore produce symbolic forms to fill the gap, to provide the missing significance.

> Man has no immediate, no purely "internal" relation to himself. His self-understanding has the structure of "self-externality".... The substantial-ism of identity is destroyed; identity must be realized, it becomes a kind of accomplishment, and accordingly there is a pathology of identity.... Man comprehends himself only by way of what he is not. It is not only his situ-

---

23. Allen Mandelbaum has called my attention to Meister Eckhart's analogous thirst metaphor and D. H. Lawrence's radical extension of this theology of desire. According to Eckhart, the best evidence for the existence of God is humankind's desire: the stronger the thirst, the more present and persistent the image of the drink. In pushing this idea to its logical extreme, D. H. Lawrence seems to dispense with the image or object altogether and make the desire an end in itself: "God is my desire in me."

24. Rushdie's turn to Islam in the aftermath of the *Satanic Verses* affair serves as a re-minder that the beholder of this metaphor determines the significance of its vacuum. Rushdie did not need to abandon the figure of speech, only to shift his understanding of it: "I used to say: 'there is a God-shaped hole in me'. For a long time I stressed the absence, the hole. Now I find it is the shape which has become more important" (qtd. in Faulks 17). See also his "Is Nothing Sacred?" in which he speaks of literature offering perhaps "a secular definition of transcendence," serving as "some sort of replacement" for the love of god, and being "the art most likely to fill our god-shaped holes" (103–4, 107).

25. For Blumenberg's use of the term *Mängelwesen*, which he borrows from Arnold Gehlen, see his "Anthropological Approach." See also his "Pensiveness" and, on the devel-opment of his philosophical anthropology, my "Metaphors for Mankind."

ation that is potentially metaphorical; his constitution itself already is. ("Anthropological Approach" 456)

The goal of this *Mängelwesen*, then, is to establish an appropriate fit between needed meaning and symbolic form, between question and answer; optimizing this fit can allow the *Mängelwesen* to feel provisionally at home in the world, to secure its identity by supplying its lack. The most common method to accomplish this is by revising or replacing answers, but occasionally—as when a god-shaped vacuum calls for an inordinate expenditure of human effort—the underlying questions may come under critical scrutiny. In both cases the goal is to balance the present "budget" of human needs and knowledge.

Haushalt is the German word Blumenberg uses for what is translated here as "budget." While "household" might be a more literal translation, it is not as close in meaning as the German *Haushalt* is to the Greek notion of *oikos*; the word "household" has now lost some of the economic associations it once had and "budget" captures more of the sense of belonging to a dynamic domestic economy. Blumenberg uses *Haushalt* in this important passage from *The Legitimacy of the Modern Age* without calling attention to its status as a metaphor, and in light of Pecora's analysis of the persistence of an *oikos* ideal deep in nineteenth and twentieth-century thought, it is worth considering whether the same nostalgia creeps into Blumenberg's reflection on humanity's deepest epistemological needs. It could be argued that he sometimes associates pre-Christian antiquity with the anthropological equilibrium that is his ideal, but for the most part he, like Said, dispenses with any nostalgia that functions as a rejection of modernity. His ideal does not depend on an imagined return to an earlier state of affairs, to a home located in some other time or place. But in contrast to Said he does not embrace exile as an alternative; rather, he acknowledges that culture is fundamentally an effort to be at home in the world. This acknowledgment comes even as his anthropological term *Haushalt* succeeds in distancing the notion of home from the theological-transcendental influences found in Novalis and Lukács. He would place less emphasis on the *everywhere* in Novalis's formulation about the desire to be at home in the world, since his anthropological model gives less weight to the concept of totality. In short, Blumenberg succeeds (like Lukács) in acknowledging the force of the drive to be at home while also avoiding (like Said) the pitfalls of a modernity-bashing nostalgia.

Blumenberg's accomplishment is not without a certain self-imposed limitation that is made evident by juxtaposition with writings by Pratt, Said, and Jameson. As the passages from Blumenberg that I have cited suggest, he understands modern self-assertion primarily in epistemologi-

cal terms, and his discussion of the causes and consequences of this reoccupation focuses primarily on psychological and anthropological aspects
of existence. To the extent that his work invokes or evokes a sense of community, it is an intellectual community dispersed through time, with individuals receiving texts from the past and anticipating a future reception.[26]
His impressive narratives of intellectual history tend to steer clear of
moral and especially political philosophy, and he is reticent about elaborating on the socio-economic consequences of modern reoccupation. In
applying the reoccupation model to literary history, however, one finds
that it is these consequences that come to the fore. Matthew Arnold's career offers an example. When he moderated his Hellenism and increasingly advocated the use of poetry as a substitute for religion, he was pro-
moting a reoccupation that had less to do with epistemology than with
social and moral influence. An attempt to distinguish the epistemological
consequences of reoccupying the god-shaped void from social and political phenomena can appear arbitrary, as Pratt's centrifugal/centripetal
model suggests. Indeed, we have learned from Foucault to view structures of knowledge as structures of power. Said has demonstrated that
one particular field of knowledge/power, Orientalism, arose in part as "a
reconstituted theology," as "a secular post-Enlightenment myth whose
outlines were unmistakably Christian" (*Orientalism* 114–15). The application of Blumenberg's theory to modernist literature necessitates therefore
an attempt to expand his focus on intellectual history to social, political,
and economic contexts. Specifically, it necessitates addressing questions
we have encountered in the work of Said, Joyce, and Jameson about the
elusiveness of community in the modern age, the role of nationalism in
constituting identity, and the viability of imperialism as an economic and
cultural totality.

When Blumenberg's analysis is expanded in this fashion, it in turn suggests an innovative way to theorize modernism and imperial culture as,
respectively, one episode and one arena in the process of reoccupation.
The source of this innovation is Blumenberg's unique analysis of the historical genesis of the concept of totality, an analysis tempered by the
recognition that we cannot summarily dispense with the desire to imagine
the whole: "Questions about the totality of the world and history" are
among the intellectual legacies of Christian theology that "cannot simply
be 'set aside' again." His historical critique of the totalizing impulse leads
him to reject any teleology, such as the Hegelianism evident in Lukács's

---

26. I have described Blumenberg's work as positioning itself in this sort of historical
continuum or community—and have examined some of the anxieties associated with such
a positioning—in "Ökonomie der Rezeption."

theory of the novel and the historical materialism in Lukács's later work. Yet his appreciation of the lasting force of this impulse enables him to embrace Lukács's description of the novel as the epic of a godforsaken world. In the light of Blumenberg's historical analysis, both the novel and Lukács's theory of it now appear to indicate a longing less for Greek immanence than for Judeo-Christian transcendence, since central to both the genre and Lukács's theory is the intention toward an ideal totality of the world.

This historicizing critique of the concept of totality highlights furthermore the extent to which not only modernist culture but also theories of modernism have been shaped by reoccupation. We have already seen, for example, the extent of Jameson's commitment to the concept of totality. And Said's apparent equation of secular and anti-nationalist criticism finds fuller justification when it is recognized that the "imagined political community" of nationalism is shaped by a reoccupation, as Benedict Anderson hints in observing that the nation "is imagined as *sovereign* because the concept was born in an age in which Enlightenment and Revolution were destroying the legitimacy of the divinely-ordained, hierarchical dynastic realm" (7). Thus in developing their respective critiques, Jameson and Said both view modernism, despite their energetic insistence on the importance of historicizing, in the context of synchronic systems—the capitalist "mode of production" or the hegemonic *episteme* of "imperial culture." Such conceptual constructs serve as replacement totalities, entangled in the process of reoccupation in a way that leaves the critic unaware of his and modernism's relation to the diachronic evolution of the desire for totality. By historicizing the concept of totality, Blumenberg opens the way for a reconsideration of the modernist novel's relation to metaphysics, to nationalism, and to imperialism.

At the same time, the anthropological underpinning of Blumenberg's historical analysis explains the stubborn persistence of the need to imagine the whole, and thus he exposes the limitations to theories that claim too quickly to have renounced totality (these are often theories—Jean-François Lyotard's, for example—celebrating the supposed achievements of postmodernism). The attempt to view *Ulysses* as a celebration of cultural multiplicity and internationalism proves premature precisely because Joyce's novel displays a mimesis pointing toward various possible totalities. Similarly, Said's praise of exile underestimates the force of the impulse toward totality that contributes to nationalism. It is in part this force that lies behind the problem he laments of affiliations that are meant to be local and anti-authoritarian but are co-opted by the dominant social totality. My use of Blumenberg suggests that such co-optation might have an anthropological as well as an ideological motive.

In each of the following two sections I describe a way in which Blumenberg's theory of modernity can fruitfully be expanded to explain aspects of colonial-odyssey fiction and modernist culture not fully accounted for in postcolonial and Marxist theories. The first of these applications blends Blumenberg's analysis of the totalizing impulse as a site of reoccupation with Jameson's analysis of imperialism as an absent totality in order to reflect on the modernists' perception that the world had become fully occupied. The second explores the melancholy consequences of calling on human faculties—memory, in particular—to assume responsibility for redeeming humankind. Both of these examples reveal the modernist colonial odysseys to be late-modern, for these novels belong to a late stage in the process of reoccupation when the futility of answering reoccupied questions has become evident, though the questions remain—and the result is a sense of impotence. These two examples of belatedness interact in an often complex fashion. Sometimes the relationship is compensatory: imperial exploits offer an opportunity to reclaim a sense of power after human attempts at total redemption have failed. More often the relationship is shaped by transference: anxieties deriving from the failed reoccupation of redemptive functions blend with and reinforce anxieties about the possession of empire. In the modernist odysseys it is this last relationship that predominates, as anxieties about the individual's relation to the absolute are projected onto colonial settings.

Colonial Occupation as Failed Reoccupation

In sorting out the various levels on which the colonial-odyssey novels reflect imperialism, one might usefully reiterate the fact that these works are not about encounters with individual colonies. This fact is all the more striking given that the authors were not lacking in first-hand experience of travel to particular British possessions. Forster traveled twice to India and, though *A Passage to India* invests its Indian setting with modern European concerns, this novel is perhaps the most realistic of the modernist colonial odysseys, the most conscientious in representing the social world of the colony. Conrad's extensive travels are well documented: the better part of two decades spent on the sea, most of them with the British merchant marine, included multiple trips in the 1880s to the East, where much of "Karain" and *Lord Jim* are set, one journey up the Congo, in 1890, on a trip that inspired *Heart of Darkness*, and the briefest of encounters with the Caribbean and South America. Waugh too anticipated his characters' wanderings: he traveled through Africa in 1930–31, just before writing *Black Mischief*, returned there twice prior to writing *Scoop*, and visited South

America in 1933, where he wrote "The Man Who Liked Dickens," the short story on which a portion of *A Handful of Dust* is based. (Woolf is the one author who had the least direct personal experience of colonial travel, and *The Voyage Out*, though in many respects an autobiographical novel, is least so in its selection of South America as Rachel Vinrace's destination.) That such extensive collective experience in the field contributed mostly incidentals when transmuted into fiction can be attributed to the fact that the significance of colonialism for the British had little to do with the relation to particular colonies; the significance rather was more insular, shaped by domestic concerns. Nothing determined this significance more than the process of reoccupation.

The first two levels on which colonialism is drawn into the process of reoccupation overlap with familiar analyses of imperial culture. On one level, the epistemological ambitions of the Enlightenment, inflated by the pressures of reoccupation, helped shape the arrogance of Europe vis-à-vis its Others. The centripetal force of modernity described by Pratt, the belief in the universal applicability and consequent virtue of human reason, served as justification for Europe's domination of people in other parts of the world. A second level is evident in the transformation of overseas colonies into objects of nostalgia. I have associated this nostalgia with Hellenism in its many guises, although the discussion of Lukács has shown that the use of Greece often masked what is more profoundly understood as a response to the waning of Christian theology. Evident in contexts as diverse as adventure-tradition triumphalism and the fatigued yearning for renewal in Tennyson's "Ulysses," this colonialism-as-nostalgia reoccupies questions about happiness and paradise. These two aspects of imperial culture—its involvement with both Enlightenment ideology and Romantic nostalgia—appear contradictory. We first encountered their paradoxical conjunction in the popular adventure tradition, but the concept of reoccupation gives a fuller explanation of the paradox, revealing that both elements share a totalizing impulse. Though they take different routes, both are shaped by the need to imagine an integrated whole. One sees salvation as the *telos* of history, heralded by modern European thought; the other seeks salvation in the primitive past and on the periphery. The more precise diagnosis of each that is made possible by the concept of reoccupation creates a more sympathetic understanding but also the potential for a more effective critique.

Both of these influences of reoccupation on colonialism long preceded modernist culture, and both had long been subject to various sorts of critique. So it is not surprising to see both influences treated ambivalently in the modernist odysseys. These novels scorn Enlightenment ideology even as they share its centripetal arrogance in projecting European preoccupations onto other lands and in characterizing non-Europeans as savage.

And these novels offer primitivism as the best hope for the escape and renewal of the "heart," even as they ultimately recognize the darkness of the heart's chthonic forces. The traces of both Enlightenment optimism and nostalgia have grown faint in these works, which succumb to a grave morbidity that is explained by the third level on which reoccupation influenced colonialism. This third level, in contrast to the first two, emerged for the first time with New Imperialism and early modernist culture, for at this stage of development new prospects for occupying territory and acquiring colonies disappeared: there was no more *nova terra*. Rather than promising undiscovered opportunities for an expansion of influence and renewal of energy, the empire now revealed itself to its fullest extent. The culmination of colonial occupation appeared to complete a successful reoccupation, suddenly fulfilling the intention toward the totality of reality.

Although Jameson suggests in "Modernism and Imperialism" that the economic system was the totality from which modernists were alienated, since portions of it were transferred overseas in the era of New Imperialism, he also acknowledges elsewhere that "totalities are *always* absent" ("Absent Totality" 122, emphasis added), and clearly the export of components of the means of production began long before the late-nineteenth century. If the perception of England's relation to imperialism changed at this time, I would argue that it came less from the absence of totality than from its momentary realization, less from the disappearance of a completely perceivable economic system than from the sense, following the Scramble for Africa, of a geographical completion. For the first time, the world was filled up, maps were filled in, the earth was fully occupied. In *Heart of Darkness*, Marlow, recalling his boyhood "passion for maps," observes that "there were many blank spaces on the earth," even the largest of which, at the heart of Africa, "had got filled since my boyhood with rivers and lakes and names" (11–12). Conrad's reminiscences show that Marlow's boyhood passion is autobiographical, as both *A Personal Record* and "Geography and Some Explorers" describe his youthful attraction to the blank white spaces soon to be filled in on maps of the world (*Personal Record* 13; "Geography" 144–47). Again, Lenin, writing in 1916 but using turn-of-the-century statistics, announces:

> The characteristic feature of the period under review is the final partitioning of the globe—final . . . in the sense that the colonial policy of the capitalist countries has *completed* the seizure of the unoccupied territories on our planet. For the first time the world is completely divided up. (*Imperialism* 254)[27]

27. The emphasis is Lenin's. He emphasizes the notion of completion again in a brief recapitulation of his theory of imperialism in the opening pages of "Imperialism and the Split in Socialism," one of his attacks on Kautsky written later the same year.

If such completion suggested momentarily the possibility of a new compensatory power, a new extensive totality—a possibility realized in the world of the adventure romances and reflected in late-Victorian exuberance about imperial dominance—it also confirmed before long the illusory nature of this worldly compensation. The consoling and redemptive influence of this geographical totality did not prove equal to that of the transcendent totality of Christian theology. Thus when the colonial-odyssey novels explore whether the empire offers an opportunity to recover the extensive totality of the epic, they demonstrate the opportunity to be illusory both through their relation to the history of the genre and through their preoccupation with the mortality of their adventuring protagonists. They illustrate Lukács's suggestion that the novel is the epic in an age still thinking in terms of totality, but with the added twist that the hope of recovering a lost meaning through geopolitical domination can lead only to demonic madness or deepened disillusionment.

While the psychological benefits of this third and late-Victorian form of reoccupation were short-lived, they nevertheless exacted a high price in the form of heightened anxieties. The geographical totality placed new burdens on the English in their dual role as reoccupiers and occupiers. On the most superficial level, arrival at the zenith of empire produced anxiety about its decline; almost simultaneous with this moment of completion, the empire did in fact begin the gradual process of disintegration. The period spanned by modernism, from the 1890s through the 1930s, moves from the culmination of the second major period of British expansion through the initial stages in the subsequent waning of Britain's imperial influence. By the time of Victoria's 1897 Diamond Jubilee, following Britain's last acquisitions in Africa, the empire comprised approximately one-fourth of the world's population and one-fourth of its land mass. Doubt and criticism accompanied Britain's New Imperialism throughout and were strengthened by events like the disastrous Second Boer War (1899–1902), but the First World War was perhaps the first major step in the decline of the empire. Although several new British "mandates" were added at its conclusion, the Great War sapped much of the moral arrogance and cultural energy with which Britain had assumed the mantle of empire; moreover, it altered the balance of power with the colonies, which contributed substantially to the war effort. The change in relations already emerging at Versailles, where the self-governing dominions and India were represented individually, was codified by the 1931 Statute of Westminster, which transformed the empire into a Commonwealth of Nations. The increasing assertiveness and restlessness of the colonies throughout the interwar period presaged the independence movements and the further disintegration of the empire after World War II. So the culmination of geographical expansion led directly to the experience of a steady erosion of power.

Beyond the feared loss of power associated with the management of empire, however, lurked another burden deriving from the realization of a worldly totality. As a phenomenon shaped by reoccupation, the geographical completion of the empire placed the English in the position of God, as Mrs. Moore observes in *A Passage to India*. One of the functions of the Judeo-Christian God had been not merely to exercise authority over subjects, but to redeem them. When Kipling spoke of the White Man's burden, he identified a very real anxiety, even though he counterproductively mistook its source. The process of reoccupation produced a White Man's burden—a human assumption of divine responsibility for total redemption—that does not derive from empire but rather is projected onto and at times perhaps intensified by empire. This additional consequence of reoccupation, and the modernist perception that such total redemption is beyond the reach of humankind, help further explain the fixation on unredeemed death in the colonial-odyssey novels.

Literature as Redemptive Memory

Neither a Foucault-influenced historicism nor a Neomarxist materialism can adequately explain the modernist preoccupation with making literature redemptive. Conrad famously pronounces in his nonfiction that restoration is the primary obligation of the writer, and his fiction returns repeatedly to the same theme, as does the work of the other colonial-odyssey novelists. What makes the obligation so formidable at this particular juncture in history is its link to the concept of totality, resulting in the drive to redeem all of history and all of the peoples of the world. Forster is the one who seems temperamentally least inclined to succumb to this compulsion, and yet it contributes to his drift away from Hellenism in the writing of his final novel. In 1915 he wrote to Forrest Reid: "My defence at any last judgment would be 'I was trying to connect up and use all the fragments I was born with.' " This formulation lacks the urgency and desperation of similar expressions by others but nevertheless hints at the conjunction of redemption as a re-membering of fragments and the intention toward the totality of life ("all the fragments"). The redemptive ideal that Forster endorses here finds its fictional analogue, as we have seen, in *A Passage to India*: "How indeed is it possible for one human being to be sorry for all the sadness that meets him on the face of the earth . . . ? The soul is tired in a moment" (275).

The challenge of making literature redemptive is immeasurably heightened by the loss of community in the modern age, for the absence or inadequacy of communal rites of memory and mourning leaves the individual author isolated in the attempt to fulfill such a responsibility. This explains perhaps why Joyce stands apart from his London contemporaries on the question of literature's redemptive value, as much as in his use of the various components of the odyssey plot. While *Ulysses* points beyond any identifiable turn-of-the-century national or Dublin community, Joyce's unique position as author-in-exile of what was said to be the British empire's second city nevertheless gives his work a local focus, an attachment to a sense of community, however imaginary or utopian that community may be. Through his imaginative representation of Dublin, Joyce comes closer to realizing a total social and linguistic world than do any of the authors centered in London, which may explain why he does not exhibit the same drive for total redemption. When it comes to the question of a reoccupied redemptive faculty, he imagines himself the object rather than the agent: he famously expressed the desire "to give a picture of Dublin so complete that if the city one day suddenly disappeared from the earth it could be reconstructed out of my book" (qtd. in Budgen 67–68). Because he aims and claims to realize the totality of Dublin life in the present, he projects its imagined reconstruction into the future.

The role of community in remembering and redeeming is one of the social aspects of modernity that Blumenberg does not confront directly, and yet his model of reoccupation is necessary to explain fully Europe's late-modern burden of redemption, which derives not merely from the loss of community but from the questions left behind after the collapse of theology. The excessive scope of the individual's desire to redeem is a reoccupation of Christianity's desire for the total redemption of history; the redeeming subject is drawn into the vacated position of the redeemer of all humankind. And the best tool the modern age can summon for such a responsibility is human memory, often in the form of narrative. Much of the remainder of this study is devoted to analyses of the ways in which Conrad's colonial odysseys are shaped by a conjunction of the drives for totality and for redemption, and in anticipation of these readings I would like to highlight two of the more notable examples of the late-modern compulsion for a total secular redemption, examples found in the work of Nietzsche and Freud. Conrad's relation to Nietzsche has received significant critical attention in the past (in particular from Said), but the affinity between them has not been articulated in relation to this fundamental problematic.

Nietzsche's writing is full of passages that define this redemptive burden and show him attempting to fulfill or escape it, but one of the most compact and compelling is Zarathustra's sermon "On Redemption." Zarathustra's insistence on "willing backwards" involves the conviction that the past is not completed, but he fears that humankind is not yet capable of this willing backward, because the will is still in "fetters":

> "It was"—that is the name of the will's gnashing of teeth and most secret melancholy. Powerless against what has been done, he is an angry spectator of all that is past. The will cannot will backwards; and that he cannot break time and time's covetousness, is the will's loneliest melancholy. (251)

This unliberated will is a will to "revenge": "that time does not run backwards, that is his wrath" (251). Willing can liberate, however, when it recognizes that the past acquires its meaning from its place in the whole of history, and its meaning is therefore still incomplete: "All 'it was' is a fragment, a riddle, a dreadful accident—until the creative will says to it, 'But thus I willed it.' Until the creative will says to it, 'But thus I will it; thus I shall will it' " (253). This redemptive act of re-creating "it was" into "thus I willed it" is what Zarathustra means by "willing backwards," a secular act of redemption that is to be one of the talents, apparently, of the *Übermensch* (overman, superman).

Nietzsche's *Übermensch* belongs to a line of belated figures characterized by the inhuman demands placed upon them: the *Übermensch*, like Freud's *Über-Ich*-burdened ego and Walter Benjamin's angel of history, carry within their names an indication of the extra-human nature of their desire to exercise a redemptive memory. The melancholy and horror to which each succumbs is a symptom of the human will divided against itself, unable to fulfill its desire to make whole the accumulating wreckage of history.

During the years in which the concept of the *Über-Ich* (Over-I, superego) was crystallizing—the years of World War I and its aftermath—Freud came to a full realization of the futility of willing backward and, more generally, of the pathology of humankind's relation to the absolute. This is the period in which he generated his conceptions of melancholy, the uncanny, the repetition compulsion, and the death drive, all of which suggest in one way or another the bind in which the subject desires or is defined by that which would destroy it; all of which also contribute to the evolution of his theory from its earlier focus on infantile sexuality to the reflections on civilization in the 1920s. The essay on mourning and melancholy—from 1915, the year Lukács wrote *The Theory of the Novel* and Woolf published *The Voyage Out*—views melancholy as a pathology, as interrupted mourning, but by the time of *Beyond the Pleasure Principle* (1920), the concept of ambivalence central to Freud's understanding of mourning has been generalized into the supposition of two primary drives in humankind, Eros and Thanatos. With the latter, "silent" drive, he in effect suggests that all humans are inherently melancholy. In *The Ego and the Id*

(1923), he transforms the analogous concepts of the "ideal ego," the "critical instance," and the "conscience"—all describing a critical agent in the genesis of melancholy—into their final and fuller form in the concept of the *Über-Ich*, and in *Civilization and Its Discontents* (1930) one finds the culmination of Freud's metapsychology in the recognition of the oppressiveness of community. "It almost seems as if the creation of a great human community would be most successful if no attention had to be paid to the happiness of the individual" (21: 140).

Also belonging to this critical development in his thought is the essay "Das Unheimliche" (1919), which offers us yet another variation on the home motif in the modernist period. According to Freud, "the uncanny [*Unheimliche*, unhomey] is that class of the frightening which leads back to what is known of old and long familiar" (17: 220). When he turns to dictionaries in his attempt to uncover the "secret [*geheime*] nature of the uncanny [*Unheimlichen*]" (241), he discovers a semantic coincidence of opposites and concludes,

> We can understand why linguistic usage has extended *das Heimliche* ['homely'] into its opposite, *das Unheimliche;* for this uncanny is in reality nothing new or alien, but something which is familiar and old-established in the mind and which has become alienated from it only through the process of repression. This reference to the factor of repression enables us, furthermore, to understand Schelling's definition of the uncanny as something which ought to have remained hidden but has come to light. (241)

Thus the *Unheimliche* describes the psychological structure of the colonial-odyssey novels, which project the European subject's discontents onto foreign settings to confront them there as something unfamiliar, unsettling, unhomey.

Although linguistic and literary examples play an important role in the essay on the uncanny, Freud follows his usual practice of attributing his discovery of the concept to his experience as an analyst. He reports that many neurotic men find

> something uncanny about the female genital organs. This *unheimlich* place, however, is the entrance to the former *Heim* [home] of all human beings, to the place where each one of us lived once upon a time and in the beginning. There is a joking saying that 'Love is home-sickness'. . . . In this case too, then, the *unheimlich* is what was once *heimisch*, familiar; the prefix '*un*' ['un-'] is the token of repression. (17: 245)

In this passage Freud's theory, though still cast in sexual terms, has already begun to transform those terms into metaphors—in this case, a metaphor for nonexistence. The drive and the repression he associates here with the *Unheimliche* have less to do with Eros than with the negation of existence that would result by pushing the concept of *nostos* to its logical extreme. "Whatever reminds us of this inner 'compulsion to repeat,' " he argues in this essay, "is perceived as uncanny" (238)—and in *Beyond the Pleasure Principle*, written a short time later, he explicitly links the repetition compulsion to the death drive. The new theory of drives introduced in *Beyond the Pleasure Principle* is less specific about the "home," presenting the pattern of estrangement and return not in relation to female genital space but in relation to death—individual existence is an odyssey with nonexistence the point of departure and the destination. "The inanimate state was here earlier than the living state," he writes. The "former home of all human beings" implied by his analysis of the *Unheimliche* is not so much the womb as death. These two characterizations of home are not mutually exclusive, of course, and often in colonial-odyssey fiction we find them thoroughly integrated, as in Conrad's "Karain" or Woolf's first novel. But in such cases, as in Freud's postwar theory, the sexual problematic then falls under the influence of the reoccupation that shapes the reflections on the absolute.

For this study, Freud serves as a convenient contemporary of the modernist novelists. His thought exemplifies an acute, late-modern sense of the impossible burden resulting from reoccupation, and out of this sense of crisis he shapes the beginnings of a terminology capable of diagnosing the phenomenon. The *Über-Ich* is a product of reoccupation—it becomes the repository of responsibility for history's accumulated woes—and the *Unheimliche* describes the experience of the living who must confront this burden. While Blumenberg's analysis suggests this is an historically conditioned phenomenon, Freud gives it the generality and closure of myth, specifically the circular closure of the odyssey myth. Psychoanalytic theory demonstrates that in the modernist period the centrifugal odyssey tradition finds its underground centripetal force in Thanatos: death is home. The will to death has subsumed the will to power.

3

Conrad's Weariness

Let us go on, as if all arose from one and the same weariness, on
and on heaping up and up, until there is no room, no light, for any
more.

—SAMUEL BECKETT, *Molloy*

Conrad explores the limits of the will to power and, like Freud, he finds
it unable to resist the will to death; instead of resisting, it ends up
serving the will to death. To understand fully the death drive manifested
repeatedly in Conrad's characters, we must perceive not only Conrad's
borrowings from the odyssey tradition and his ambivalence about European imperialism, but also the ways in which his work is a product of reoccupation. He would like his art to compensate for the absence of an omniscient and beneficent deity. This desire is reflected in the large number
of Conradian characters who "like posing as gods" (as Forster's Mrs.
Moore says of the British). Queen Victoria, who makes a brief but significant appearance in "Karain," is perhaps Conrad's most acutely paradoxical figure of reoccupation, but Kurtz, "Lord" Jim, and *Nostromo*'s Charles
Gould—to name only the most prominent examples from works I plan to
discuss here—all pose as gods, reoccupying the position of the West's ab-
sconded deity. In his nonfiction, Conrad indicates that he shares this impulse with his characters—he would like to step into the breach by using
fiction to provide the redemptive meaning that he no longer expects from
a divine source.

His inability to fulfill this desire leads to a wearying melancholy manifested, again, both in his nonfiction and in his fictional characters. In their
roles as would-be deities, the characters repeatedly lead us into distor-
tions and horrors, into the demonic rather than the divine. Karain, Kurtz,

Jim, and Decoud all evidence a relationship to death and the dead that is particular to the late-modern period of failed reoccupation. Their burdensome relationship to the dead shapes Conrad's use of the odyssey motif: echoes of the Hades episode predominate.[1] While he was clearly well versed in the epic tradition, his melancholy, hell-bound characters are signs of this tradition's fatigue. (In contrast to Forster and Woolf, he is free of the influence of Cambridge Hellenism.) One lexical marker of the fatigue is Conrad's fondness for various forms of the word *weary*. Derived from the Old English *wérig*, it names the effects of a journey that has lasted too long. Etymologists explain that it is related to the Old English *wórian*, meaning "to wander, go astray," and in corresponding Old Norse and Old High German words its early semantic range extended to "bewildered," "stupefied," "mad," and "intoxicated."[2] From its beginning, in other words, "weary" indicated mental as well as physical fatigue, and the *OED* informs us that in "modern times" the sense of mental fatigue only grew in strength and gravity. Always already an exhausted metaphor, "weariness" eventually serves to express an age's sense of its own disorienting belatedness: Conrad and his weary characters manifest the late-modern sense that history has gone astray.

Conrad uses *weary* in its various forms with increasing frequency throughout the first decade of his writing career; by the time of *Nostromo* his use can seem indiscriminate. (It is attached, for example, not only to Decoud, the Goulds, and Dr. Monygham, as one might expect, but to Nostromo himself at a stage of his career when he still shows no sign of weariness.) The word surfaces repeatedly and revealingly in scenes involving Conradian protagonists who have felt the pressure to pose as gods. In the following pages I cite some of these scenes without commenting on every appearance of the word, but its repetition in crucial passages arises from the defeat of Conrad's most profound artistic ideals. The weariness resulting from failed attempts to fill the god-shaped void is what links Karain and Karain's Victoria, Marlow's Jim and Kurtz (and sometimes Marlow himself), and Charles and Emilia Gould—and this weariness is what links these characters in the final analysis to Conrad himself.

By remembering the etymology of *weariness*, "wandering," we also gain insight into its complement and onetime antithesis, *home*. The weariness of Conrad's protagonists is a function of the complex sense of crisis

---

1. On modernist *katabasis* as an allegorical representation of the past, see Pike.
2. The entries in the *OED* and in the etymological dictionaries by Ernest Klein and Walter Skeat are all in basic agreement about the etymology and semantic range of "weary."

associated with their notions of home.[3] He founds his colonial fiction on the paradox that, despite the exotic settings and international cast of characters, the weariness derives primarily from experiences closer to home. In making such an assertion, one needs to acknowledge the difficulty of determining what and where home is for Conrad, and this determination may prove especially difficult for Anglo-American readers, even though Conrad wrote in English. Ford Madox Ford claimed that Conrad never felt at home in England, and Edward Garnett wrote that Conrad "had the Continental tradition in his blood and his nerves in a way no Englishman has." Zdzisław Najder, the leading Polish expert on Conrad, has observed that this continental component manifests itself in Conrad's notion of home; Najder notes as an example that the significance of the hero's relation to his home in *Lord Jim* can best be understood "within the conceptual framework of the Polish tradition" ("Joseph Conrad").[4]

The Polish notion of *ojczyzna* carries a mystical and moral weight that is lacking in the word "homeland" or "fatherland" or any other possible English equivalent. *Ojczyzna* has an affinity with an untranslatable term from another central-European language: *Heimat*, derived from the root *Heim*, or home, evokes a similar, profoundly Romantic sense of the identity-shaping influence of one's place of origin.[5] *Heimat* is related etymologically to, among other words, *heimisch* (native or domestic), *heimlich* (secret or familiar), *Geheimnis* (secret or mystery), and *unheimlich* (uncanny). The common etymology does not necessarily indicate, of course, any essential or substantive identity among the terms. But the linguistic link does at least invite speculation about a possible historical and psychological coincidence of opposites: mystery and familiarity, strangeness and domesticity, exoticism and homeliness. In Freud's discovery of something *geheim* and *heimisch* in the *Unheimliche*, we have found an affinity to the insight that had already emerged in Conrad's colonial fiction, namely, that the earth's most exotic and troubling mysteries are domestic, found in one's own home and homeland. The numerous physical displacements in Conrad's life and work reinforce and often mask the sense of metaphysical estrangement that was generated from within Europe and is central to

3. George has usefully examined the politics of this crisis (65–88).
4. The revised version of Najder's comments appears in *Conrad in Perspective* (173–74). I first presented my interpretation of Conrad's notion of home (in relation to the *Narcissus* preface) at the same conference.
5. The most literal translations of *ojczyzna*—and in many instances probably the most appropriate translations—are *Vaterland* in German and "fatherland" in English. *Ojczyzna* is related to *ojciec*, "father."

Conrad's vision. Nowhere is the sense of weariness stronger for Conrad than when he contemplates the elusiveness of a metaphysical home.

I focus my attention here on texts Conrad wrote and published between 1897 and 1904. In this period he produced the majority of his colonial odysseys, and in this period he focused most intensively on the consequences of the failure of reoccupation. "Karain" (1897), *Heart of Darkness* (1899), and *Lord Jim* (1901) explore the psychological, moral, and political implications of the imperial subject who feels compelled to fill the god-shaped void through his own actions. Though departing in important respects from the colonial-odyssey subgenre, *Nostromo* (1904) carries Conrad's reflections on the political implications of reoccupation a long step beyond the earlier works, demonstrating that the challenge of reoccupation is beyond the capabilities of the modern state as well as the modern subject. Neither individually nor collectively, Conrad suggests, can moderns accomplish the superhuman task of transmuting all suffering into meaning, all remorse into desire fulfilled.

"Remorse and Power":
Karain and the Queen

Are there spectres moving in the darkness?
    —ALFRED TENNYSON, "On the Jubilee of Queen Victoria"
                                                (1887)

I have lived during many days with the faithful dead.
        —JOSEPH CONRAD to Edward Garnett, 20 April 1897

In the opening chapter of "Karain: A Memory" the narrator declares that the most one can expect from life is the knowledge of "remorse and power." This pairing points the story's reflection on the psychology of rule in a particular temporal direction: toward the past. The narrator links remorse and power while describing Karain and, more particularly, while imagining Karain's death: "He was an adventurer of the sea, an outcast, a ruler—and my very good friend. I wish him a quick death in a stand-up fight, a death in sunshine; for he had known remorse and power, and no man can demand more from life" (8–9). The story is focused so completely on the past that we never learn what Karain's fate is—he may no longer be alive at the time the narrator offers us this description. Nor does the reader know at this point in the narrative the particular source of Karain's remorse. One might jump to the conclusion that remorse arises from the exercise of power over others, but the ambiguity of the conjunction "and" leaves the relation between remorse and power enigmatic. In fact, in Karain's case, as we learn later in the story, remorse precedes and contributes to power. Here, in the first chapter of the story, the omission of particulars gives the comments about Karain a general validity. "No man can demand" a different experience: there is remorse, there is power, and then there is death. For Conrad's most comprehending British readers, ruled by a morose monarch widely viewed as a symbol of British imperial power, such a message could not have been comforting.

Conrad wrote "Karain: A Memory" in the early spring of 1897, between completion of *The Nigger of the "Narcissus"* (in January) and composition of its famous preface (in August). It is the story that initiated his fortunate five-year affiliation with *Blackwood's Magazine*, which would serialize *Heart of Darkness* two years later. It also represents an important step toward the discovery of Marlow, for it contains Conrad's first use of one narrator (unnamed) to frame the story of another (Karain), a framing that allows him to distance the cruder forms of imperial ideology while engaging the underlying psychological dynamic of imperial culture. Despite its virtues as a work of fiction and its important position in Conrad's corpus, "Karain" received comparatively little critical attention prior to this past decade, when postcolonial approaches in particular have begun to find it one of the more useful of Conrad's Malay stories.[1] The earlier neglect may be attributable in part to the negative judgment of Albert Guerard, who criticized the story for ending in "trivial anecdote." Hinting at the difficulty of identifying with the protagonist Karain, whom he calls a "superstitious native," Guerard comments that "it is as though Conrad did not yet want to admit that Lord Jim with his crime was 'one of us' " (91).[2] This comment has fed into a tradition of viewing the tale as exotic, whether the exoticism is characterized as Polish, deriving most specifically from Adam Mickiewicz's ballad *Czaty* (see Busza 209), or as Malay, a discovery from Conrad's days in the merchant marine. While not wishing to reject such analyses, I hope to show how the exotic material also mirrors domestic

1. My claims to offer new historical information about the story's gilt Jubilee sixpence and a new theoretical orientation emphasizing the theological underpinnings of the story's exoticism are based on a survey of the following "Karain" criticism. Articles on the story have been published by Johnson ("Conrad's 'Karain' "; see also *Conrad's Models* 28–29), Herbert, Naipaul, La Bossière ("Marvellous Thing"; also *Joseph Conrad* 95–96), Humphries, Drouart, Conroy, GoGwilt ("Alien Genealogies"; also *Invention* 43–63), Dryden, DeKoven ("Conrad's *Unrest*"), Krajka ("Betrayal" and "Making Magic" are largely the same; also *Isolation* 85–88), Fothergill, and Brown and Sant. Other works commenting on "Karain" include those by Bendz (44–46), Gordan (247–52), W. Wright (25–27), Geurard (89–92), Andreas (31–34), Boyle (63–65), Busza (209–15), Fleishman (*Conrad's Politics* 120–21), Resink (305–23 passim), Stein (5–8), Graver (29–34), Lee (23–34), Dowden (31–33), Gillon (*Conrad and Shakespeare* 44–46 and *Joseph Conrad* 33–35), Gekoski (48–50), Bruss (47–57), Weiand (122–24), Bonney (22–24), Schwarz (29–30), Tarnawski (162–63), Wilson (63–64), Fraser (38–47), Lester (56–57), Wollaeger (42–51), Hervouet (49–52), Ambrosini (70–79), Bongie (159–61, 164–65), Erdinast-Vulcan (*Joseph Conrad* 31–33 and *Strange Short Fiction* 62–76), Watts ("Conrad" 21–22), McLauchlan (61–62), Hampson ("Topographical Mysteries" 161–63 and *Cross-Cultural Encounters* 121–28), Billy (121–29), Tagge (108–9), and Roberts (49–56). The earliest reviews of *Tales of Unrest* (1898) are collected in Sherry, *Conrad: The Critical Heritage*.

2. Guerard's otherwise insightful Conrad criticism continues to have a deservedly long shelf life. His nicely formulated observation that Lord Jim is anticipated in "Karain's desperate attempt to leave in space what travels with him in time" has proved a fruitful stimulus for a number of later Conrad critics (91). My own interpretation can be seen partly as an attempt to elaborate on this description while transferring it to the British.

concerns that are best understood as the search for a spiritual or psychic power sufficiently robust to conquer a form of remorse unique to the modern age. By identifying the specific historical model for the gilt coin at the center of the tale, I intend to explore both the nature of the remorse projected onto Karain and Conrad's pessimism about the possibility of alleviating it.

Guerard's comment about Karain's otherness points to one significant way in which this story diverges from the colonial-odyssey subgenre, namely that, as the primary Odysseus figure, Karain is not a European and his journey does not begin in the West. As I hope to show, however, he is nevertheless "one of us," and the ways in which he is marked as different are merely an indication of the discomfort caused by the identification. The narrator presents him indeed as a superstitious native, lacking in rational understanding, subject to delusional horrors and able to escape them through the use of counterfeit talismans; but in this regard the narrator is only half reliable, for he misleadingly opposes Karain's belief and behavior to Western civilization. One of the story's central points, demonstrated repeatedly, is that Europeans are no less superstitious and no less criminal. Like Karain, they prove to be haunted by the voices of the dead; their power, like Karain's, is not free of remorse; and their hopes for relief take a form no less mystical. The parallels between East and West are reinforced by the ambiguous subtitle, "A Memory," which refers both to Karain's memory of the friend he murdered and to the narrator's memory of Karain. The story not only exploits but also undermines the opposition between Western enlightenment and Eastern superstition by treating the English narrator's rationalism ironically. In particular, through the ironies of the closing scenes, which are anything but trivial anecdote, the story shows how the burden of remorse helps shape the culture of empire. By demonstrating this in a semi-comic fashion, "Karain" exposes the empire's inability to carry the burden.

The story's exploration of British New Imperialism takes place within the larger context of Conrad's ambivalent reaction to modernity, which finds a nice one-sentence crystallization in this story. It is a sentence in which the narrator excuses his destructive and illegal selling of guns to Karain by claiming that he and his compatriots at least tried to make their customer, suffering from "profound ignorance of the rest of the world," view their exchanges more broadly: "We tried to enlighten him, but our attempts to make clear the irresistible nature of the forces which he desired to arrest failed to discourage his eagerness to strike a blow for his own primitive ideas" (18). The sentence moves from enlightenment to primitiveness, at first aligning the former with the Europeans and the latter with Karain. Their opposing desires bring together the opposed ideas:

we hear of the Europeans' "attempts" concentrated in one direction, and of Karain's desire and "eagerness" focused in the other. The result of these contradictory trajectories is suggested first by the term "irresistible," attributed to the forces for which the Europeans speak, but by the end of the sentence that attribute has migrated to Karain's primitive ideas, which have successfully resisted enlightenment; the Europeans' attempts have "failed," much as, we assume, Karain is doomed to destruction.[3] The momentum of the sentence and its complex use of the word "force," fluctuating between intellectual influence and physical violence, link civilization to barbarism. It is one of many passages in "Karain" where the narrator speaks more profoundly than he knows; Conrad's pessimism emerges here from beneath the surface of the narrator's self-justification.[4]

If the story insists on the parallels between enlightenment and primitiveness, this does not mean the remorse of the British and Karain is identical. Karain's guilt is traceable to a particular act—his murder of his friend Matara—and in the end his culpability becomes a cipher for, or projection of, the guilt of the British. Their guilt, however, is overdetermined. It derives first of all from their colonial activities. Although the *Spanish* rule the territory where Karain and the British operate, and although a *Dutchman* is at the center of the initial betrayal (he elopes with Matara's sister, sending Matara and Karain on their quest for revenge), these details may be seen as minor displacements, for, as in *Heart of Darkness*, Conrad gives the offending parties roots on the continent and thus superficially insulates the conservative readership of *Blackwood's* from the need to identify too closely with the culprits. And yet in the context of European

3. The logic of Conrad's sentence resembles the logical pattern of a marvelous parable by Kafka: "The crows claim that a single crow could destroy heaven. That is undoubtedly so, but it proves nothing against heaven, because heavens mean precisely: the impossibility of crows" (32). Although it would not preserve the shrewd shifting between singular and plural forms in Kafka's parable, the following might serve as a paraphrase of the underlying argument of Conrad's sentence: "The enlightened claim that enlightenment could destroy primitivism. That is undoubtedly so, but it proves nothing against primitivism, because primitivism means precisely: the impossibility enlightenment." The necessity of eventually construing the word "force" in Conrad's sentence to mean imperial violence encourages Conrad's reader to acknowledge the persistence of barbarism in civilization.

4. Many critics have credited the narrator of "Karain" with more understanding and insight than I do, a discrepancy evident especially in readings of the story's final scene. This variation in responses is easily explained as the result of an inconsistency in Conrad's characterization: despite his ironic treatment of the narrator's narrowness, Conrad cannot avoid sometimes speaking through him. Given the ignorant comments the narrator sometimes makes and Conrad's distance from them, I have chosen to view the narrator as consistently uncomprehending and to see his wiser and more unsettling observations as authorial intrusions. In some passages, such as the sentence discussed here, the limitations of the narrator and the insights of Conrad are evident on different levels, and thus coexist to great effect.

colonial activity in the East, these culprits—white, European, imperial-ist—are indistinguishable from the British. It is understandable that Karain believed his three British visitors "to be emissaries of Govern-ment" (12), for there are signs Conrad wants us, as well, to view them as representatives of European imperialism. In their role as gunrunners sup-plying Karain for his local wars, they are as culpable as anyone. The isola-tion of Karain's land made it possible for them "in comparative safety" to "break the law against the traffic in firearms and ammunition with the na-tives" (7). However, when Karain tells them his story of remorse, they are making their final delivery, since "the game was becoming at last too dan-gerous; . . . the risks were too great." They are fully aware that their smug-gling is speeding Karain on his way to an "honourable disaster" (19). Such disaster then becomes the stimulus for the narrator's memory of Karain: years after their encounter, the narrator begins his recollection when he reads in the newspapers "of various native risings in the Eastern Archi-pelago" (3). The activities of Karain's three white acquaintances thus typ-ify the not uncommon imperial practice of pursuing material gain—espe-cially gain from the sale of weaponry—even at the price of instability and "disaster" for the local population.

If the activities of the Europeans provide objective grounds for British guilt, it is also possible to see such guilt as entirely uncanny, generated from within and projected onto imperial experiences rather than deriving from them. This dynamic is evident when Karain serves as a stand-in for the Europeans, when his guilt, haunting memories, and superstition prove to be theirs. From this perspective, the story's use of allusions to Hades—and other references to the presence of the dead among the liv-ing—reveal another source of European melancholy beyond imperialism, a source of remorse not derived from power. This agonistic relation to the past emerges in the figure of Karain as a convergence of epic heroism, im-perial fantasy, and spiritual weariness.

Hades and the Burden of the Past

Karain is never without a protective or haunting spirit, and the succes-sion of spirits—seductive phantom, murdered friend, Queen's effigy—di-vides his career into three periods, with each spirit not only replacing but displacing its predecessor. First he is accompanied by the beguiling image of the sister of his "only friend," Matara. After she flees from her home with the Dutch trader, Karain and Matara wander in search of them for years, committed to making them pay with their lives for the dishonor she has done her family and people. But during the years of pursuit and deprivation, memory of this woman's beauty begins to haunt Karain until he feels himself accompanied by her at all times:

> She swam on the sea to follow me. . . . In the silence of foreign countries she spoke to me very low in the language of my people. No one saw her; no one heard her. . . . I saw her! The consoler of sleepless nights, of weary days; the companion of troubled years! I saw her! . . . —a faithful wanderer by my side. (34–35, 37)

Lest her relation to Athena not be obvious already, the narrator soon makes the Homeric parallel explicit in speaking of Karain's "wanderings, of that obscure Odyssey of revenge" (40). But the sister is a bewitching Circe more often than a benevolent Athena. We twice hear of her "extreme" beauty, "silencing the reason and ravishing the heart of the beholders" (30, 36). Her spell is broken and Karain's self-deception exposed only after he and Matara actually find the sister and Karain sacrifices Matara to save her life. She rewards Karain by denying any knowledge of him—"No! I never saw him before" (39)—and with this denial she disappears from his life forever, ending the first phase of his spiritual odyssey.

The last whispered words of the betrayed and murdered friend now echo endlessly in Karain's ears: "you are my friend—kill with a sure shot" (37).[5] It is this second phase of Karain's career that imparts to the story its "gloomy" atmosphere and provides its central problem. Karain must find a charm "to silence the lifeless voice" of his friend in order to free himself, "the slave of the dead" (43). During the time when Karain first conquered and ruled his small land and for most of the two years that the narrator knew him, an old man served this function, always remaining directly behind Karain to keep away the haunting spirit, but the death of this old man exposes Karain again to the "reproachful shade" and drives him to the Europeans to tell his story and ask for help. Of the three gunrunners who hear his story on board their ship—Hollis, Jackson, and the narrator—the narrator is the least sympathetic character: he shows the least sympathy for Karain and thus receives the least from Conrad and the reader. When he complacently asserts to Karain that "there is forgetfulness in life. Even the dead cease to speak in time," Karain reacts "with bitter resentment" and the narrator's comment on this resentment betrays the extent of his condescension: "He startled me. It was amazing. To him

5. In the altered context—with Matara rather than the Dutchman as the object of "kill"—these last words echo Christ's taunting encouragement of Judas, though of course Matara utters them unaware of the fatal implications. The parallel to an older Biblical story—that of Cain and Abel—has been observed in earlier Conrad criticism. See Erdinast-Vulcan (32); GoGwilt, *Invention of the West* (55–56); Conroy, "Ghostwriting" (5).

his life—that cruel mirage of love and peace—seemed as real, as undeniable, as theirs would be to any saint, philosopher, or fool of us all" (43–44). The comment not only exposes the narrator's limitations but also emphasizes Karain's representative position, for once allowances are made for the narrator's lack of comprehension, the ironic reversal of his amazement leaves one associating Karain affirmatively with "any saint, philosopher, or fool of us all" and perceiving us all to be living a "cruel mirage of love and peace." The narrator has succeeded here, despite his obtuseness, in identifying the central problem of the story: the problem of forgetfulness, of silencing the voices of the unrestful, unplacated dead.

This central problem is represented by an epic image borrowed from book 11 of *The Odyssey* and presented piecemeal throughout the story: the image of the living wanderer descending into Hades to converse with the dead. The first borrowing comes as Conrad's narrator, in introducing the mysteriousness of Karain and his surroundings, describes a moment when it appeared as if "the earth had indeed rolled away from under his land, and he, with his handful of people, stood surrounded by a silent tumult as of contending shades"—and the narrator promptly connects this image to the still unexplained "memories" that haunt Karain (8). The second appearance of the image also associates Karain with Odysseus, but this time it is invoked by Karain himself, who recalls the blood thirst of Homer's dead. At the moment of his greatest madness and anger while relating his story to the Englishmen on board their schooner, he jumps up, shouting, "By the spirits that drink blood: by the spirits that cry in the night: by all the spirits of fury, misfortune, and death, I swear—some day I will strike into every heart I meet—I . . ." (43). These passages make clear that Karain is an impoverished Odysseus: he lacks the means to exploit—or simply to control and contain—the dead.

This impoverishment and the image through which it is communicated are not reserved only for Karain and his people, as Conrad's subsequent uses of this Homeric episode draw the Europeans into the charmed circle. For instance, in response to Karain's confession the narrator himself comments that "we felt as though we three had been called to the very gate of Infernal Regions" (45).[6] The story's final and most important adaptation of

---

6. The sentence in full reads: "We felt as though we three had been called to the very gate of Infernal Regions to judge, to decide the fate of a wanderer coming suddenly from a world of sunshine and illusions" (45). While casting Karain as the wandering Odysseus on his descent to Hades, this oddly casts the three listeners in the role of the dead whom Odysseus visits. The closest correspondence in Homer is Tiresias, whom Odysseus seeks out for advice about the future, but again the correspondence only highlights the distance. Tiresias is able to advise Odysseus, but the narrator invokes this precedent at a moment when he and his companions are clueless about how to assist Karain: "We did not know what to do[,] . . . could not find one word to the purpose among us."

the image comes when Hollis devises Karain's cure, which momentarily cures the narrator, as well. Hollis rummages through his small box to retrieve mementos from his recent "dash home through the Canal," and the narrator perceives

> that the cabin of the schooner was becoming filled with a stir invisible and living as of subtle breaths. All the ghosts driven out of the unbelieving West by men who pretend to be wise and alone and at peace—all the homeless ghosts of an unbelieving world—appeared suddenly round the figure of Hollis bending over the box . . . —they all seemed to come from the inhospitable regions of the earth to crowd into the gloomy cabin, as though it had been a refuge and, in all the unbelieving world, the only place of avenging belief. . . . (47–49)

The narrator then reports that the spirits "all disappeared" the moment Hollis produced "something small that glittered between his fingers. It looked like a coin." A coin indeed: "He held it up. It was a sixpence—a Jubilee sixpence. It was gilt; it had a hole punched near the rim" (49). Thus Conrad provides another sign that the haunting memories (and their cure) belong as much or more to the Europeans as they do to Karain.

Hollis is initially worried that the coin's "engraved image"—the likeness of the Queen—may prevent Karain from accepting the sixpence (48), but in fact the Queen and the empire she rules are instrumental to the coin's effectiveness. Earlier, the narrator recalled that Karain began each visit by inquiring about the Queen:

> He was fascinated by the holder of a sceptre the shadow of which, stretching from the westward over the earth and over the seas, passed far beyond his own hand's-breadth of conquered land. He multiplied questions; he could never know enough of the Monarch of whom he spoke with wonder and chivalrous respect—with a kind of affectionate awe! Afterwards, when we had learned that he was the son of a woman who had many years ago ruled a small Bugis state, we came to suspect that the memory of his mother (of whom he spoke with enthusiasm) mingled somehow in his mind with the image he tried to form for himself of the far-off Queen whom he called Great, Invincible, Pious, and Fortunate. (12–13)

As he presents the token to Karain, Hollis says in Malay that "the image of the Great Queen" is "the most powerful thing the white men know," and then comments in English to his companions—as if they are the ones he must convince—that the Queen

> commands a spirit, too—the spirit of her nation; a masterful, conscientious, unscrupulous, unconquerable devil . . . that does a lot of good—inci-

dentally . . . a lot of good . . . at times—and wouldn't stand any fuss from the best ghost out for such a little thing as our friend's shot. (49–50; ellipses in original)

The three affirm their "faith in the power of Hollis's charm efficiently enough" (51) that it appears to work on Karain, restoring to him the "illusion of unavoidable success" (52) as he returns to shore and passes "out of our life forever" (53). In the third and final phase of his career, then, it is the Queen who becomes his guiding spirit, the Athena who is always at his side. The form in which she works her magic, her effigy on the Jubilee sixpence, is thus asked to carry a lot of meaning—perhaps too much meaning—in the context of the story. Her supposed ability to silence the clamor of the dead is worth examining in detail.

Gilt Sixpence, Golden Jubilee

The coin and the historical event with which it became associated provide an economical way for Conrad to evoke a complex semantic field. The Jubilee sixpence was a common coin for contemporary readers, who would have immediately associated it in specific ways with Britain's imperial activities and the Queen's role in them. If "Karain" has a major weakness, it is that so much of its significance is condensed into so trivial an object. Such a strategy has its advantages, as much of the story's meaning and humor derive from the incommensurability between the sixpence and what the sixpence is called upon to represent. However, there is the risk that much of the meaning will remain uninterpreted or underinterpreted, for the story finds no other means of earning the payoff contained in the symbol of the sixpence. It is thus understandable that when V. S. Naipaul, in an essay titled "Conrad's Darkness," wants to illustrate the quality in Conrad that he calls puzzling, elusive, obscure, and impenetrable, he turns to "Karain": "The simple yarn is made to carry a lot" (190). He explains further that its

truths . . . are difficult ones. The world of illusions, men as prisoners of their cultures, belief and unbelief: these are truths one has to be ready for, and perhaps half possess already, because the story does not carry them convincingly within itself. (191)

The difficulty of such truths may well account for the extremity of the condensation they undergo in the sixpence; their "difficulty"—a term with affinities, in this context, to the psychoanalytic notion of resistance—

is transferred and transformed into the challenging rhetorical strategies of the truth-concealing fiction. And yet, because of a very different but overlapping sort of difficulty, I think Naipaul exaggerates the inaccessibility of this story. As an instance of Conradian darkness, the opacity of "Karain" is a problem that has worsened with time, for certain facts about the gilt sixpence and its potential range of symbolic associations lay more readily at hand for Conrad's contemporaries. The coin was first issued in the year of Victoria's Golden Jubilee (1887), Conrad's story in the year of her Diamond Jubilee (1897). Thus in turn-of-the-century Britain, the coin could have worked its literary magic subliminally if not intellectually; the story, in other words, would have carried its truths more convincingly within itself. To reveal the intensity of the condensation at work in the story and simultaneously to minimize the opacity accumulated through historical distance, I propose examining both coin and Jubilees in some detail.

Criticism on "Karain" to date has said little about the historical basis for Conrad's sixpence, nothing about the literary significance of the gilt.[7] The Jubilee issue was in fact the standard British coinage for six years, and it represents one stage in a numismatic history that in certain details reflects the growing imperial consciousness of the period. For example, as Peter Seaby explains, well before the Jubilee

> the abbreviation *brit:* [inscribed on coins] is changed to *britt:*, the doubling of the last letter of a contraction being the classical method of indicating an abbreviation of a plural form (*Britt.* is the contraction of *Britanniarum*—"of the Britains"—meaning "of Great Britain and the British colonies overseas"). (100)

7. Graver commented much earlier, though inaccurately, that the "coin is a Jubilee sixpence minted in 1888 to celebrate Victoria's fifty years as sovereign" (33). Robert Lee suggests that the sixpence is "worth about eighteen cents" (33). GoGwilt speculates that it "is, one assumes, a coin from the 1887 Jubilee celebrations" (*Invention* 62). Drouart follows GoGwilt in describing the sixpence as "produced to celebrate fifty years of Victoria's reign" (146). (Drouart draws on an earlier version of GoGwilt's chapter that appeared in *Mosaic* in 1991.) Dryden devotes one sentence to the coin's gilt, misleadingly suggesting that "this sixpence is not even the real thing" (*Joseph Conrad* 130; cf. her "Karain" 46n28)—as a sixpence the coin is perfectly genuine.

Without citing a published source, Dryden attributes her knowledge of the gilt's significance to Cedric Watts. After publishing my interpretation of "Karain" as a journal article (*Modern Fiction Studies* 47 [2001]: 723–52), I learned in correspondence with Professor Watts that he had noted the fraudulent status of the coin in an endnote to his edition of the tale in *Heart of Darkness and Other Tales* (259n83). The note has apparently gone unremarked in "Karain" criticism; interpretations appearing after his edition of the story have not exploited Conrad's selection of the gilt coin any more than those appearing earlier. Professor Watts informs me that he might offer his own interpretation of the gilt sixpence in a new introduction to his edition (forthcoming in a new printing).

This feature was perpetuated in the Jubilee issue (see figure 2) but was not enough to satisfy the Queen, who began to lobby for inclusion of what she called "one of her proudest titles," Empress of India, within the inscription circling her portrait. She insisted that the challenge of finding sufficient space on the coins was not insurmountable, a disingenuous argument since the real obstacle was the 1876 bill that granted her the title but included the limitation that it be used only in India or in matters directly related to India. Her lobbying was eventually successful, in apparent defiance of the law, for when the Jubilee coinage was discontinued in 1893 in favor of a design with a more popular image the Queen, the new coins included the inscription IND.IMP for *Indiæ Imperatrix*.[8]

No coinage of the period was more strongly associated with Britain's New Imperialism and its champion Queen Victoria than that which Conrad introduces into his story. It was linked to the yearlong celebration in 1887, highlighted by a royal procession through London in June, to mark the fiftieth anniversary of her accession to the throne, although the coinage was not initially intended as a Jubilee issue and bears no reference to that event or her accession. The need to update the Queen's effigy had long been recognized; nearly fifty years into her reign, coins were still decorated by a portrait of her dating to the time of her accession in 1837 at the age of eighteen. A new design was delayed long enough to be issued in conjunction with the 1887 celebration. Although the public snatched up the coins as Jubilee mementos, the portrait of the Queen was widely condemned, especially her small, crooked crown and limp veil. The design had other problems as well, problems which explain Conrad's selection of the sixpence over other Jubilee denominations for use in "Karain." Since values were not indicated on the Jubilee coins, they could be distinguished only by size, design, and material. This was an unpopular design feature, but it was a problem especially for the sixpence and half-sovereign. Identical in size and design, differing only in material, these two coins were an invitation to fraud. As one writer explained in *The Times* on June 22, the day after the Jubilee processions, "I think it is a great blunder that the new sixpence should be precisely the same in size and pattern as the new half-sovereign and that it bears no indication of value. It will be very easy to gild these coins and pass them through banks for

8. See Seaby 101 and Lant, "Jubilee Coinage" 139–40. Rawlings's 1898 history of British coinage presents a different interpretation of the Royal Titles Act of 1876 (126). In language that is reminiscent of the Queen's and Karain's theatricality, thus giving a second meaning to the term "half-sovereign," Rawlings also explains that a Jubilee sixpence could be "dressed in a gilt coat" and made "to personate a half-sovereign, a fact which was immediately taken advantage of by the dishonest" (125).

Figure 2. The withdrawn-type Jubilee sixpence of 1887. © The British Museum.

half-sovereigns" (qtd. in Lant, *Insubstantial Pageant* 182 and "Jubilee Coinage" 137). The fear was justified: the coins were gilded for substantial profit. Before the end of the year the original Jubilee sixpence was withdrawn and its reverse was replaced with an earlier design clearly indicating its value.

Conrad provides an unequivocal clue that Hollis's coin is the withdrawn-type Jubilee sixpence when he has his narrator announce that "it was gilt." Conrad has carefully placed this disclosure, a kind of warning about inflated value, immediately before Hollis's boast to his white companions that "the thing itself is of great power—money, you know" (49). For some memento collectors and readers, the fact that the coin was gilt would not necessarily alter its symbolic value. One can imagine such collectors knowingly buying the counterfeit half-sovereign, with pendant-hole already punched, from entrepreneurs engaged in what George Gissing calls "Jubilee speculation"; but such readers miss the finest ironic touch in a story filled with irony. The deflation of value through the suggestion of deception and fraud reflects not only on Hollis's claim regarding the power of British money, but on the Queen and her two Jubilees and all that they represent.

The Jubilees represented first and foremost progress. Victorians were quick to observe that the two celebrations acknowledged Britain's accomplishments more than Victoria's, that she herself was primarily a symbol of the nation's progress. In Gissing's *In the Year of Jubilee* (1894), a character claims the Golden Jubilee is not only for the Queen, but "far more, it's to celebrate the completion of fifty years of Progress. National Progress, without precedent in the history of mankind! One may say, indeed, Progress of the Human Race" (51).[9] At the Diamond Jubilee, Mark Twain

---

9. Though the speaker is Samuel Barmby, a character dismissed as fatuous by the heroine and treated with scorn by Gissing, the fatuity here lies in his unabashed enthusiasm for Progress rather than his observation about the purpose of the Jubilee. The language of Gissing's Jubilee-day letter to his sister anticipates his heroine's description of Barmby: "As for this same Jubilee, after all it is something to have seen the most gigantic organized exhibition of fatuity, vulgarity & blatant blackguardism on record. Anything more ignoble can scarcely be conceived. Prithee, what is it all about? What has this woman Victoria ever done to be glorified in this manner? The inscriptions hung about the streets turn one's stomach. It is very clear to me that England is very far indeed from the spirit of republicanism. Well, I don't object to that, but it certainly degrades humanity to yell in this way about a rather ill-tempered, very narrow-minded, & exceedingly ugly farmer's daughter, just because she cannot help having occupied a *nominal* throne for half a century. But the vulgarity of the mass of mankind passes all utterance" (*Collected Letters* 3: 125). At the next Jubilee, Keir Hardie expressed a similar scorn for the celebration, though with more hope in the masses: "Millions will go out on Tuesday next to see the Queen. What they will see will be an old lady of very commonplace aspect. That of itself will set some a-thinking. Royalty to be a success should keep off the streets" (qtd. in Judd 135).

described the Royal procession as a "symbol" standing "for English history, English growth, English achievement," for "sixty years of progress and accumulation, moral, material, and political" (193–94, 209).[10] His essay on the event devotes several pages to reviewing all the moral, material, and political advances in Victoria's lifetime. As commemorations of progress, the Jubilees—especially the 1897 event—also celebrated the related phenomenon of empire. Twain reports that during the procession "the Queen Empress . . . was received with great enthusiasm. It was realizable that . . . in her the public saw the British Empire itself. She was a symbol, an allegory of England's grandeur and the might of the British name" (209). Imperial ideology, though deeply rooted in 1887, became more entrenched by 1897 and more explicitly associated with the monarch. Thus the Diamond Jubilee was a grander affair, calling attention more deliberately to the size, diversity, and strength of the empire. In a study of the commercial exploitation of the 1887 Jubilee, Thomas Richards observes that "if the image of Victoria in the year of the Golden Jubilee had been a domesticated image, in the year of the Diamond Jubilee it became an imperial image" (32). Victoria's refusal to invite any "Crowned Heads" in 1897, although initially a cause for disappointment, led to Chamberlain's inspired idea of inviting the Premiers, with military escorts, from all of the colonies. This transformed the Jubilee procession from a display of the extended family of European royalty (as in 1887) into a colorful demonstration—with Victoria at its center—of the extent and variety of the empire.

While Conrad and most of his contemporary readers certainly would have been familiar with the Jubilee of 1887 and its withdrawn sixpence, they most likely derived their understanding of the significance of a Jubilee from the event more immediately at hand, the celebration of the Dia-

---

10. Although Twain's admiration is evident, the essay is not without some of his redeeming humor. He comments on the extent of the "mighty estate" of British dominion in the world, then adds: "I perceive now that the English are mentioned in the Bible: 'Blessed are the meek, for they shall inherit the earth' " (206).

Given the concern in "Karain" with the presence of the dead, it is perhaps worth noting that Twain's essay begins and ends by commenting on their physical absence and haunting presence in notable historical processions. His conclusion reflects on the men who contributed to the greatness of the empire but did not participate in the Jubilee procession ("one could supply the vacancies by imagination"), but the essay's most remarkable passage is the introduction, in which he recalls his and others' reactions to Civil War veterans from New York marching in faded uniforms up Broadway with great gaps in their ranks, "an eloquent vacancy where had marched the comrades who had fallen and would march no more!" (210, 193). First sight of the veterans provoked enthusiastic cheering, followed abruptly by silence as people perceived the eloquent gaps. Accompanied by this narrow wave of cheers, leaving a stunned silence in their wake, the depleted troops marched through the city.

mond Jubilee. (When the Queen endorsed the term "Diamond Jubilee," the earlier event became known retrospectively as "Golden," and so for Conrad's readers in 1897 the gilt would have given the coin a further association with the Jubilee, one unavailable when the coin was gilded in 1887.) Conrad conceived of the idea for and wrote "Karain" in the early months of 1897, when preparations for the June ceremonies were in full swing; the story was published in November of the same year, when commemorations had not yet ceased.[11] In other words, Hollis's comments making the Queen into a symbol of imperial strength did not require a great deal of invention on Conrad's part; such comments had many models and echoes in Jubilee discourse and would have in fact sounded commonplace in that context.

Emasculating Specters

In emphasizing Victoria's symbolic status, her subjects often seemed to be registering their perception of the incongruity between the person and the prestige. This incongruity, paralleling the tension between power and deception represented in Conrad's sixpence, assumed two distinct forms: both her sex and her mournful reclusiveness introduced discordant elements into her role as titular imperial sovereign.

"Karain" confronts the first of these through its display of anxiety about the power of women. The seductive threat represented by Matara's sister, in the story Karain tells, gives way to the supposedly benign influence of the Queen in all that the narrator remembers. One common late-Victorian strategy for making the queen's power appear benevolent was to name her the mother of her people. Lytton Strachey's biography refers to the "double sentiment" of Victoria's subjects at the time of the Golden Jubilee: "The Queen was hailed at once as the mother of her people and as the embodied symbol of their imperial greatness" (280). Even a cursory survey of literary and journalistic texts of the period supplies ample evidence for this filial sentiment; Conrad's description of Karain mingling "the memory of his mother . . . with the image he tried to form for himself of the far-off Queen" (13) would have seemed as commonplace as Hollis's presentation of her as a symbol of British might. And yet the sentiment did not prevent her male subjects from reacting with hostility to having a woman be "the most powerful thing the white men know" (49). In the year of the Diamond Jubilee, an act of sublimated hostility toward the ruling sex

---

11. On the timing of his conception and composition of the story, see Conrad's letters from February to April of 1897 (*Collected Letters* 1: 338–39, 342–52).

highlighted the irony that the Queen could be accorded the highest honors, while women were denied the vote. With the third reading (and potential passage) of a Woman's Suffrage Bill scheduled for June 23, one day after the Jubilee procession, the House of Commons decided to declare the 23rd a national holiday, preempting consideration of the bill (Stevens 111–12). The attempt to obtain genuine political power for women was thus foiled by an act of homage to the symbolic power of the Queen.

An analogously hostile homage is enacted in Hollis's treatment of the sixpence image of Victoria retrieved from his small leather box. Among the items in the box are, as the narrator explains,

> a bit of silk ribbon, dark blue; [and] a cabinet photograph, at which Hollis stole a glance before laying it on the table face downwards. A girl's portrait, I could see. There were, amongst a lot of various small objects, a bunch of flowers, a narrow white glove with many buttons, a slim packet of letters carefully tied up. Amulets of white men! Charms and talismans! (48)

Hollis cuts a piece from the glove to sew around the coin and uses the ribbon to fashion it into a pendant "like those Italian peasants wear" (50), leading William Bonney to suggest that these "trophies of erotic involvement" contribute to the "potency" of the sixpence and its effect on Karain (23).[12] In terms of sexual politics, however, these trophies have the opposite effect, making the notion of conquest function in two opposing directions. Although the Queen commands the spirit of her nation, Hollis nevertheless encloses her image in the glove leather, sign of his own sexual conquest, his own command of the opposite sex. As a result he becomes, the narrator tells us, "masterful and compelling" and "powerful"; with "a skin that gleamed like satin," he usurps aspects of royal spectacle (50).

In the end, however, sexual power proves no more liberating than imperial power for the white men. This becomes evident when Conrad ties the fear of an emasculating feminine power to the Hades motif and the problem of remembering the dead. The sixpence scene reveals that many of the haunting spirits afflicting both Karain and the English are female.

---

12. The sexuality of this scene has produced a striking diversity of interpretations, reflecting perhaps the ambiguity in Conrad's handling of it. Johnson observes that the objects in the box are "souvenirs of love and apparently of disappointed love" ("Conrad's 'Karain' " 18). Mark Conroy accounts for the coin's effectiveness by noting that the "fusing of genders" (Victoria as ruler) coordinates with a "fusing of mythologies" in Karain's mind (his family romance and the imperial one) ("Ghostwriting" 7; see also his n. 5). Dryden views the use of Victoria's maternal image as a response to the "fear of feminine domination" in the form of the "Oriental *femme-fatale*" ("Karain" 45). See also Billy (251n17), the Lacanian reading by Brown and Sant, and Roberts' analysis of Karain's masculinity (49–56).

"Every one of us," Hollis tells his English companions, "every one of us, you'll admit, has been haunted by some woman" (47). First on the narrator's list of examples of the "ghosts driven out of the unbelieving West" and into the cabin of the schooner are "all the exiled and charming shades of loved women" (48). The power relations between the living men and the haunting women remain as ambiguous as Hollis's relation to the Queen. If "Karain" anxiously explores the impotence of the British imperial imagination in relation to the dead, as I am arguing, then it also positions itself alternately to blame that impotence on women, and to transfer it to them. The female specters provoke a sense of guilt about the subjection of women, and they provoke fear, making the men feel that even in spectral form—or especially in that form—the women possess a threatening power. In her black mourning clothes at the center of empire, Victoria is a very visible reminder that men's most domineering acts against women, like their most daring exercises of imperial power, cannot free them from the threat of the emasculating ghosts of the past.

Jubilee Redemption

The second discordant element in Victoria's symbolic power, besides her sex, was her obsessive public mourning, which touched directly on Conrad's concern with the problems of power and remorse. In her he found a symbol of power incapacitated by remorse, a figure of progress riveted to the past. Like the supposed Jubilee half-sovereign shrinking in power when exposed as a gilt sixpence, the glittery trappings of state enfolding a perpetually mourning sovereign served as a reminder that the accumulated power of empire could not compensate for a deficiency in Britain's rites of memory. The imperial pageantry remained haunted at its core by the dead who would not rest.

The grandest spectacle in each of Victoria's Jubilee celebrations was the royal procession through London on the anniversary of her accession in June. But if these processions were the most spectacular displays of power witnessed in imperial London, they also made the melancholy Victoria visible to more of her subjects than ever before. This incongruity comes through in an entry titled "Diamond Jubilee Day" in the journal of fifteen-year-old Virginia Woolf:

> At 12.30 a Captain Ames, & the sailors appeared & then followed troop after troop—one brilliant colour after another. Hussars, & Troopers & Lancers, & all manner of soldiers—then Indian Princes, & at last carriages with the little Princesses & the big ones—Finally the cream coloured

ponies were sighted: every one stood up & waved: shook their pocket handkerchiefs, & stamped their feet—the Queen was lying back in her carriage, & the Pss. of Wales had to tell her to look up & bow. Then she smiled & nodded her poor tired head, & the whole thing moved on. (*Passionate Apprentice* 103–5)

At both Jubilees, Victoria frustrated the determined efforts of her family and ministers to get her to travel the processional routes in full robes of state, choosing instead black dresses that perpetuated her mournful ways. She remained obsessively focused on the loss of Prince Albert in 1861, and she would never cease to make mourning her foremost duty—for forty years, to the day of her death, she had fresh water delivered and clothes laid out in the bedchamber for her deceased prince. After viewing two colorful Jubilee processions in which she wore black silk, Conrad's audience must have thought of her when they read of Karain's "strange obsession that wound like a black thread through the gorgeous pomp of his public life" (12).

The contrast between pompous power and Victorian fatigue is most acute, and its relation to mourning most clear, when its theological underpinnings are recognized. But this requires a reversal of the perspective common in analyses of the sacred aspects of political power in the modern age. Such analyses have tended to see the sacred as a means to establish or to represent an ultimate political authority. Clifford Geertz, for example, has argued that royal progresses "locate the society's center and affirm its connection with transcendent things by stamping a territory with ritual signs of dominance" (125). His essay on the "symbolics of power" compares monarchs from Britain, Java, and Morocco to demonstrate "the inherent sacredness of sovereign power" and "of central authority" (123, 146). Providing (like many of the other contributors to *The Invention of Tradition*) a more historically specific explanation than Geertz, David Cannadine has characterized the expanded symbolic and ceremonial function of Victoria as "the secular magic of monarchy," but this too focuses on the political uses of "magic" (102). Strachey's 1921 analysis nicely captures the English flavor of this secular magic in discussing the final years of Victoria's reign, her "years of apotheosis" (297):

During the last fifteen years of the reign . . . imperialism was the dominant creed of the country. . . . The English polity was in the main a commonsense structure; but there was always a corner in it where common-sense could not enter. . . . Naturally it was in the Crown that the mysticism of the English polity was concentrated—the Crown, with its venerable antiquity, its sacred associations, its imposing spectacular array. But, for nearly two centuries, common-sense had been predominant in the great building. . . .

Then, with the rise of imperialism, there was a change. For imperialism is a faith as well as a business; as it grew, the mysticism in English public life grew with it; and simultaneously a new importance began to attach to the Crown. The need for a symbol—a symbol of England's might, of England's worth, of England's extraordinary and mysterious destiny—became felt more urgently than ever before. The Crown was that symbol: and the Crown rested on the head of Victoria. (301–303)

In part, Strachey's analysis is additional evidence for my early assertion that the English are no less superstitious, mystical, and believing than Karain. But Strachey's suggestion that tradition was invented or adapted for imperial purposes does not account as fully as it might for the sharp contradictions in Victoria's role. He describes political uses of the monarchy without fully accounting for their failure, for the incongruities and anxieties associated with Victoria as a symbol of empire.

To supplement the recognition that sacred associations serve political purposes, I would like to reverse the perspective and view Victoria's symbolic power as serving particular spiritual purposes. In reflecting on the range of associations inspired by Hollis's sixpence, one should not neglect the extent to which the notion of "Jubilee" in the context of Victoria's reign is an instance of what Blumenberg describes as a human reoccupation of positions vacated by God. Because functions once attributed to God—including redemptive remembering of the dead—did not simply disappear from the catalogue of human needs in the modern age, human agents stepped in to take them over—and be shaped by them. A variety of details collectively indicate that this theological background shaped Victorians' notion of "Jubilee." For example, the title of Gissing's novel, *In the Year of Jubilee*, recalls the Biblical roots of the concept and thus explains why Victoria's transcendent connections were affirmed not only by the one-day royal processions but by a full year of celebration. In February 1887, in a further reminder of Biblical precedent, *The Times* reported "that one hundred debtors had been set free, their liabilities being discharged by the government" (qtd. in Chapman and Raben). Ten years later, many hesitated to call the 1897 commemoration a "Jubilee" because, as the Home Secretary explained to the Queen's private secretary, " 'Jubilee' has got its meaning from the old Jewish law & is certainly inseparably connected with a notion of 50 years" (qtd. in Lant, *Insubstantial Pageant* 216). Such details help place Victoria in the impossible position of a redeemer.[13]

---

13. The economic principles of Jubilee, including emancipation, restoration, and redemption, are laid out in Leviticus 25. Isaiah 61 then uses Jubilee terminology metaphorically to announce the "good news" in a passage that the New Testament invokes in presenting Jesus as the fulfillment of the prophets' teaching (see, for instance, Luke 4; also see

In offering reasons beyond political expediency for Victoria's sacred associations, the concept of reoccupation explains why her obsessive mourning seems so appropriate to the age and how the incongruities in her symbolic status became so acute. Humankind's assumption of the superhuman responsibility for redemption settled on her "poor tired head," and thus the monarch who was expected to redeem what had been lost appeared the greatest victim of loss, the greatest slave to the past. In this regard, Karain is more like the Queen than like any of her subjects; like her, he becomes bearer of his people's burden. "Some ten years ago he had led his people—a scratch lot of wandering Bugis—to the conquest of the bay, and now in his august care they had forgotten all the past, and had lost all concern for the future" (8). It seems to the narrator "as if a dead world had been laid to rest" in Karain's conquered land (26). Because the past is *not* weighty for his people, they seem to exist in an earthly paradise: "It appeared to us a land without memories, regrets, and hopes; a land where nothing could survive the coming of the night, and where each sunrise, like a dazzling act of special creation, was disconnected from the eve and the morrow" (5). As we have seen, this state is possible because the burden of memories and regrets is carried by Karain and his protector, the wise old man, who "was there on duty, but without curiosity, and [he] seemed weary, not with age, but with the possession of a burdensome secret of existence" (5). (The image of the always-attendant old man, "part of our friend's trappings of state" [19–20], has an affinity with the numerous surviving photographs of Victoria's Indian servants waiting on her in the later years of her reign. See, for example, figure 3.) The wearying secret does not belong exclusively to the old man; upon his death the "tormented weariness" passes back to Karain (23). And in the end, like all of Conrad's characters who participate in the mysteries of modern existence, Karain lacks the power to conquer his own remorse.

As Karain liberates his people (at least temporarily) from the burden of memory, so too the Queen and the empire she rules are offered as anti-

---

C. Wright's article in *The Anchor Bible Dictionary*). In moving to consolidate the Roman Catholic church's authority over the idea of Jubilee, Pope Boniface VIII instituted the first church-sanctioned Holy Year in 1300. Dante probably witnessed the crowds of pilgrims at this first Catholic Jubilee: he compares (with deliberate irony?) the bi-directional movement of scourged crowds in the eighth circle of hell to the pedestrian traffic in Rome "in the year of Jubilee" (*Inferno* 28: 25–33; see also *Purgatorio* 2: 98–99 and the corresponding note in the Mandelbaum translation), an image that Gissing closely (though perhaps unknowingly) imitates in an epistolary description of the 1887 Jubilee: "at night, all the great streets were packed from side to side with a clearly divided double current of people" (*Letters* 3: 127). The *OED* cites secular uses of the term throughout the post-Dante modern age, but the pattern of citations suggests such use accelerated in the nineteenth century, when it first became customary to apply the term to the reigns of monarchs.

Figure 3. Queen Victoria with Mustafa and Chidda, 1896. Photograph courtesy of The Royal Archives © 2002 Her Majesty Queen Elizabeth II.

dotes to Karain and the British. Conrad and his fictional English gunrunners perceive the empire (with Victoria at its head) as an organization of spiritual energy meant to counteract an inherited malaise. Karain's haunting problem is merely a projection of Britain's own, his state a microcosm of the empire. Conrad's story thus offers a diagnosis of "the White Man's burden" far more honest than—and directly opposed to— that of Kipling, who gets the cart before the horse in thinking that the malaise derives from the possession of empire. The redemption of Karain and his people comes cheaply enough, costing only a sixpence (and an evening of storytelling)—not much of a "burden." "Karain" demonstrates that the source of unrest lies closer to home, among the discontents of modernity. Perhaps this is part of the reason Conrad expresses the malaise far more indirectly than Kipling, projecting it onto Malayan Karain and his kingdom so that, as in a dream (to use one of Conrad's favorite metaphors for his fiction), uncomfortable truths can come to light. The truths are uncomfortable in part because the story does not display great confidence in the success of the cure, repeated assertions of the Queen's "invincible" power notwithstanding. Reminders of Victoria's sex and mournful obsession could only have reinforced the fear that she was an inadequate protective deity, as suggested by her counterfeit coin. Although the gilt charm is effective initially for both Karain and the narrator, we are left to assume that it helped sweep the former along to his destruction. More ominously for contemporary British readers, the spirits haunting the narrator and Jackson, spirits that suddenly dissipated at the appearance of the sixpence, return with a vengeance. The Queen proves only a temporary cure, and the narrator's unreliability further undermines the supposed efficacy of his imperialist sentiments in controlling the ramifications of memory.

The concluding scene of the story, set in England seven years after our last sight of Karain, begins with the assertion: "But the memory remains" (53)—a provocative warning that even the spirit of the nation cannot save one from the ghosts of the past; indeed, this spirit (the nation) is constituted to a large extent by those spirits (the dead, the past). The narrator runs into Jackson in the Strand just after Jackson has returned from a voyage, and a passage that ranks among Conrad's best offers a retrospective image of their relation to Karain:

> Jackson gazed about him, like a man who looks for landmarks, then stopped before Bland's window. He always had a passion for firearms; so he stopped short and contemplated the row of weapons, perfect and severe, drawn up in a line behind the black-framed panes. I stood by his side. Suddenly he said—

"Do you remember Karain?"

I nodded.

"The sight of all this made me think of him," he went on, with his face near the glass . . . and I could see another man, powerful and bearded, peering at him intently from amongst the dark and polished tubes that can cure so many illusions. (53–54)

While the guns are a reminder of English guilt vis-à-vis Karain, Jackson's reflection in the glass offers a visual analogy for the kind of projection underlying the entire tale. Both the origin and the victim of this specter are English. The self-haunting it suggests is the result of a self-estrangement, a doubling that brilliantly encapsulates the uncanny nature of Jackson's predicament. The image reminds us that his return to London is not a true homecoming; the narrator unwittingly suggests that death, the gift of the firearms, is the only homecoming available to Jackson.

Throughout the remainder of this final scene, the narrator persists in a defensive preservation of the opposition between home and abroad, truth and illusion, enlightenment and superstition, West and East, but Conrad's irony indicates more strongly than ever that these are false or superficial oppositions. As the two men proceed to speak of Karain, they oppose the visible, material world of the street where they are standing to Karain's specter-companion, the dead friend Matara. "Only look at all this," urges the narrator, insisting on the physical reality of the street scene and on a materialist dismissal of Karain's superstitions (54). " 'Yes; I see it,' said Jackson, slowly. 'It is there; it pants, it runs, it rolls; it is strong and alive; it would smash you if you didn't look out; but I'll be hanged if it is yet as real to me as . . . as the other thing . . . say, Karain's story.' " And then the final sentence of Conrad's story offers the narrator's reaction to Jackson: "I think that, decidedly, he had been too long away from home" (55). Here again, ironic treatment of the narrator undermines the supposed insularity of his "home." In fact, an intervening description of the street scene, in which one hears Conrad's voice more than the narrator's, invests even the local crowd and buildings under the hard light of day with a shadowy, spectral quality—even the sun and sky seem to contribute to the "underlying rumour" of "panting breaths, of beating hearts, of gasping voices" (54). England is simply not, as Karain and the narrator imagine, a "land of unbelief, where the dead do not speak," where people "understand all things seen, and despise all else!" (44). In London one cannot feel "as if a dead world had been laid to rest," nor as if the homeless ghosts of this dead world had been driven out of the West. The England the narrator calls home is haunted by specters, and not even the Queen can resist such suitors.

Gilt Lettering; or, Writing and Redemption

While struggling to revise "Karain," Conrad wrote a letter in which he extended the Hades imagery to his own activity: he complained about "that infernal story" (*Collected Letters* 1: 346). The recipient of the letter, Edward Garnett, having already read a draft of the story, was in a position to appreciate the punning equation of Conrad's affliction and the characters'. Conrad's playfulness hints that fiction can extend the infernal regions to its author and perhaps to its audience, a hint that prepares the way for the ambitious argument in his nonfictional writings that fiction must redeem human suffering. He wrote his most famous proclamation of this obligation, the preface to *The Nigger of the "Narcissus,"* in August of 1897, just months after completing "Karain."

When Garnett promoted his friend's work by publishing an anonymous article on *Tales of Unrest*, the 1898 volume in which "Karain" is the lead story, he took up Conrad's theme of redemption and stripped it of Conrad's pessimism:

> Whenever the artists are absent—in enormous tracts of life, that is—human nature appears to the imagination absolutely uncanny and ghost-like. But wherever the artist has been there the life of man appears suddenly natural and comprehensible. (Sherry, *Conrad: The Critical Heritage* 105)

Given the inappropriateness or impotence of Queen and empire when it comes to banishing the ghosts of modernity, it falls to the artist (according to both Garnett and Conrad) to attempt the exorcism and restore humankind to the world. Does "Karain" possess a charm the Queen lacks? Does art practice a magic stronger than empire?

In contrast to Garnett's assertions, "Karain" appears to supply negative answers to these questions. Mark Wollaeger has observed that the story itself introduces the printed word as a theme. For example, the tale is framed by references to the press: not only are the narrator's recollections of Karain stimulated by a newspaper article about the Eastern Archipelago ("sunshine gleams between the lines of those short paragraphs . . . [and] the printed words scent the smoky atmosphere of to-day faintly" [3]), but the concluding scene in the Strand includes a hawker of newspapers ("a ragged old man with a face of despair yelled horribly in the mud the name of a paper" [55]). While the earlier passage depends on "the evocative resources of language" and "solicits the imagination to close the gap between the verbal and the real by making us see," the concluding description of London has the feel of "language adrift": "Contrary to the narrator's intentions, the words seem not to represent an actual scene at all but rather to call attention to their own status as writing" (Wollaeger 44–45). The newspaper begins by creating the illusion of a representational whole and ends by having its name shouted in despair in the mud.[14]

If we take the references to the printed word to be self-referential, then one other such passage is perhaps especially relevant to Conrad's art. Among the disjointed images that are supposed to convince Hollis of the reality of London street life is this one: "gold letters sprawling over the fronts of houses" (54). Now language itself has become gilt, and it too has little value when so dressed. Aside from what one can surmise from the location of these letters, no indication is given of their meaning or their purpose. The most important thing we know about them is that they are colored gold. The gold itself becomes the message as well as the medium here, and we have already seen that in this story gold is a sign of delusion and inflated value. The fact that the letters are "sprawling" suggests a touch of disorder; the fact that they are so deployed on houses brings the delusion home, so to speak. When contrasting this image to the opening scene in which words are so effective at evoking a visible world, one might almost conclude that Conrad is working with a variation of the epic's traditional distinction between horn and ivory: the images that pass through the black-and-white smudge of newsprint are more truthful than ones presented in gilt letters. But, in fact, the coherence and solidity of the world the narrator remembers is as illusory as his perception of the London street. Conrad offers us no dreams from the Gate of Horn in this story, for he knows not how to wake us from the nightmare of history that has been displaced onto Karain. Only dreams from the Gate of Ivory are to be found here—the glittery gilt charms that sooner or later lose their luster and expose the deficiency they were meant to hide. Neither Queen, empire, nor fiction has the power to perform the redemptive role once belonging to the Christian God; none can conquer the remorse stirred up by the restless dead of the West.

14. Conrad's use of newspapers draws much of its significance from his contemporaries' view of the press as a symbol and agent of progress, a view handled quite differently in Gissing's novel and Twain's essay. Among the Victorian innovations Twain most admires is the creation of an inexpensive "public educator—the newspaper" (203), while Gissing has his scorned Barmby praise newspapers as the most outstanding feature of the "Age of Progress," marking the "difference between civilisation and barbarism" (52).

Redemption and Belatedness in *Lord Jim* and *Heart of Darkness*

A second time? why? man of ill star,
Facing the sunless dead and this joyless region?
      —Tiresias to Odysseus in EZRA POUND, *Cantos*

How do you shoot a spectre through the heart, slash off its spectral
head, take it by its spectral throat?
      —JOSEPH CONRAD, *Lord Jim*

In August of the Diamond Jubilee year, seven months after completing
The Nigger of the "Narcissus," Conrad composed the story's preface, destined to become his most famous declaration of his artistic intentions. The
preface states his claim that literature should be redemptive and, in fortunate moments, can be redemptive. This seems to contradict the bleak assessment of narrative's redemptive power found in "Karain," a story completed only three months earlier. In turning to the preface now, I hope to
show that in fact it confirms the bleak assessment in "Karain" by including sufficient clues that the project it lays out is not feasible. The preface
outlines the epistemological assumptions at work when colonial odysseys
attempt to muster the power to redeem, and it hints at the inevitable failure of this attempt, leaving such fiction trapped in a hellish belatedness.
The preface thus foregrounds issues central to two colonial odysseys that
Conrad would begin writing the next year: *Lord Jim* and *Heart of Darkness*.

Rescuers in Need of Rescue (Conrad's Nonfiction)

In one of the most frequently quoted lines from the *Narcissus* preface,
Conrad insists that the artist's primary purpose is "to make you hear, to
make you feel—it is, before all, to make you *see*" (xiv). He resists the idea

that fiction should edify, console, amuse, frighten, or shock its audience; the task of the writer is rather to render justice to the "visible universe" (xi). Despite this insistence, however, Conrad cannot limit himself to this visible universe for long. He is quick to acknowledge that conveying an impression through the senses is not an end in itself but merely the writer's only means of appealing to the reader's temperament, since "temperament, whether individual or collective, is not amenable to persuasion" (xiii). Literature is an appeal from one temperament to another "conveyed through the senses" (xiii); in other words, a writer renders justice to the visible universe "by bringing to light the truth, manifold and one, underlying its every aspect" (xi).

This concept of a single but manifold truth is Conrad's primary tool for reconciling a series of oppositions presented in the preface. He asserts that the successful writer must yoke a particular place and moment to eternal truth, surface appearance to moral depth, and the isolated, suffering individual to all other individuals, past, present, and future. Other critics have rightly observed that Conrad's theoretical statements are neither detailed nor rigorous, that his answers to these stubborn philosophical questions remain incomplete and vague. But that is not to say that his theory lacks clear parameters, the first and foremost of which is his claim that truth is both manifold and one (which appears, appropriately, at the very beginning of the preface). The claim anticipates the work of Neo-Kantian philosopher Ernst Cassirer, who also exploits the concept of *Mannigfaltigkeit* (literally, "manifoldness") in an attempt to reconcile the finite with the infinite, the individual with the whole of human history. But Cassirer's pitfall, an excessive faith in the ability of human reason to map and master truth's multiple folds, is not Conrad's. In fact one of the first tasks Conrad's preface undertakes is to distinguish the terrain of the artist from that of "the thinker" and "the scientist." Conrad's emphasis on the autonomous value of the moment reflects, as Thomas Harrison has shown, a Kantian resistance to making any moment instrumental in a theoretical order or practical scheme (51). Cassirer certainly shares this Kantian insistence on the intrinsic value of each individual independent of the individual's role in a larger historical process, and his notion of "symbolic form" acknowledges the importance of modes of thought beyond the strictly rational. However, he retains an Enlightenment perception of history as progressing from *mythos* to *logos*.

Though he remains immune to Cassirer's faith in progress, Conrad nevertheless assumes other liabilities in using the concept of a manifold truth to insist on truth's oneness. The most obvious consequence of such a concept for his encounters with foreign cultures is that he views them *a priori* as manifestations of an absolute truth that he has already encountered in cultures closer to home. This grants the various cultures an equal and fundamental value, or, to use more Conradian terminology, it recognizes that the moral and emotional atmosphere of any particular place and time, no matter how obscure, participates in an enduring truth and solidarity that binds together all humanity. This understanding of universal truth, unlike the Neo-Kantian one, avoids the condescending Enlightenment presumption that some cultures—namely Western ones—have progressed closer to that truth than others.[1] But Conrad's position, while positing a fundamental legitimacy for all cultures, is also predisposed to diminish or deflect cultural differences. The conviction that all places and times ultimately lead to the same truth, or that all visible surfaces open onto the same moral depth, encourages one to see the foreign as familiar and to assimilate unknown mysteries more readily to known ones. (In Freudian terms, Conrad, like Freud, claims the *Unheimliche* as *heimisch*, leaving little room for a *Geheimnis* that is extrinsic, or not already a part of the self.)

I have adapted this distinction between unknown and known mysteries from Northrop Frye, who was in turn extrapolating from Carlyle's distinction between extrinsic and intrinsic symbols.[2] According to Frye,

> The mystery of the unknown or unknowable essence is an extrinsic mystery, which involves art only when art is also made illustrative of something else, as religious art is to the person concerned primarily with worship. But the intrinsic mystery is that which remains a mystery in itself no matter how fully known it is, and hence is not a mystery separated from what is known. The mystery in the greatness of *King Lear* or *Macbeth* comes not from concealment but from revelation, not from something unknown or unknowable in the work, but from something unlimited in it. (88)

Conrad invokes this knowable, intrinsic mystery when he writes in the preface that the artist must appeal to "our capacity for delight and wonder, to the sense of mystery surrounding our lives" (xii). He testifies fur-

---

1. See Armstrong's comment on the term "manifold" in his discussion of monism and pluralism in Conrad's preface. Armstrong sees a greater emphasis on multiplicity in the term, while I am suggesting that Conrad and Cassirer choose it precisely because it acknowledges multiplicity *within* unity. The etymology of "manifold" suggests that a substance can have multiple, varied features—many folds—and still be one. Though I give greater emphasis to this search for unity in Conrad's preface, I concur with Armstrong when he observes that Conrad knows this search is doomed: Conrad's "intense desire to overcome contingency" is matched by "an equally compelling recognition that this can never be accomplished" (*Challenge of Bewilderment* 11–12).

2. Cf. Echeruo's discussion of the distinction between heterophoric and homeophoric symbols (terms he borrows from Watt), which is part of his analysis of race in *The Nigger of the "Narcissus."*

thermore to the intrinsic nature of such mystery when he explains that in contrast to the thinker and scientist, who plunge into ideas and facts, the artist "descends within himself," into a "lonely region of stress and strife" (xii). This type of mystery appears to take priority for Conrad over that which envelops an alien culture, which is analogous to the other type defined by Frye, the mystery associated with extrinsic truths.

Conrad works to open a path between extrinsic and intrinsic mysteries with his suggestion that truth, though manifold, is one. His conception fosters a readiness to transform the unknown secrets of foreign cultures into the intrinsic, known mystery of Western literature. For example, in the paragraph where he speaks of the artist rescuing a "fragment" or snatching "from the remorseless rush of time, a passing phase of life," he initially respects the exotic or obscure nature of these fragments by indicating that each contains its own mysterious truth. To rescue a fragment, he argues, the artist must "show its vibration, its colour, its form; and through its movement, its form, and its colour, reveal the substance of its truth—disclose its inspiring secret: the stress and passion within the core of each convincing moment" (xiv). But in the very next sentence Conrad transforms these apparently unique and obscure secrets into familiar, universal ones:

> In a single-minded attempt [. . . to rescue a fragment of life], if one be deserving and fortunate, one may perchance attain to such clearness of sincerity that at last the presented vision of regret or pity, of terror or mirth, shall awaken in the hearts of the beholders that feeling of unavoidable solidarity; of the solidarity in mysterious origin, in toil, in joy, in hope, in uncertain fate, which binds men to each other and all mankind to the visible world. (xiv)

With this claim Conrad completes an epistemological circle, showing how the most exotic, alien, and obscure fragments of human experience can become—with a little good fortune—fully accessible to artist and audience.

After closing this epistemological circle, the preface ends with a surprising and revealing twist. Conrad acknowledges that it is difficult and rare for the artist to succeed, and then concludes with the following words: "When [the task] is accomplished—behold!—all the truth of life is there: a moment of vision, a sigh, a smile—and the return to an eternal rest" (xvi). In other words, success in communicating universal truth through the rescued moment leads directly to death. Life's central secret—its intrinsic mystery—is not a presence that supports the individual life and opens up a wider range of experience; rather, it appears to be the antithesis of self-preservation, the ultimate threat to the self. In Conrad's final sentence the artist's will to create collapses suddenly into a will to die.[3]

One cause of this collapse can be found, paradoxically, in the very method by which Conrad attempts to forestall such a collapse. The preface strives to show that there is one thing short of complete darkness that can make eternity restful for mankind: namely, human memory, especially memory secured by art. Hence the prominence of the concepts of pity and solidarity in the preface. Solidarity "binds together all humanity—the dead to the living and the living to the unborn" (xii)—and therefore offers the individual his or her only means of living "within sight of eternity" (to borrow a phrase not from the preface but from the tale itself [25]). Clearly, the imagination of the whole shapes Conrad's understanding of solidarity; he manifests the unmanageable bequest from theology that Blumenberg has identified as the question "about the totality of the world and history." Laudable as the ideal of solidarity can be, when wedded to a totalizing will it becomes an enormous psychological liability (with potentially dangerous social and political consequences, as Conrad's Jim and Kurtz demonstrate in very different ways). Since the only source of rescue Conrad can imagine lies with humanity itself, the artist's endeavor becomes not only an affirmation but also a nearly impossible moral burden.[4] The artist must assume a godlike responsibility for redeeming human suffering, for rescuing fragments of human experience from oblivion.

This sense of responsibility manifests itself when Conrad departs from his usual allusions to the secret truth contained in events and suggests that events acquire their significance only through art. He refers to the artist's and audience's temperaments, the power of which "endows passing events with their true meaning, and creates the moral, the emotional

3. Hay provides a more optimistic reading in observing that the preface's final phrase echoes the antithesis in the requiem mass between *requiem aeternam* and *morte aeterna* ("Conrad Quintet" 184). See also Watt (85), Miller (*Poets* 39), and Stewart (143–44).

4. Commentary on the preface has overlooked the totalizing impulse underlying solidarity and rescue work. To cite one distinguished example, Watt's detailed discussion takes note of the "difficulty" of Conrad's existential and experiential use of the term "solidarity." But the difficulty is moral as much as existential or epistemological and it can be fully explained, I would suggest, only by reference to the totalizing impulse that lies behind it. Watt usefully links Conrad's term to Wordsworth and the Romantics, but in the end he focuses mostly on the autobiographical significance of solidarity for Conrad: "His deepest interest in the preface was to articulate the hope . . . for the only kind of human brotherhood that was available to him now that his days at sea were over" (87), and the preface "expresses in personal . . . terms, the essential continuity of spirit with which Conrad aspired to bridge the gap between the old tasks of his life and the new" (87–88).

atmosphere of the place and time" (xiii). This formulation obligates the artist not only to rescue obscure moments, but to create them, to grant them meaning through pity and solidarity. In passages such as this Conrad comes closest to matching Nietzsche's wishful insistence on the power of the creative will. The ambivalence with which one must approach such a formidable task is reflected in the way Conrad describes the purpose of the tale that follows the preface: his aim in it is "to present an unrestful episode in the obscure lives of a few individuals out of all the disregarded multitude of the bewildered, the simple and the voiceless" (xii). He manifests here a double humility, if not a double sense of futility. First, he betrays some doubt about his ability to convince readers of the worthiness of the subject matter, these few individuals leading obscure lives. This doubt surfaces over and over again in the preface as Conrad reiterates the likelihood of failure in a task that requires so much good fortune as well as talent. Second, he realizes that this task, however difficult, is confined to only the tiniest fragment of all that calls out for attention and redemption. He is nearly immobilized by the "disregarded multitude" of the voiceless, a multitude whom he feels the artist must make visible. His vision, in other words, must compensate for their silence.

Ideas and phrases from the preface echo throughout Conrad's later work. One of the most somber moments in his long dialogue with the darkness comes in his essay on Henry James (1905). Kenneth Graham observes that the essay clarifies "two of the most important features that link the two writers: the exalted view of the responsibility and potentiality of the novel as a form, and the overriding importance in art of inwardness" (208). But there are passages in the essay that say less about James than about Conrad. One such passage is worth quoting at length, for it echoes the pronouncements made over seven years earlier in the preface. Coming on the heels of Conrad's praise of James's "inextinguishable youth," it interrupts the discussion of James to offer a vivid image of belatedness:

> The creative art of a writer of fiction may be compared to rescue work carried out in darkness against cross gusts of wind swaying the action of a great multitude. It is rescue work, this snatching of vanishing phases of turbulence, disguised in fair words, out of the native obscurity into a light where the struggling forms may be seen, seized upon, endowed with the only possible form of permanence in this world of relative values—the permanence of memory. . . . But everything is relative, and the light of consciousness is only enduring, merely the most enduring of the things of this earth, imperishable only as against the short-lived work of our industrious hands.

So far, this passage is elaborating on the functions of art Conrad had explored earlier. It endorses the same audacious aims, expresses the same sense of humility-bordering-on-futility about the prospects for success; it burdens memory with responsibility for the rescue work while recognizing that memory itself is vulnerable. But in the next paragraph it turns to a Conradian vision of apocalypse:

> When the last aqueduct shall have crumbled to pieces, the last airship fallen to the ground, the last blade of grass have died upon a dying earth, man, indomitable by his training in resistance to misery and pain, shall set this undiminished light of his eyes against the feeble glow of the sun. The artistic faculty, of which each of us has a minute grain, may find its voice in some individual of that last group, gifted with a power of expression and courageous enough to interpret the ultimate experience of mankind in terms of his temperament, in terms of art. . . . The artist . . . is so much of a voice that, for him, silence is like death; and the postulate was, that there is a group alive, clustered on his threshold to watch the last flicker of light on a black sky, to hear the last word uttered in the stilled workshop of the earth. It is safe to affirm that, if anybody, it will be the imaginative man who would be moved to speak on the eve of that day without tomorrow—whether in austere exhortation or in a phrase of sardonic comment, who can guess? (*Notes on Life and Literature* 13–14)

Here sufferer and redeemer are one. Vision and voice are allied, but doomed. The final day of history, the final moment for a redeeming deity to appear, finds only an artist—perhaps—uttering "the last word," while humankind "will sleep on the battlefield among its own dead, in the manner of an army having won a barren victory. It will not know when it is beaten" (14). This image of apocalypse concentrates and intensifies Conrad's views on the role of the artist. In the position at the end of history traditionally occupied by the Judeo-Christian redeemer, the artist, surrounded by the dead, responds to acute crisis and faces inevitable failure.

Not Quite Gods (Jim and Kurtz)

Conrad's insistence on the need for art to perform rescue work shapes his conception of solidarity in ways not generally acknowledged in critical assessments of his fiction. His nonfiction makes clear that rescue work and solidarity have for him both a temporal aspect and a totalizing intention: he desires a fidelity to the past in its entirety, a solidarity with all of the dead. It is with an eye on these characteristics of Conrad's rescue work that I turn to *Lord Jim* and *Heart of Darkness* to offer readings that are partial and allegorical: partial in the sense that for reasons of economy I limit myself to evidence of reoccupation in these tales, assuming knowledge of the extensive critical tradition on which I build; allegorical in the sense that all modernist colonial odysseys adapt literary form and colonial setting to explore the cultural crisis of failed reoccupation. The responsibility Jim and Kurtz assume as colonial adventurers is a displacement of—and in literary terms an allegory for—the rescue work inherited by the modern subject, compelled to speak "the last word" at the end of time.

Conrad presents both Jim and Kurtz as artists. Jim's powerful and romantic imagination leads Marlow to pronounce him "a finished artist" (96); and Kurtz is a talented painter, writer, orator, and musician—in short, "a universal genius" (71). Most importantly, both assume the burden of the Conradian artist to perform rescue work. *Lord Jim* and *Heart of Darkness* fully exploit a parallel between the pressures of reoccupation and the effects on Europeans of encounters with colonized populations: both experiences invite one to play the role of God. The intellectual crisis at the root of secular modernity provides a profound underground pressure for Jim and Kurtz to assume godlike functions even as their journeys to native populations in the East and Africa seem to provide them with opportunities to do so. Conrad's inflation of the Malay title *Tuan* into the English *Lord* serves not only as ironic comment on the power Jim accumulates in Patusan, but as a somber warning of the power required for him to redeem himself.[5] Kurtz similarly is driven and tempted to play the role—to exercise the power—of a god among the natives. His eloquent report for the International Society for the Suppression of Savage Customs, "seventeen pages of close writing," begins with the premise that Europeans abroad assume a superhuman responsibility. Here is Marlow paraphrasing and briefly quoting from the report:

> We whites, from the point of development we had arrived at, "must necessarily appear to them ["savages"] in the nature of supernatural beings—we approach them with the might as of a deity," and so on, and so on. "By the simple exercise of our will we can exert a power for good practically unbounded," etc. etc. (50).

While Kurtz embraces this opportunity to exercise a will of "unbounded" power, Marlow recognizes that Kurtz's formulation is "ominous." But the

---

5. "They called him Tuan Jim: as one might say—Lord Jim" (*Lord Jim* 5). Conrad's contemporary Hugh Clifford objected to this translation: "The Malay word *Tûan* does not mean 'Lord.' Its exact equivalent in English is *Master*" and Conrad has raised "honest Jim thus unnecessarily to the peerage" (qtd. in Gordan 400n528). But Conrad's translation of the title suggests more about Jim's deification than it does about his class standing.

sort of moral audacity expressed in the report is precisely what leads Marlow to admire Kurtz and to side with him rather than the hypocritical "pilgrims."

Jim's and Kurtz's analogous attempts at self-deification produce quite different characters; Jim's naïveté, taciturnity, and more-than-criminal weakness contrast with Kurtz's experience, eloquence, and criminality. The comparison suggests that the two figures represent for Conrad disparate responses to a common problem. The problem finds a coded representation in Jim's leap off the *Patna*, and *Heart of Darkness* and the second half of *Lord Jim* can both be understood as responses to this irrevocable act. Readers have long felt that *Lord Jim* breaks into two parts—the psychological study of Jim's leap and the romance of his attempted redemption—and Conrad concurred, writing to Edward Garnett on 12 November 1900: "Yes! you've put your finger on the plague spot. The division of the book into two parts . . ." (*Collected Letters* 2: 302). In fact, Conrad wrote *Heart of Darkness* during a pause in his work on *Lord Jim*, during a period when he was still developing the idea for Jim's Patusan adventure. His original plan had been to write a short story limited to the *Patna* episode; a fragmentary draft of the story, written by June of 1898 and titled "Tuan Jim: A Sketch," breaks off with the *Patna* underway on its "pious voyage" (102) with "live cargo" (103).[6] Having set aside this incomplete sketch, he wrote *Heart of Darkness* between December 1898 and February 1899 before returning to *Lord Jim*, written mostly in the second half of 1899 and the first half of 1900. When the ballooning size of *Lord Jim* prevented him from

---

6. Conrad wrote this early draft in a notebook now in the possession of Harvard University's Houghton Library; a complete transcription of the "sketch" is provided in Janta's article, to which the page numbers cited here refer. Despite the unreliability of Conrad's comments on his own writing, he is plausible when he claims in his 1917 "Author's Note" to *Lord Jim* that "my first thought was of a short story, concerned only with the pilgrim ship episode; nothing more" (*Lord Jim* viii). Some critics have taken the inclusion of "Tuan" in the title of the sketch as proof that Conrad did in fact know from the beginning the importance that Patusan would play in the story. Janta's study of the manuscript indicates, however, that Conrad originally titled the draft merely "Jim: A Sketch" and returned later to add "Tuan" (on page 15 of the manuscript notebook; Janta 94). On the facing page (the back of page 14 in the notebook; Janta 95) he also added a paragraph that adumbrates the Patusan story: "Afterwards when his perception of the intolerable drove him away from the haunts of white men, the Malays of the village . . . [called] him Tuan Jim—as one might Lord Jim." Watt overlooks the fact that this is a later addition, incorrectly locating it on "the second page of the Harvard manuscript" (264). The confusion arises perhaps from the fact that Janta's transcription places the back of page 14 after page 15, the beginning of the story. Whether the addition of "Tuan" came almost immediately, as Janta argues, or not until the next year, as Hay suggests ("*Lord Jim*" 428), it seems clear that Patusan was an afterthought, a response to the moral predicament represented on the *Patna*. Well into 1900, nearly two years after writing the sketch and at a time when serial publication of the novel was far advanced, Conrad still expected the Patusan episode to constitute a relatively short conclusion for the story (see Conrad, *Collected Letters* 2: 248–49 and Najder, *Joseph Conrad* 263–64).

publishing the two tales in one volume with "Youth," he lamented their separation: *Lord Jim* "has not been planned to stand alone. *H of D* was meant in my mind as a foil, and *Youth* was supposed to give the note" (*Collected Letters* 2: 271). Thus the composition history of the two works provides some justification for linking *Heart of Darkness* to Conrad's reflections on the *Patna* episode.

The story of Jim's leap is a study in the origins of weariness, the origins of the fruitless, centrifugal wandering of Jim and Kurtz. Both suffer, though in very different fashion, the thoroughly European problem of a grand belatedness, a consequence of the modern subject's inability to perform the retrospective rescue work of a God. Applied to *Lord Jim*, the model of reoccupation highlights two features of the *Patna* episode that have not received adequate attention in the vast criticism devoted to the novel. The first of these is the fact that Jim's shame triggers his jump from the *Patna*, not the other way around. His sense of responsibility for the pilgrims' deaths precedes his jump and survives his later discovery of their rescue. The burden of solidarity—not simply a professional duty but a totalizing, redemptive identification—motivates both his jump and his subsequent flight east. The second feature is the role George plays in hinting at the source of Jim's shame, a role one inevitably overlooks when viewing the shame merely as a case of lost honor. By taking George's place in the lifeboat, Jim demonstrates that his survivor guilt is a European phenomenon: the white man's burden is his fellow white man. Thus Conrad encodes Jim's burden of belatedness by splitting it between George and the Muslim pilgrims. Jim's subsequent Patusan adventure and Kurtz's Congo exploits then appear as futile attempts to compensate for the failure of reoccupation dramatized in the *Patna* episode. Conrad transfers his darkest reflections on these compensatory impulses not to Jim's colonial odyssey but to Kurtz's. And to mediate Kurtz's more direct encounter with the god-shaped void, Conrad reinforces one of his lines of defense: Marlow. Marlow's resistance to the omnivorous imagination grows stronger as Conrad transfers him from *Lord Jim* to *Heart of Darkness*. The remaining sections of this chapter examine in order this sequence of splitting, evasion, transfer, and resistance: Jim's *Patna* behavior as a product of the totalizing imagination, his subsequent evasions and failure in Patusan, Kurtz's descent into the god-shaped void, and finally Marlow's weak imagination as a buffer against Jim's nightmare on the *Patna* and Kurtz's in the Congo.

Jim's Survivor Guilt, A "Created Terror of the Imagination"

The farcical helmsman of "Youth" must be read not only against the background of Virgil's Palinurus, as I suggested earlier, but also in relation to Conrad's Jim, "to give the note," as Conrad says. In many respects, "Youth" 's helmsman and Jim are opposites in misadventure. The former returns to a sinking ship, the latter deserts a ship afloat. Conrad employs the same humor for both situations, adapting sea lore about the intuition of rats in order to impugn the judgment of the men: in "Youth," Marlow and his shipmates observe rats fleeing the ship and agree that "the wisdom of rats had been grossly overrated, being in fact no greater than that of men" (17), while one of the employers Jim abruptly abandons tells him unwittingly, "you haven't as much sense as a rat; they don't clear out from a good ship" (195). But the humor remains comic in "Youth" while assuming tragic depth in *Lord Jim*. The grave consequences of Jim's jump overboard derive first of all from the fact that he is denied the recovery allowed his counterpart in "Youth," who reappears on deck dripping wet after his leap from the *Judea*. Jim's first thought following his leap from the *Patna* is that "there was no going back" (111). The observation is at once commonplace and foreboding, suggesting from the beginning the futility of his search for redemption in the East, the futility of any attempt to will backward.

The deed Jim cannot undo is not a crime. The outcome of the official inquiry is never in doubt and Jim does, of course, lose his certificate. But the "crime" investigated by the authorities, the crew's abandonment of their posts, does not rise to the level of Karain's and Kurtz's crimes and, most importantly, does not account in itself for the magnitude of Jim's haunting feelings of guilt. While we know Karain has killed his friend and we receive intimations of atrocities committed by Kurtz, nothing of the kind taints Jim. The pilgrims he abandons on the *Patna* survive. He is "found out, not in a crime but in a more than criminal weakness," Marlow observes (42), and thus Marlow emphasizes his naïveté and youth. Jim's lost honor, for which he pays the price of the humiliating public inquest, becomes "more than criminal" only in conjunction with a deeper moral malaise deriving from the solidarity of the living with the dead, a malaise preceding the crew's abandonment of the ship and surviving their discovery of the pilgrims' survival. Jim has killed no one and yet he, like Karain and Kurtz, is still haunted by the dead. He feels guilt for deaths he did not cause, for an irrevocable loss he did not instigate.

Jim and the *Patna*'s chief engineer both respond as if the pilgrims who were the ship's cargo had indeed perished, and it is striking how little changes in their responses even after they know that all eight hundred of their abandoned passengers have been towed safely to port. The chief engineer goes insane from the terror of thinking them drowned. The day before the opening of the official inquiry, Marlow discovers him in the hospital, where a resident surgeon reports that "the head, ah! the head, of course, gone, but the curious part is there's some sort of method in his raving" (54), a "thread of logic in such a delirium" (55). Convinced that the *Patna* has sunk "full of reptiles" (51), the chief engineer turns his hospital stay into a *Patna* voyage of sorts. He sees "millions of pink toads" lurking under his bed (52); with so many, "she won't swim more than ten minutes" (54). He asserts that he must remain quiet and let them sleep, just as the *Patna* crew quietly avoided alarming the pilgrims lurking below and on deck. Even though the pilgrims have survived, the thread of logic remaining in his raving is terror and guilt for surviving the deaths of hundreds.

The moral conviction that the pilgrims have perished shapes Jim's reaction as well. Initially, when he hears from another in the lifeboat that the ship has sunk, he feels that "to know of it and yet to have seen and heard nothing appeared somehow the culminating-point of an awful misfortune" (113). Marlow comments that this

> did not seem so strange to me. He must have had an unconscious conviction that the reality could not be half as bad, not half as anguishing, appalling, and vengeful as the created terror of his imagination. I believe that, in this first moment, his heart was wrung with all the suffering, that his soul knew the accumulated savour of all the fear, all the horror, all the despair of eight hundred human beings pounced upon in the night by a sudden and violent death, else why should he have said, "It seemed to me that I must jump out of that accursed boat and swim back to see—half a mile—more—any distance—to the very spot . . ."? Why this impulse? Do you see the significance? Why back to the very spot? (113)

Jim now desires another kind of return, not a return to the deck before the imagined loss but a compulsive return to the loss itself. Such repetition ensures that this "created terror of his imagination" stays with him.[7] He says to Marlow later of his jump, "it was like cheating the dead," and when Marlow reminds him that "there were no dead," he stubbornly and remarkably insists, "that did not matter" (134). Haunted in his imagination by the dead, Jim becomes enveloped, like Karain, in Hades allusions. "Spectres," ghosts," "shades," "shadows," "dark powers," and "infernal powers" pursue him long after the fate of the pilgrims can be his concern. Marlow refers to the *Patna*'s fate—its improbable survival after a freak, crippling collision with a submerged object in a calm sea—as an "infernal joke" played on Jim (109). Jim describes the leap itself as a descent to the

7. The one symptom that vanishes with news of the *Patna*'s rescue is the muted shouting Jim began hearing when he thought the ship was sinking. "Imagination I suppose," he says. He continues to hear the shouts, "very faint screams—day after day" (134). "It was getting worse, too . . . I mean—louder" (135). As soon as he learns of the passengers' survival, however, he "could hear nothing any more" (135).

underworld: "It was as if I had jumped into a well—into an everlasting deep hole . . ." (111).[8]

One reason the pilgrims' survival has so little effect on Jim is that they are merely, for a time, the crowd onto whom he projects his remorse, a remorse not deriving from his jump but preceding and triggering it. We can safely follow Marlow in accepting Jim's assertion that he was not afraid to die; this is what distinguishes him from the other fleeing crew members. Instead "he was afraid of the emergency" (88)—afraid of mass death and mass suffering. On his second trip to inspect the bulging, rust-eaten bulkhead, he becomes convinced the ship and most of its passengers are doomed, and he surveys them like "the silent company of the dead. They *were* dead! Nothing could save them! . . . He imagined what would happen perfectly; he went through it all . . . to the very last harrowing detail" (86). "His confounded imagination had evoked for him all the horrors of panic, the trampling rush, the pitiful screams, boats swamped" (88). He returns to the bridge to wait passively, and this is the point in his story when Marlow declares him, on the strength of his imagination of horror, "a finished artist, . . . a gifted poor devil with the faculty of swift and forestalling vision" (96); he is one of those cases "where his very Maker seems to abandon a sinner to his own devices" (97). Having asserted in his nonfiction that the artist must perform rescue work by making us see, Conrad shows us in Jim how such a burden places the rescuer in need of rescue. As a "finished artist," Jim succumbs to suffering rather than redeeming it—he is "finished" in more than one sense. (Joyce would later echo this pun when he has Stephen announce in Nighttown: "No voice. I am a most finished artist" [506; 15.2508].) It is precisely his artistic gifts that provoke his leap into an everlasting hell. The leap is not a cowardly act of self-preservation but a suicidal attempt to quiet his overly sympathetic imagination.

If the success of the *Patna* in staying afloat against all odds is part of an "infernal" joke, the ship's passengers are not infernal powers. The fact that they appear so at first—to the chief engineer, to Jim, and to Marlow—is the result of a displacement common in colonial odysseys. The Muslim passengers (and later Jim's Patusan) become substitute objects for the failed mourning and guilt originating in Europe, much as "Karain" transfers the focus of Victorian melancholy to the Eastern Archipelago and *A Passage to*

---

8. DeKoven cites this passage as an indication that Jim leaps into a maternal, deathly hole, an interpretation reinforced by the fact that Conrad uses similar wording in a later scene when Marlow stares into Jewel's eyes: "I could see . . . the big sombre orbits of her eyes, where there seemed to be a faint stir, such as you may fancy you can detect when you plunge your gaze to the bottom of an immensely deep well" (DeKoven, *Rich and Strange* 156; *Lord Jim* 307).

India projects an English muddle onto India. *Lord Jim* contains a clue about this transference in the figure of George, who becomes the *Patna's* intriguing cadaver, its "interesting corpse" (137–38, 142). He is the only person who actually dies on this voyage. Jim's sense of guilt emerges most immediately from his relation to this dead, white shipmate, and only secondarily from the betrayal of the ship's cargo of pilgrims. "A haggard, white-faced chap," George dies of a "weak heart" while helping to lower the boat, just before he can abandon ship. The other escaping crew members do not see him collapse on deck, and they call repeatedly for him from the boat below. In response to their shouting of George's name, Jim finally jumps, impulsively; through this act he identifies himself with George.

Jim exhibits Freudian melancholy in relation to George. It is a phenomenon that psychologists have more recently termed "survivor guilt" or "identification guilt."[9] Survivor guilt consists of a sense of shame for surviving when another does not, as if one survives in place of the other. This is precisely the way Jim's survival is dramatized as he steps over George's legs and, hearing George summoned, occupies his place in the boat. When others in the boat realize after some delay that Jim rather than George is accompanying them, they treat him, Jim feels, like a "tree'd thief," as if he had stolen George's life (117). Later he comments to Marlow on George's death in a way that half-consciously emphasizes his own proximity to the dead man:

> Weak heart. The man had been complaining of being out of sorts for some time before. Excitement. Over-exertion. Devil only knows. Ha! ha! ha! It was easy to see he did not want to die either. Droll, isn't it? May I be shot if he hadn't been fooled into killing himself! Fooled—neither more nor less. Fooled into it, by heavens! just as I . . . Ah! If he had only kept still; if he had only told them to go to the devil when they came to rush him out of his bunk because the ship was sinking! If he had only stood by with his hands in his pockets and called them names! (107)

Jim concludes by describing this episode as "a joke hatched in hell"—referring now not to the ship's collision and survival, but to George's

9. Robert Jay Lifton introduced the terms to describe a condition he found repeatedly in his work with survivors of the Holocaust and Hiroshima (see *Death in Life* and "The Concept of the Survivor"). The survivor's sense of having survived in place of another is not dependent on situations such as a Nazi death camp in which a limited number of survivors were selected from the ranks of the doomed. Lifton speaks of the Hiroshima survivor's "unconscious sense of an organic social balance which makes him feel that his survival was purchased at the cost of another's" (*Death in Life* 489). This sense of an organic social balance is analogous to Conrad's "faith with the community of mankind," which I discuss below. Lifton's terms have now been applied to survivors of a wide variety of traumatic events, including natural disasters and the events of 11 September 2001.

death—and he exclaims, "Weak heart! . . . I wish sometimes mine had been." Marlow's answer:

> "Do you?" I exclaimed with deep-rooted irony. "Yes! Can't *you* under-stand?" he cried. "I don't know what more you could wish for," I said, an-grily. He gave me an utterly uncomprehending glance. This shaft had also gone wide of the mark. (108)

Jim's failure to recognize the pun on "weak heart" that is so obvious to Marlow and the reader makes possible Jim's adventure and Marlow's tale, which depend on Jim's naïve hope that he can still prove the strength of his heart.

Jim's desire for a physically weak heart so that he, too, might have died on board the ship exemplifies the death drive that is a major component of survivor guilt. The perception that one has survived in place of another leads quickly to the conviction that one should now join the dead. "I wished I could die," Jim says of his feeling immediately after jumping (111), and he and Marlow reiterate in numerous ways the conviction that he would be better off dead. George by himself, however, is clearly not an adequate object for Jim's robust death drive. Conrad in fact goes out of his way to make of George a pathetic figure, thereby heightening the ironic ef-fect when Jim becomes identified with him. But the characterization of George also reflects, I believe, Conrad's reluctance or inability to represent the magnitude of Jim's psychological guilt, which precedes and tran-scends his relation to George. With his totalizing redemptive impulse, Jim has taken the place not just of George but of God, a reoccupation that de-termines, when he fails, the magnitude of his shame. One could describe the need for reoccupation in the modern age as trauma on a grand scale unfolding over an extended period of time, the trauma of the retreat from the world of the Judeo-Christian God. The moderns mourn for this God in a double sense: they mourn his death and, in coping with the resulting cri-sis in rites of memory and mourning, they take his place in the attempt to impart meaning to human death. Thus survivor guilt deriving from a spe-cific traumatic experience and the late-modern sense of belatedness deriv-ing from failed reoccupation are homologous and can potentially rein-force each other—these are not mutually exclusive explanations of a particular psychological phenomenon. But the scope of Jim's remorse ex-ceeds any particular person or event. The meanness of George as a charac-ter serves as a reminder of his smallness as a symbol in relation to what he represents. He is a meager synecdoche for all of the unrestful dead, and, indeed, for all those human creatures whose common fate, as Marlow re-peatedly reminds us, is death. "The real significance" of Jim's jump, Marlow suggests, "is in its being a breach of faith with the community of mankind, and from that point of view he was no mean traitor" (157).

Indeed, Jim's death drive precedes his leap and George's death. In a crucial passage speculating on Jim's state of mind on the bridge shortly before the leap, Marlow corroborates the suggestion that Jim's leap represented not a flight from but a drive toward death:

> He might have been resigned to die but I suspect he wanted to die without added terrors, quietly, in a sort of peaceful trance. A certain readiness to perish is not so very rare, but it is seldom that you meet men whose souls, steeled in the impenetrable armour of resolution, are ready to fight a losing battle to the last, the desire of peace waxes stronger as hope declines, till at last it conquers the very desire of life. Which of us here has not observed this, or maybe experienced something of that feeling in his own person—this extreme weariness of emotions, the vanity of effort, the yearning for rest? (88)

The "added terrors" Marlow refers to are the sufferings of the drowning pilgrims in the imagination of Jim, the "finished artist"; and the "yearning for rest" they provoke is reminiscent of the "eternal rest" Conrad named in his earlier preface as the reward for the struggles of the artist. The pilgrims are indispensable for understanding Jim's guilt, for in their multitude they hint at its magnitude. Jim's anguish, which so often exceeds both Jim's and Marlow's capacities for understanding and expression, finds its representation in the *Patna* episode through a splitting of its elements. The core problem of death and arrested mourning originating among white men lies buried in Jim's relation to meager George, while the scope and gravity of this problem are deflected onto Jim's relation to the Muslim passengers. He betrays them as much as the code of the profession, and his relation to them, like his relation to the "community of mankind," is largely a product of his imagination. The imagination, shaped in the scope of its intention by reoccupation, affirms solidarity with the totality of humankind, but such a grand dream transforms itself at times for Jim, always for Conrad, into a terrifying nightmare. This is a notion of solidarity so grand as to be always already corrupted by betrayal. Jim is indeed "no mean traitor," but in this regard he is "one of us," for in the face of such an ideal of solidarity, as Marlow also says, "nobody is good enough" (319).

In short, Conrad uses Jim's jump from the *Patna* to represent his protagonist's burdensome and not entirely justified sense of obligation to the dead. Jim and Kurtz both respond to such a temporal burden by giving it a spatial dimension, transferring the object of their debt from the dead to other races and regions. The one escapes to exotic locales naïvely hoping for cancellation or discounted redemption of the debt whereas the other descends to chthonic regions in an attempt to face down the burden, but both, in the end, merely confirm the inadequacy of the imperial imagination to conquer weariness and restore the modern subject to itself.

The Mad Lie of Rejuvenation in the East

Like Tennyson's Ulysses, who seeks rejuvenation through his colonial voyages, Jim travels to Patusan in an attempt to recover—or merely preserve—his youth. Conrad had already embraced this paradox in "Youth," where Marlow arrives in the East "weary beyond expression" and finds it "silent like death, dark like a grave" (38), yet also comes to associate it with his "youth and the feeling that will not come back any more—the feeling that I could last for ever . . . ; the triumphant conviction of strength" (36–37). By reflecting on Jim's youthfulness rather than his own youth, the Marlow of *Lord Jim* remains farther removed from the naïve enthusiasms of the adventurers to the East. But the ambiguity of the East in the earlier story carries over to remote Patusan, which becomes associated both with Jim's youthful vigor and with a failure culminating in his death. "I remember," Marlow says, "as I unfolded our precious scheme for his retreat, how his stubborn but weary resignation was gradually replaced by surprise, interest, wonder, and by boyish eagerness" (230)—and yet the rediscovered boyishness leaves him still vulnerable to haunting spirits from another world, confirming his deficiency and ensuring his defeat.

Of this fatal search for rejuvenation, Marlow says that "what I could never make up my mind about was whether his line of conduct amounted to shirking his ghost or to facing him out" (197). Jim faces out his ghost only to the extent that he accepts his failure at the moment of death, when he presents himself to Doramin to be shot for failing to protect Doramin's son: "It may very well be that in the short moment of his last proud and unflinching glance, he had beheld the face of that opportunity which, like an Eastern bride, had come veiled to his side" (416). Perhaps in this emasculating consummation he successfully faces the inadequacy of his own will without resorting to the *ressentiment* epitomized in Gentleman Brown, the unsavory agent of evil who, like Jim, is "haunted by an almost imperceptible suspicion of sighing, muttering ghosts" (399) and flees the metaphorical embrace of "a spectre."[10] But it is not clear from Jim's death scene that he recognizes the nature of the ghost that defeats him (Marlow himself qualifies the idea with the word "may"). In Marlow's formulation

---

10. Brown's fear is, in fact, of a Spanish prison. The thought of being locked up inspires in him "the sort of terror a superstitious man would feel at the thought of being embraced by a spectre" (354).

the metaphor of an "Eastern bride" still veils the opportunity Jim beholds, suggesting that both men, like the gunrunners in "Karain," remain inclined to blame their melancholy on—and seek its cure from—women as well as the East.[11] Jim's behavior in Patusan, in other words, consists of shirking his ghost, assuming we understand this ghost to be the failed attempt at redemptive solidarity represented in the *Patna* episode. Conrad has Kurtz confront this ghost more directly, immersing him in rescue work that is both indispensable and impossible. After exploring a face-off with the terror vicariously through Kurtz, Conrad returned to Jim and explored in the second half of the novel a different response, an unsuccessful attempt to shirk the problem.

Despite sympathy for Jim's idealism and a desire to see him succeed, Marlow himself gives us plenty of clues that Jim's Patusan adventure, built on a shadowy dream, is doomed to fail. One such clue resonates most for readers aware of the counterfeit coin in "Karain": describing Jim's appearance at the time of the inquiry, Marlow says "he looked as genuine as a new sovereign, but there was some infernal alloy in his metal" (45) contributing to Marlow's "doubt of the sovereign power enthroned in a fixed standard of conduct" (50).[12] More elaborate clues come in Marlow's response to Stein, his trustworthy adviser who at 60 remains "unwearied" (202), manifesting an "intrepidity of spirit" (203). Stein, in labeling Jim "romantic," provides the most concise and encompassing diagnosis of his character, and Stein prescribes the trip to Patusan as a way of letting Jim indulge his romanticism. Stein too is a romantic, as his love of butterflies demonstrates. While conversing with Marlow he admires one rare specimen for its "accuracy," "harmony," and reflection of "perfect equilibrium" (208)—this dark bronze butterfly throws into sharp relief humankind's restlessness and discontent. Stein's romanticism and the butterfly's self-sufficiency have elicited much commentary, and Stein's charming oracular authority has in a few instances led commentators to privilege his perspective.[13] A more critical view emerges when we use him

11. DeKoven's *Rich and Strange* provides the most thorough exploration of the conjunction of the maternal and the East in *Lord Jim*, but see also Mongia's interesting essay.

12. See Seidel's discussion of sovereignty and soundness in *Lord Jim*, part of a study of Conrad and exile.

13. Charmed by Stein, many critics have overlooked the ways in which Marlow and Conrad undermine his philosophy. Batchelor, for example, comments on Conrad's triple identification—with Jim, Marlow, and Stein—and perceives Conrad as author to be closest to the latter: "Stein is, in a sense, Conrad as he actually was[:] . . . an exotic stranger speaking broken English, a wise foreigner with an adventurous past" (110). Kirschner's discussion of Conrad's relation to Goethe concludes that the real tragic hero of *Lord Jim* may be Stein rather than Jim (79). Tanner's influential analysis of Stein and his butterflies similarly perceives a "powerful authority" in Stein's comments, though Tanner also considers Marlow's and Conrad's skepticism about Stein (*Conrad* 43; see also his "Butterflies and Beetles"). And Parry's reading concludes that "although doubt does attach to Stein's prescrip-

and his butterflies to link human deficiency and lepidopteran perfection more specifically to two concerns central to this study: the human drive to totalize and the task of the artist in remembering the dead. In relation to these themes, Stein's romanticism appears less exalted, Marlow's resistance to it more appealing.

Stein's elaboration of the human/butterfly antithesis associates restlessness with a desire for the totality of life: " 'We want in so many different ways to be,' he began again. 'This magnificent butterfly finds a little heap of dirt and sits still on it; but man he will never on his heap of mud keep still' " (213). For Stein, desiring many ways of being corresponds to a desire to occupy every place, and he makes it clear that such ambition derives from weakness rather than strength, from lack rather than plenitude. A profound homelessness afflicts humankind in this world and gives rise to the drive to be at home everywhere: "Sometimes it seems to me," he explains, "that man is come where he is not wanted, where there is no place for him; for if not, why should he want all the place?" (208). He describes here the psychology underlying the colonial odyssey, in which a sense of profound loss, of transcendental homelessness, motivates a futile ambition for a total, compensatory conquest.

Stein not only describes the colonial-odyssey psychology, he exemplifies it in his life story. His passion for insects and his entrepreneurial drive, which lead him east and keep him there, reveal an agitated acquisitiveness. The butterflies not only provide an object for this avidity—he "never failed to annex on his own account every butterfly or beetle he could lay hands on" (206)—but in their still perfection they also offer him a momentary, vicarious fulfillment and silencing of his desire. He concludes the story of his capture of the rare specimen by observing: "On that day I had nothing to desire. . . . What I had once dreamed in my sleep had come into my hand" (211). He quotes Goethe's *Torquato Tasso* in describing the moment of capture:

> So halt' ich's endlich denn in meinen Händen,
> Und nenn' es in gewissem Sinne mein. (211)
>
> [So then finally I hold it in my hands
> And call it in a certain sense mine.]

tions, his posture is not repudiated by the fiction" (95). A more critical account comes from Conroy, who observes that Stein's butterfly collection is analogous to his wealth, both being the result of sacrificial rituals that transform living beings (laborers, butterflies) into fixed objects of value. Capital accumulation, in other words, contaminates Stein's romantic ideals, much as the greed of Chester, Cornelius, and Brown contaminates Jim's endeavors (*Modernism and Authority* 111). Roussel argues that Conrad rejects Stein's retreat from the world (92–97). See also Thorburn's analysis of Conrad's romanticism, Winner's reflections on Conrad's irony, and Dodson's discussions of the sublime in Conrad.

This reveals a possessiveness not unlike that of Kurtz, who frequently repeats the first-person singular possessive pronoun in laying claim to the ivory, station, river, and Intended. The butterfly, perfect in death and associated with Psyche of Greek mythology, connects Stein's aspiration for totality to the rescue work Conrad expects the artist to perform for the dead. The scene of the butterfly's capture evokes the Greek personification of the soul, for Stein first perceives the butterfly as he watches the face of a dying man whom he has just shot: "As I looked at his face for some sign of life I observed something like a faint shadow pass over his forehead. It was the shadow of this butterfly. . . . I raised my eyes and I saw him fluttering away" (210). Like the man, the butterfly becomes Stein's victim. In taking possession of the psyche of this man, and of humankind generally, Stein kills it. This irony empties Stein's hands at the moment of possession, and thus it fills Goethe's phrase, *in gewissem Sinne,* because in a certain sense the essential eludes Stein, who destroys more than he redeems. In more than one sense, he too is "finished."

Demonstrating the elusiveness of human self-possession, the butterfly becomes in death once again the antithesis to human discontent; its inhuman or superhuman harmony accompanies it from life into death. Immobilized in Stein's glass case, it displays "a splendour unmarred by death" (207). It makes no claim on survivors; its plenitude does not depend on the retrospective rescue work of any artist. This is because the butterfly is already the product of an artist figure more accomplished than Jim or Kurtz, more accomplished than any human. The butterfly's splendor, an immunity of sorts to death, identifies it as a "masterpiece of Nature—the great artist" (208). "Man," by contrast, "is not a masterpiece," and so by implication has a more troubled relation to death—and to Nature. "Perhaps the artist was a little mad. Eh?" Stein wonders (208). For a man who has held his dream in his hands, the idea of humankind as the product of a mad artist comes startlingly close to the Gnostic notion of an evil demiurge as creator of this world, a dualism that would find its starkest formulation in Kafka's suggestion to Max Brod that humans "are nihilistic thoughts that came into God's head" (Brod 75). But the idea of a mad, imperfect creator works well as a comment on the attempts of the modern subject at self-definition and self-redemption. Having reoccupied the position of a God, Jim and Kurtz assume a mad task and inevitably fail at it.

Stein's theology is marginally less surprising in a man for whom success is momentary and long past—for this is one perspective on Stein that Conrad provides us. The time when he held the object of his dream in his hands has itself dissolved into a dream: "But for the reality of sorrow [over the death of his wife and daughter] which remained with him, this strange part [of his existence] must have resembled a dream" (207). He now responds feebly and sentimentally to his homelessness by planning to bequeath his collection of insects ("Something of me. The best.") to his "small native town" (205). His recognition of the fleeting nature of desire's fulfill-ment and the persistent reality of remorse tempers his advocacy of imagi-nation and dreaming, and his own reservations prepare the way for Mar-low's skeptical response to him. Marlow does not dispute the diagnosis of Jim as romantic but he is critical of the romanticism that Stein shares with Jim. In Marlow's narrative, the views of the German trader have suffered a fatal blow even before he makes his first appearance. We have seen that in the *Patna* episode imagination—the romantic's most important tool—cre-ates terror rather than alleviates it, increases the clamor of the dead rather than calms it. Stein recognizes that the imagination can be destructive and he implies simultaneously, through his famous metaphor equating dream-ers and swimmers, that one cannot simply climb out of the dream but must learn to float in it: "In the destructive element immerse" (214)! As he con-tinues this line of thought, he provokes in Marlow a reaction that dismisses the possibility of successfully inhabiting the dream and thus questions the benefits of such immersion. Stein concludes: "That was the way. To follow the dream, and again to follow the dream—and so—*ewig—usque ad finem.* . . ." And Marlow immediately comments:

> The whisper of his conviction seemed to open before me a vast and uncer-
> tain expanse, as of a crepuscular horizon on a plain at dawn—or was it,
> perchance, at the coming of the night? One had not the courage to decide;
> but it was a charming and deceptive light, throwing the impalpable poesy
> of its dimness over pitfalls—over graves. . . . That was the way, no doubt.
> Yet for all that the great plain on which men wander amongst graves and
> pitfalls remained very desolate under the impalpable poesy of its crepus-
> cular light, overshadowed in the centre, circled with a bright edge as if sur-
> rounded by an abyss full of flames. (214–15)

No passage in the novel is more important for assessing Stein's convic-tions and Jim's adventure in Patusan. Confusing dawn and dusk, East and West, Marlow uses the heliotrope in a way reminiscent of its appearance in the centrifugal odysseys of Dante's and Tennyson's Ulysses, and he pro-vides the novel's pivotal Hades allusion, a memorable image of the dark earth ringed by a glowing horizon, like an island suspended in "an abyss full of flames." The image offers a sobering assessment of Stein's project. The romantic imagination in which Stein wishes to immerse Jim casts a charming yet dim and deceptive light; "crepuscular" and "impalpable" are each repeated twice within the paragraph to emphasize the thinness of Stein's "poesy" in action. The inability to distinguish between dawn and dusk creates a momentary balance between hope and despair, but this quickly tips over into despair when the hope that Stein's romantic vision might cast a redemptive light on the earth disintegrates in the face of death: first, the light cannot diminish the desolation of earth's "pitfalls" and "graves" (each of these words is also repeated twice); second, the light it-self transforms from charming poesy into hellish fire as Marlow's line of thought leads inexorably to the abyss. In the end it makes little difference whether the light is waxing or waning in the vista opened by Stein's con-victions; no sun illuminates this landscape, for the earth remains in the grip of hell. Thus Marlow has warned us in advance that sending Jim to Patusan to follow his dream, to immerse himself in the element of his own imagination, cannot free him from desolate wandering among graves.[14]

As it turns out, the practical effect of the Patusan "opportunity" is not to give Jim's imagination freer reign, but to constrict its sympathies. Subtly but unmistakably, Conrad uses Patusan to transform the struggle within Jim's imagination into a conflict with Islam. Thus the second half of the novel strengthens the repression and displacement only half accomplished in the *Patna* episode. Conrad emphasizes Jim's sense of solidarity with the Muslim pilgrims while on the ship and even in the act of leaping, but when such sol-idarity becomes too oppressive then Islam becomes the enemy.[15] Conrad in-troduces Sherif Ali as "a wandering stranger, an Arab half-breed, who, I be-lieve, on purely religious grounds, had incited the tribes in the interior (the bush-folk, as Jim himself called them) to rise, and had established himself in a fortified camp on the summit of one of the twin hills" (257). Jim's initial conflict with the Sherif is similarly religious, beginning with the Sherif's

---

14. This passage has the potential to prejudice every subsequent use of the heliotrope in the novel. For example, the scene in which Marlow has his last sight of Jim in the East standing against the background of a darkening West comments on Jim's moral rigor and youthfulness: "He was white from head to foot, and remained persistently visible with the stronghold of the night at his back, the sea at his feet, the opportunity by his side—still veiled. What do you say? Was it still veiled? I don't know. For me that white figure in the stillness of coast and sea seemed to stand at the heart of a vast enigma. The twilight was ebbing fast from the sky above his head, the strip of sand had sunk already under his feet, he himself appeared no bigger than a child—then only a speck, a tiny white speck, that seemed to catch all the light left in a darkened world" (336). Although Marlow professes uncertainty here, his earlier image for Stein's romanticism suggests Jim has little hope in the darkness. Admittedly, however, the active involvement of the reader is necessary to preserve the sobering effects of Marlow's earlier image so far into the story of Patusan, be-cause Marlow often succumbs, despite himself, to the romance of Jim's adventure. See also the passages where Marlow subsequently qualifies this parting image of Jim (342, 393).

15. The contrast with Jim's earlier sense of sympathy for the pilgrims appears more de-liberate on Conrad's part when one notes the changes he made to his source material for the *Patna* episode, the abandonment of the *Jeddah* by its crew in 1880. Fighting broke out on the *Jeddah* between the European officers and the pilgrims, and one officer died not from a weak heart but because the pilgrims cut the falls of the boat in which he was trying to es-cape. The details are reported in Sherry, *Conrad's Eastern World* 52–54.

plot against Jim's life: "Jim was to be murdered mainly on religious grounds" as "a simple act of piety"—at the time he did not seem to pose any political threat (310). The eventual defeat of the Sherif makes Jim himself the dominant religion of the land, securing his "racial prestige and the reputation of invincible, supernatural power" (361); he becomes the "creed" of the people (393). Not until Jim's demise does Islam reappear in Patusan, reasserting itself with a vengeance. On the night Jim gives Brown free passage out of Patusan only to have him ambush Dain Waris, the fires throughout the village reflect off the river, Tamb' Itam reports, "as on a night of Ramadan" (394). Dain's body is returned to the home of his father, where Jim will shortly report to die, in a scene accompanied by "the high sing-song voices of two old men intoning the Koran" (412). In Patusan, in other words, Jim struggles less with his own imagination and will toward solidarity, for Conrad has provided the "Arab half-breed" as an object on which to hang much of the guilt that Jim had earlier taken upon himself.

This contraction of Jim's sense of solidarity is apparent in his heroic behavior in the battle against the Sherif. In contrast to his terror-stricken identification with the pilgrims on the *Patna*, he turns indifferently from smoldering corpses, victims of his attack on the Sherif's stockade:

> The rout, it seems, had been complete. . . . In Patusan the excitement was intense. Jim told me that from the hill, turning his back on the stockade with its embers, black ashes, and half-consumed corpses, he could see time after time the open spaces between the houses on both sides of the stream fill suddenly with a seething rush of people and get empty in a moment. . . . "You must have enjoyed it," I murmured, feeling the stir of sympathetic emotion.
>
> "It was . . . it was immense! Immense!" he cried aloud, flinging his arms open. . . .
>
> Immense! No doubt it was immense; the seal of success upon his words, the conquered ground for the soles of his feet, the blind trust of men, the belief in himself snatched from the fire, the solitude of his achievement. (271–72)

In the introduction to his edition of the novel, Cedric Watts has commented on the "too cursory a notation of the 'half-consumed corpses' on which Jim turns his back" and contrasts the passage revealingly with the sympathy Jim shows to passengers on the *Patna* (17). Jim's method of rehabilitation-through-conquest in Patusan betrays the human community far more than his leap from the *Patna*.

In turning his back on the dead in Patusan, however, Jim does not completely shed reminders of the original need for his supernatural power, the need for solidarity with the unredeemed dead. Conrad plants doubts about Jim's conquest analogous to the skepticism about Stein's romanticism. Jim's assault on the Sherif's hill dramatizes his rehabilitation spatially, as an ascent from the depths of hell to a conquest of the secular world. If the leap from the *Patna*, his lowest moment, plunges him "into a well—into an everlasting deep hole" (111), his period of dominance in Patusan is assured by his storming of the hill overlooking town and forest. He returns to the hill with Marlow and they gain a view of the surrounding forest, "the dark waves of continuous tree-tops": "A brooding gloom lay over this vast and monotonous landscape; the light fell on it as if into an abyss. The land devoured the sunshine" (264). The gloomy forest devoid of sunshine is a *topos* belonging to epic descents to Hades: Homer's Odysseus encounters the thick, tall, black groves of Persephone and the sun-deprived Cimmerians (211, 217), Aeneas passes through "darkened groves" and "shadows" like one who journeys in a forest on a "black night" (6: 320, 341, 356, 359–62), and Dante begins his story lost in "a shadowed forest," a "savage forest, dense and difficult" (1: 2, 5). Conrad had adapted the *topos* already in his first novel, revealing an inclination to see in the forests of the Malay Archipelago an abysmal image of human history. In *Almayer's Folly* (1895), Dain Maroola "skirted in his weary march the edge of the forest . . . with its unrelieved gloom where lay entombed and rotting countless generations of trees, and where their successors stood as if mourning in dark green folliage, immense and helpless, awaiting their turn" (125). Mourners immense and helpless, awaiting their death immersed in the unrelieved gloom of the dead—this describes Karain, Jim, and Kurtz, products of a failed reoccupation.[16]

The forest's "corruption of countless ages" (*Almayer's Folly* 125) constitutes the secular gloom[17] that Jim as Lord momentarily seems to conquer. On the hill Marlow observes that Jim

16. As the passages cited in this paragraph indicate, Conrad turns many of his earthly landscapes (not only the Africa of *Heart of Darkness*) into Hades scenes. He compares the stream running through Patusan to the underworld's mythical rivers at least twice, calling it "as black as Styx" (312) and observing that the houses on the bank "were like a spectral herd of shapeless creatures pressing forward to drink in a spectral and lifeless stream" (246).

17. In appropriating Conrad's phrase "secular gloom," I want of course to emphasize the theological implications of the word *secular*. The same does not appear to be true always for Conrad, who often uses the word in the sense of the French *séculaire*, "ancient." While I would be happy to view my use of "secular gloom" as a creative twisting of his phrase, I find it hard to imagine that he was not often thinking of the theological associations in the English word, as in the French *séculier*, "secular," or in the Polish nouns *sekularyzacja*, "secularization," and *sekularysta*, "free thinker," both of which were in use in nineteenth-century Poland. Conrad uses the term in both *Lord Jim* and *Heart of Darkness* as part of a literary *topos* associated with the descent to Hades, and the theological sense works well—though paradoxically—in this context. Hades is otherworldly, and "secular" often means worldly; yet in the absence of a redeeming God the world itself, for Jim and Kurtz, has become a hell.

> dominated the forest, the secular gloom, the old mankind. He was like a figure set up on a pedestal, to represent in his persistent youth the power, and perhaps the virtues, of races that never grow old, that have emerged from the gloom. I don't know why he should always have appeared to me symbolic. Perhaps this is the real cause of my interest in his fate. I don't know whether it was exactly fair to him to remember the incident which had given a new direction to his life, but at that very moment I remembered very distinctly. It was like a shadow in the light. (265)

Marlow imagines here that this lord symbolizes the youthful power of his race and so, by extension, the *Patna* incident Marlow remembers represents the malaise of the entire race. Jim supposedly dominates the secular gloom, and yet the shadow of solidarity still hangs over him, landing a counter-blow for the gloom. A short time later, after listening to Jim tell his story on the hill, Marlow describes the effect of Jim's unwearied voice on the Patusan landscape much as he had earlier imagined Stein's impalpable poesy illuminating an expansive plain of graves: Jim's military victory over the Sherif has led him

> through death into the innermost life of the people; but the gloom of the land spread out under the sunshine preserved its appearance of inscrutable, of secular repose. The sound of his fresh young voice—it's extraordinary how very few signs of wear he showed—floated lightly, and passed away over the unchanged face of the forests like the sound of the big guns [on the morning of his victory]. (269)

Though Jim preserves his youth and proves his strength, he does so not through solidarity with the community of humankind, but by adding smoldering corpses to the shadowy groves of "countless generations."[18] The opportunity greeting him in the East, when unveiled, reveals the "unchanged face" of a secular gloom that he cannot conquer.

Jewel, Jim's companion in Patusan, provides a cue for an appropriate

---

18. A specter-filled grove haunted the domestic life of the Conrad family, and Conrad's response to this crisis is instructive. Conrad's son John recalls reading a copy of Æsop's fables illustrated by Arthur Rackham with "awe-inspiring" drawings of trees: "One morning I was playing by the moat after an evening of reading Æsop when I chanced to look up and saw a most horrible 'face' in the bark of the willow tree in front of me. I rushed into the house where my parents were talking in the kitchen, grabbed my father round his legs and burst into tears. . . . My mother considered that it had been rather thoughtless to have shown me so many Rackham drawings but JC did not agree, saying that I had to get used to having an imagination and not to be frightened by it, 'After all he'll have to use it in the future' "(20). *Lord Jim* and *Heart of Darkness* suggest that Conrad was not always so confident that the uses of the imagination could outweigh its terrors; he was not always so certain that the "imagination" was susceptible to "soothing" (*Heart of Darkness* 70).

final word on Jim despite her incomprehension of the larger world from which Jim brings his burden. "You are mad or false," she tells him as he heads off to his death, seduced away from her by an ideal she does not understand (412). In fact he is both, having embraced an ideal of redemptive solidarity mad in its scope (as the *Patna* episode demonstrates) and then having betrayed this impossible ideal—and having betrayed her in the process. After his death she repeats both charges against him and adds "cruelty" to the list (349–50). Her accusations implicitly identify him with two foils who display madness and falsity in more concentrated forms: the chief engineer and Gentleman Brown. While listening to Brown, Marlow observes "how much certain forms of evil are akin to madness, derived from intense egoism" (344)—and thus he names a common link among the three characters, the common thread in their idealism, madness, and evil. Jim, the hopeful Lord, suffers the "intense egoism" of a subject shaped by reoccupation. As Jim reels away from the *Patna* episode, however, Conrad deflects the potential for madness and evil in such egoism onto the chief engineer and Brown—and onto Kurtz. In Kurtz we find all three aspects of intense egoism concentrated in one character.

Mournful Africa

More than any other work of Conrad's, *Heart of Darkness* confronts the moral and psychological depths to which the modern subject's reoccupied redemptive task can lead. Kurtz is the character whose attempts to perform rescue work land him in the most dire need of rescue himself. More quickly and thoroughly than "Karain" or *Lord Jim*, *Heart of Darkness* strips away any illusion of preserved innocence or possible success. Redemption requires that the prospective redeemer descend into history's pain and suffering, and such an act of total identification leads the human subject to a perception and condemnation (and perhaps appropriation) of the horror. Like Nietzsche's Zarathustra, humbled into silence in the attempt to will backward and transform "it was" into "thus I willed it," like Benjamin's angel of history, mouth agape at the sight of the mounting wreckage of history, Kurtz loses his "magnificent folds of eloquence" (67) at a "supreme moment of complete knowledge"—at a moment, in other words, when he recognizes the extent of the wreckage of history. In place of his resonant voice and eloquence, he can summon at this moment merely a whisper: "The horror! The horror!" (68). While Marlow watches Jim chase the "sovereign power" of an ideal to his death, he finds in Kurtz someone ready to pronounce judgment on the hollowness and corruptibility of the ideal when it is confronted with the reality it must transform.

While "Karain" and *Lord Jim* hint that charms against the horror (Victoria's Jubilee sixpence, Stein's ring) can be effective at least temporarily, *Heart of Darkness* readily pronounces such "charms" and "gifts of witchmen" (60) to be "powerless" (75).[19]

Like Jim, Kurtz responds to the psychological phenomenon represented in the *Patna* episode, the imagined suffering and death of multitudes. One who approaches the horror as "an emissary of pity" (*Heart of Darkness* 28) risks becoming an agent of horror, a troubling truth that *Heart of Darkness* confronts more directly than *Lord Jim*. The latter examines the potential for cruelty and abomination in Jim's exalted egoism only in passing, for example when Marlow wonders whether all of "mankind" is not "driven by a dream of its greatness and its power upon the dark paths of excessive cruelty" (349–50). On another occasion Marlow describes the situation on the lifeboat on a pitch-black night—"no law, no sounds, no eyes" (120)—when Jim's antagonism with the *Patna* crew might result in a disaster without a trace: "It is as if the souls of men floating on an abyss and in touch with immensity had been set free for any excess of heroism, absurdity, or abomination" (121). But Jim and his companions survive this unusual situation and for the most part *Lord Jim* touches only tentatively on the conjunction of dream and cruelty, of heroism and abomination. In the figure of Kurtz, Conrad offers a more sustained examination of "a soul that knew no restraint" (66), an "unlawful soul beyond the bounds of permitted aspirations" (65); Kurtz in the wilderness, like Jim momentarily in the lifeboat, has "nothing either above or below him. . . . He had kicked himself loose of the earth." In coaxing him from the wilderness back to the steamer, Marlow cannot "appeal in the name of anything high or low" but can only "invoke him—himself" (65). While details of Kurtz's abominations are not plentiful, Conrad's rhetoric—and the heads on the stakes surrounding Kurtz's house—make clear that Conrad's pause in composing *Lord Jim* allowed him to examine more intensively in Kurtz the potential for atrocity when the human subject aspires to a godlike omnipotence.

To explore the potential for evil in the exalted egoism induced by reoccupation, Conrad structures *Heart of Darkness* around one of the central scenes from the odyssey tradition: the *katabasis*. While he uses Hades imagery piecemeal throughout "Karain" and *Lord Jim* to suggest a haunting belatedness, in *Heart of Darkness* he employs it in a more systematic fashion to structure the entire tale. One strand in the critical reception of *Heart of Darkness* has acknowledged this debt, reading the novella as a descent to hell modeled on Virgil's *Aeneid* and Dante's *Divine Comedy*. Lillian

19. These are the charms worn by the African woman and thus may well be gifts from Kurtz.

Feder initiated this line of criticism in 1955 with a study of Virgil's influence, Robert Evans shifted the focus to Dante in 1956, Bruce Stark identified the Intended in the Sepulchral City with the Horror of the inner circle of the Inferno in 1974, Thomas Cleary and Terry Sherwood heightened the emphasis on irony in Conrad's appropriation of the epic tradition in 1984, and in 1995 Kelly Anspaugh hit on the insight, indispensable for my purposes, that Kurtz corresponds not so much to Dante's Satan, as earlier commentators assume, but to God—Kurtz is himself, in short, a hollow God.[20] Marlow prepares the way for the ironic God by ironically comparing the vegetation to a "temple" (29) and the tremor of drums in the wilderness to "the sound of bells in a Christian country" (23)—these clues accompany pre-Christian *topoi* as Marlow passes through a "multitude of secular trees" (67). While the underworld imagery in *Lord Jim* could have been drawn largely from pagan Hades, *Heart of Darkness* is closer in spirit to Dante's Inferno; the focus shifts, in other words, from shades to demons. Virgil knew well the cruelty and violence that accompany imperial power, but it is the Christian God whom Kurtz ironically—unsuccessfully, abominably—replaces. Dante presents a Christianized image of hell and evil that incorporates the modern subject's exalted egoism (witness his Ulysses crossing the bounds of permitted aspirations).

Throughout the epic tradition, the descent to hell has served as a way for the epic adventurer (and the artist) to confront his dead predecessors and work through his relationship to them. When this process is most successful, it expresses something of the arrogance of the living in relation to the dead (and when it is a question of poets confronting their predecessors, the arrogance often seems to counter or to mask what Harold Bloom has called the anxiety of influence). In the *Odyssey*, the encounter with Achilles and Agamemnon in Hades is in part a way for Odysseus to distance himself from the heroic ideal established in the *Iliad*. Similarly, Aeneas separates himself from the Greek heroes (and Virgil from Homer) in adjusting the heroic ideal to imperial Rome. Then it is Virgil's turn, after accompanying Dante through the Inferno, to miss out on the Christian paradise at the conclusion of Dante's journey. The encounters with predecessors are necessary, in other words, not only to acknowledge a debt but also to create a certain distance. In each of these cases, the descent enables the living adventurer to map a path "home," and eventually each reaches a home that marks his distance from the dead predecessor: Odysseus

20. Note also the article by Yarrison. The opening pages of Anspaugh's article provide a brief overview of this critical tradition. Collectively these articles provide an extensive catalogue of the numerous correspondences between Conrad's text and its epic predecessors, freeing me from the need to provide one here, where my purpose is merely to show how Conrad adapts the epic *topoi* to reflect on the phenomenon of failed reoccupation.

finds his way to Penelope and Ithaca, Aeneas to Lavinia and Latium, Dante to Beatrice and God. Thus a successful encounter with the dead produces prophecy, giving the adventurer (and the reader) a glimpse of the future as well as the past. When the working through is less successful, however, Hades becomes an image for a haunting past and offers no vision of the future—it suggests, indeed, that human history is at an end. The women become haunting figures of absence and impotence. The living wanderer is unable to distance predecessors, unable to escape the shadow of the dead, unable to capture the arrogance of the living.

Conrad's fiction, *Heart of Darkness* in particular, exemplifies this second, unsuccessful type of descent, in which the traveller fails to work through the legacy of the past and discovers no viable future. The failure accounts for two related and recurring motifs in his work: the idea that the human heart or mind encompasses both past and future in their entirety, and the perception that humanity, without hope, has reached the end of history. The first idea surfaces in the *Narcissus* preface, the second in the apocalyptic scene sketched in the essay on Henry James. In *Nostromo*, Emilia Gould is worn down by "the care of the past and of the future" (521). The two ideas are linked to one another in both *Lord Jim* and *Heart of Darkness*. In the former, Marlow comments that "the human heart is vast enough to contain all the world" and then confesses to the "strange and melancholy illusion" that Patusan had "passed away out of existence, living only for a while longer in my memory, as though I had been the last of mankind"— to this illusion he attributes his need to tell the story (323). In *Heart of Darkness*, he asserts that "the mind of man is capable of anything—because everything is in it, all the past as well as all the future" (38). Kurtz explores this capability of the mind of man extensively enough that he can comment as if he were at the end of history: Marlow admires him for having "pronounced judgment" and "summed up." (He sums up not only his own behavior, as some have assumed; his judgment is "wide enough to embrace the whole universe, piercing enough to penetrate all the hearts that beat in the darkness" [69].) When Marlow imagines what his own dying words might be, he anticipates the alternatives for the last artist that Conrad would later sketch in the essay on James: "sardonic comment" or "austere exhortation" are the options for this artist on the eve of that day without tomorrow; Marlow similarly imagines choosing either "a word of careless contempt" or "an affirmation, a moral victory paid for by innumerable defeats" (70).

One might speak most accurately of this use of odyssey *topoi* not as a failed descent but as a failed ascent: it has the effect of suggesting that hell is inescapable. Marlow senses that the tall dark forest will "bar the way for our return" (37). Thus the *katabasis* becomes the only episode on the journey, not one among many; the encounter with all of the past and all of the future is not an isolated, revealing, harrowing experience, but a constant condition of existence; the tumult of the dead is no longer something that can be forgotten on earth or sealed off from the earth. The effect in *Heart of Darkness*, in other words, is to break down the boundaries between this world and the underworld—this world *is* hell. "The earth seemed unearthly," Marlow reports (37), and yet there is no other place for humankind: "The earth for us is a place to live in, where we must put up with sights, with sounds, with smells too, by Jove!—breathe dead hippo so to speak and not be contaminated" (50). Kurtz's great daring is to sum up and pass judgment on a history that stinks of rotting flesh. Kicking himself loose of the earth is thus a heroic act as well as an abomination. He wishes, indeed, to destroy this hell-on-earth, for he not only kicked himself free but "kicked the very earth to pieces" (65), and Marlow twice speaks of him opening his mouth voraciously as if "to swallow all the air, all the earth, all the men before him" (59), "to devour all the earth with all its mankind" (72). Kurtz responds to a situation in which questions about the totality of history are no longer confined to other worlds (whether Hades or heaven) that play a judicatory role in this world; the final adjudication takes place now in this world, in the mind or heart of the artist, of every person. In his readiness to kick this world to pieces, Kurtz exhibits a Manichean dualism that Conrad flirted with but rejected. The horror for Conrad is not merely the corruption of this world but also, paradoxically, the readiness to discard this world without certainty of something better.

The totalizing impulse reflected in the conflation of life on earth and life in hell helps collapse the boundaries between other worlds as well—between the world of Europe and the world of Africa, for example. Marlow reminds us in a famous line that "all Europe contributed to the making of Kurtz" (50), who is the epitome of the darkness located in the heart of Africa. *Heart of Darkness* makes Europe's participation in the discontent more visible than Conrad's other colonial odysseys. Beginning his tale with an analogy between Roman Britain and Africa, and then describing Brussels as a "whited sepulchre" (13), "city of the dead" (14), and "cemetery" (72), Marlow consistently incorporates Europe into the Inferno. So when he reports—in his last line before moving his tale on from Brussels—that "for a second or two I felt as though instead of going to the centre of a continent I were about to set off for the centre of the earth" (16), we are aware that he is in fact already at the center of the earth, already coping with an unsettling past. His departure from Brussels is also an occasion for him to insist unconvincingly on a boundary between the worlds of men and women. A visit to his aunt convinces him that women "live in a world of their own," "out of touch with truth," and yet the "humbug" he hears from her is common European (and male) ideology about the virtues of colonialism, ideas he has often seen in print (16). He would like similarly to characterize the Intended as living in a world of her own, and yet he equates her domestic mourning not only with the sorrowful African woman but with Kurtz's horror. In a hallucinatory experience, he hears her despairing words "I have survived" simultaneously with Kurtz's dying words of judgment (73). For both woman and man, mere survival is a horror.

The collapse of boundaries between worlds and the resulting pervasiveness of hell partially account for the similarities between home and colony, but *Heart of Darkness* still uses the conflation of epic episode and imperial setting to project the source of domestic anxieties onto Africa. Just as "Karain" and *Lord Jim* transferred to the Malay Archipelago Britain's discontent with its own rites of memory and mourning, so *Heart of Darkness* transfers this discontent to King Leopold's Congo. The mourning and guilt, and thus the process of transference, remain more mysterious in *Heart of Darkness* because there is no *Patna* episode to represent their source. They therefore become more firmly attached to, and find their most intense manifestation in, the geographical heart of darkness. Marlow insists that hell is located in Africa, and the disturbing dead he encounters on his descent are mostly Africans. The racism of Conrad's tale results from this superimposition of epic and imperial geography. In *Heart of Darkness*, Chinua Achebe observes, "Africa is to Europe as the picture is to Dorian Gray—a carrier onto whom the master unloads his physical and moral deformities so that he may go forward, erect and immaculate" (128). The last part of this claim is not persuasive: Conrad and his characters do not emerge "erect and immaculate" (not even Jim, whom we first see "apparelled in immaculate white from shoes to hat" [3]). But *Heart of Darkness* does associate the greatest deformities with Africa. If this distancing of deformity produces a form of racism, it also allows Conrad to probe the deformities behind the racism, to represent the discontent that motivates the transference. He fails to reach beyond the constraints of European thought and prejudice, but he goes far in understanding the "accursed inheritance" (37) at the root of this thought, and so in this respect, too, the story demonstrates the intimate, delicate relation between cruelty and heroism.

While much Conrad criticism has joined Achebe in observing the various deformities common to Conrad's Europe and Marlow's Congo, it has yet to recognize the extensive signs of a monumental, arrested mourning—the result of failed reoccupation—that the Inferno structure transfers to Africa. Marlow's first experience on African soil, during his approach to the company's first station, leads him into the "grove of death" (22): "no sooner within than it seemed to me I had stepped into the gloomy circle of some Inferno" (20). The "black" and "moribund shapes" he finds crumpled in the shade—native workers whom the imperial enterprise has exhausted and left to die—become the dead who haunt Marlow, emblems of the past with which he and Kurtz cannot come to terms. Associated with "pain," "abandonment," "despair," "disease," "starvation," "gloom," "weariness," "massacre," and "pestilence," the "phantom[s]" reclining in the shade highlight not only the excesses of colonial endeavor but all of Europe's unsettled past (20–21). One of the men wears a necklace of white thread that may be intended, like Karain's sixpence pendant, as "a charm," but it has no effect other than to startle Marlow and provoke the first appearance in the story of the word "horror," for Marlow stands "horror-struck" (21). When he reports that these phantoms are "not of this earth," he not only calls attention to the subterranean position of the Inferno but also hints at the phantoms' *unheimlich* status as superficially alien, profoundly familiar figures of loss.

The grove of death is characteristic, not unique; as Marlow ventures upriver, he finds the wilderness to be a site of pervasive mourning. The approach to Kurtz provokes "a tremulous and prolonged wail of mournful fear and utter despair as may be imagined to follow the flight of the last hope from the earth" (47). Farther upstream the boat comes under attack from the shore and Marlow again hears a "very loud cry as of infinite desolation," a "complaining clamour," a "tumultuous and mournful uproar" (41). This is sorrow, not savagery, and he is baffled. He registers an "inexplicable note of desperate grief in this savage clamour" (43), and he latches onto the idea that grief lies behind all of the natives' actions, their attack on the boat as well as the uproar. The cries

> had given me an irresistible impression of sorrow. The glimpse of the steamboat had for some reason filled those savages with unrestrained grief. The danger if any, I expounded, was from our proximity to a great human passion let loose. Even extreme grief may ultimately vent itself in violence. (44)

They are grieving over the imminent loss of their god, Kurtz, and thus they are much like Kurtz, who has attempted to fill the void left by the retreat of *his* God. In explaining their violent attack on the steamer, Marlow offers a tentative, anticipatory explanation of Kurtz's abominations: "unrestrained grief" lies behind the famous lack of restraint in Kurtz's character, for "extreme grief" can "vent itself in violence."

Marlow next comes upon the native woman, who serves in her grief as a synecdoche for the grief of the natives, of the land, and ultimately of Kurtz and Europe. Like Karain, she is a native version of Queen Victoria: mournful, associated with charms of dubious value, and "stately in her deliberate progress." She is "the image," Marlow says, of the "tenebrous and passionate soul" of life in that "sorrowful land." Her supposed savagery, like that of the warriors who attack the steamer, turns out to consist of "wild sorrow" and "dumb pain" (60). The mourning of the Africans becomes an allegory for—an intensified, projected version of—Europe's own affliction. They mourn the death of God.

Marlow's Renunciation

Conrad betrays profound ambivalence about Jim's and Kurtz's ambitions as godlike artists, and nothing reveals this ambivalence more fully than his use of Marlow. Marlow, too, is an artist, and sometimes he postures as a minor deity. He repeatedly discusses his own storytelling in terms Conrad used in the *Narcissus* preface—solidarity, rescue from oblivion, responsibility to make one *see*—and he poses as a Buddha, an idol, one in a position to sum up. But he does not embrace these roles as unreservedly as Jim and Kurtz do. Possessing an open-eyed skepticism about his ability to fulfill the task of the redeeming artist, Marlow is resigned to failure.

The primary objects of his rescue work are, of course, Jim and Kurtz, rescuers in need of rescue. He often perceives them as haunting spirits, and the descriptions of Hades-like landscapes most often represent his perceptions, not Jim's or Kurtz's. For example, while acknowledging his solidarity with Jim—"he is one of us"—Marlow comments that sometimes Jim "passes from my eyes like a disembodied spirit astray amongst the passions of this earth, ready to surrender himself faithfully to the claim of his own world of shades" (416). Kurtz similarly is "indistinct like a vapour exhaled by the earth" (64). Marlow frequently describes both as mysterious, but they are mysteries of the unknown type: inscrutable, impenetrable, inexpressible, insoluble, dark, elusive. Conrad's *Narcissus* manifesto depends on the assumption that human mysteries are known or knowable and rescue work succeeds by communicating the mystery. Marlow's skepticism about understanding Jim and Kurtz—and getting his audience to understand them—calls the imperatives of the earlier preface into question.

The preface itself provides hints, I have argued, that its imperatives cannot be fulfilled, but it shows no sign of backing away from them. Marlow seems to be on the verge of taking this extra step from doubt to renunciation. An ambiguous sentence in *Lord Jim* on the occasion of Marlow's visit to Patusan might be interpreted as an expression of the desire to cast off the artist's redemptive responsibility. Gaining a moment of solitude outside Jim's house one night, Marlow perceives a Hades-like gloom engulfing the town, marking it as one of the obscure fragments of history destined for oblivion, and he feels himself to be the only one whose memory and words might keep it alive. (As he says elsewhere of Jim, "it is only through me that he exists for you" [224].) The landscape he describes is otherworldly: illuminated by the rising moon, by a "mournful eclipse-like light" that is punctuated with the "heavy shadows" of dark "stumps of felled trees," the scene contains a "solitary grave" garlanded with "flowers gathered by no man, grown not in this world, and destined for the use of the dead alone" (322). This is the moment when he imagines himself, like the last artist in Conrad's essay on Henry James, at the end of time: "when I stood still all sound and all movements in the world seemed to come to an end" (322) and "it was a great peace, as if the earth had been one grave" (323). The recurring idea of the artist's total comprehension appears with an ambiguous addendum: "The human heart is vast enough to contain all the world. It is valiant enough to bear the burden, but where is the courage that would cast it off?" (323).

How precisely does he imagine casting off the burden? Perhaps through suicide, for which Marlow does not have the courage, but the idea is in keeping with reflection he indulges in at other times on death as a "blessed finality" (176), a release from woe. Perhaps through homicide, an option Marlow cannot entertain as seriously as Kurtz, who begins exterminating the brutes in an attempt to kick the earth to pieces. Another, less expected, more intriguing possibility, however, is that Marlow would like to renounce the responsibility of the artist, renounce the search for meaning in Jim's life and death in order to escape Jim's specter and be better able to go on living. Roy Roussel observes that Marlow fears his responsibility as author of Jim's story, because Jim illustrates how "fellowship has been transmuted into something destructive" (86). As Mark Conroy notes, "ironically, Marlow may become as much a buffer against meaning in this novel as he is an instrument for transmitting meaning" (*Modernism and Authority* 93).[21] If such buffering is what Marlow intends when he speaks

21. Conroy makes this observation parenthetically while observing that Conrad's texts, like Kurtz, "give the aftereffect of being resonantly 'hollow at the core' " (93). But Conroy's concern is to show that Conrad uses Marlow in an attempt to overcome this perplexing absence and "to find or to found an audience" (87). Not until *Nostromo* and *The Secret Agent*, Conroy suggests, does Conrad abandon his nostalgia for a more immediate communion, or solidarity, between writer and public. In speaking of Marlow's renunciation, I am pointing to evidence that Conrad had in fact begun to move beyond this nostalgia already in the earlier Marlow stories.

of casting off the burden, this would not be the only time he wished to un-load Jim. He views the whole Patusan scheme as a way to get Jim out of sight, to "let him creep twenty feet underground and stay there," as Brierly puts it (before committing suicide himself). Marlow confesses that he decided on the Patusan plan at a time when he needed to "dispose of" Jim so he could return home to England with a "clear consciousness," not overly burdened by his belief "in the solidarity of our lives" (221–24).

Disavowal of solidarity with "all the world" might paradoxically have salutary ethical consequences as well as psychological and anthropologi-cal benefits. The modern subject could perhaps set aside the redemptive burden, dissipate the created terror of the imagination, relinquish respon-sibility for the past and future—and thus practice a less exalted egoism, a less ambitious solidarity. If one hopes to cast off the burden of universal solidarity, then the elusiveness of knowledge and inscrutable nature of the darkness provide cause for hope rather than despair. Pushing this idea to an absurd extreme for a moment, one might perceive in Marlow's asser-tion that "we live, as we dream—alone . . ." more a sigh of relief than a lament. It comes in an aside to his audience as he acknowledges the diffi-culty of making them understand Kurtz:

> Do you see him? Do you see the story? Do you see anything? It seems to me I am trying to tell you a dream—making a vain attempt, because no re-lation of a dream can convey the dream-sensation. . . .
> No, it is impossible; it is impossible to convey the life-sensation of any given epoch of one's existence—that which makes its truth, its meaning—its subtle and penetrating essence. It is impossible. (30)

Considering what happened to Kurtz when *he* encountered the darkness, Marlow might very well perceive the isolation of his living and dreaming to be a necessary defense. Similarly, his repeated insistence that he has a weak imagination (in comparison to Jim) may be a point of pride, consid-ering the terror that Jim creates for himself with his powerful imagination.

I have been conflating two Marlows, but the impulse toward a renunci-ation of knowledge is not equally strong in both. One way to identify the difference is indirectly, through their objects of inquiry: Jim is brightly il-luminated in his immaculate white clothes, while Kurtz is shadowy, dis-embodied, lacking substance. Despite Marlow's uncertainty about what is beneath Jim's surface, Kurtz and his actions remain the lesser known mys-tery with the result that the focus in *Heart of Darkness* is more on Marlow's own quest. The novella, intruding into the composition of *Lord Jim*, is less concerned with the finished artist than with the ambivalent one, and the darker evil of Kurtz gives Marlow more reason to feel conflicted about his artistic endeavor. Albert Guerard describes Marlow's ambivalent relation to Kurtz—an isolated man committing himself to one even more isolated—as an act of solidarity for the purpose of a distancing catharsis. "The double is exorcised," he concludes (48); the ghost is laid to rest; the solidarity, in other words, is eventually severed. This is an overly optimistic account of what happens when Marlow returns to the sepulcher city, but it accurately captures his desire to break free from the specter and suppress its story.

Marlow attempts to free himself by literally disowning Kurtz—by liquidating possessions he has received from Kurtz. Kurtz's own possessiveness revealed his need for mastery, providing Marlow with a negative example: " 'My Intended, my ivory, my station, my river, my . . .' everything belonged to him" (49). Marlow decides conversely on a strategy of dispossession:

> All that had been Kurtz's had passed out of my hands: his soul, his body, his station, his plans, his ivory, his career. There remained only his memory and his Intended—and I wanted to give that up too to the past, in a way—to surrender personally all that remained of him with me to that oblivion which is the last word of our common fate. (71)

So he heads off to visit the Intended to lay the ghost to rest. He finds, however, that the specter of Kurtz's memory is not easy to shake: "He lived then before me, he lived as much as he had ever lived—a shadow insatiable of splendid appearances, of frightful realities, a shadow darker than the shadow of the night, and draped nobly in the folds of a gorgeous eloquence" (72). He is incredulous when the Intended laments that nobody will ever see Kurtz again: "Never see him! I saw him clearly enough then. I shall see this eloquent phantom as long as I live" (75). The most conclusive evidence of his failure is the fact that he later finds himself telling Kurtz's story, as if compelled against his will to preserve Kurtz's memory—or compelled repeatedly to attempt to shake Kurtz's memory. As the Marlow of *Lord Jim* says about Jim narrating the story of his terror on the *Patna*, "he could no more stop telling now than he could have stopped living by the mere exertion of his will" (100). To live is to tell: the only way to cast off the burden is, after all, suicide. Like Coleridge's ancient mariner, the living artist compulsively repeats the tale without hope of relief or release.

Marlow's frustrated desire to renounce the responsibility of the artist says much about Conrad's view of language, which to him parallels the imagination in its duplicity as both tool and plague of the artist. On his visit to the Intended, Marlow associates the hauntingly vivid images of

Kurtz with Kurtz's eloquence ("gorgeous eloquence," "eloquent phantom"). He had earlier noted the "unbounded power of eloquence—of words—of burning noble words" in Kurtz's report on savage customs (50), but the nobility is quickly obliterated by Kurtz's brutal postscript. In these instances language is not a tool for rescue work but has itself become a savage custom. In *Lord Jim* Marlow observes that "a word carries far—very far—deals destruction through time as the bullets go flying through space" (174). These temporal bullets fall ineffectually to the ground only when one tries to turn them against the phantoms. Marlow also asserts that "words . . . belong to the sheltering conception of light and order which is our refuge" (313),[22] but then a short time later, wondering how to kill off a specter, he concludes that for such an enterprise "the bullet is not run, the blade not forged, the man not born; even the winged words of truth drop at your feet like lumps of lead. You require for such a desperate encounter an enchanted and poisoned shaft dipped in a lie too subtle to be found on earth" (316).

Conrad would like to cast aside the imperatives of his own *Narcissus* preface as dangerously burdensome. But the imperatives are the expression of needs that cannot be negated by an act of will. No individual heroism can restrain the aspiration to make history whole; no silver bullet or golden words will kill off the impulse to reoccupy the god-shaped void. Only a subtle lie can slowly, almost imperceptibly, dilute such impulses over time, and Conrad suggests that no such subtlety will be found on earth. Perhaps he is right; but it is also possible that his own fiction, a subtle reminder of the danger of reoccupation, contributes to the gradual process of persuading the human heart that it need not rescue all of the past from oblivion. Perhaps his stories contribute to the creation of an "unconscious subtlety which could draw consolation from the very source of sorrow" (*Lord Jim* 235). These words are borrowed, I confess, from a description of Jim in his naïve enthusiasm for the Patusan scheme, and it may be that the search for such subtlety constitutes a futile attempt to stay afloat in a destructive element. The question persists: can the imagination lie subtly enough to cure its own affliction?

22. In this passage Marlow speaks also of his "conception of existence" as "that shelter each of us makes for himself to creep under in moments of danger, as a tortoise withdraws within its shell" (313). The concept of language as a shelter lends itself to comparison not only with tortoises, but with the beetles Stein collects. Insects of the order *Coleoptera* are characterized by their tough, protective covers, or sheaths. The counterfeit gilt lettering of "Karain" carries over to Stein's laboratory to suggest that the value of language as shelter and refuge is exaggerated. In Stein's study, above the dead earthbound beetles, "the word *Coleoptera* written in gold letters glittered mysteriously upon a vast dimness" (204).

Conrad soon extends his reflection on possible cures into other realms. Late in 1902, two years after the publication of *Lord Jim*, he began work on *Nostromo*, in which he turns to consider whether the state can cure the affliction. In this form the lie is not subtle but violent, and on the question of its effectiveness Conrad will prove as pessimistic as ever.

A State of Terror: *Nostromo*'s Dynamite

In Russia, the land of spectral ideas and disembodied aspirations, many brave minds have turned away at last from the vain and endless conflict to the one great historical fact of the land. They turned to autocracy for the peace of their patriotic conscience as a weary unbeliever, touched by grace, turns to the faith of his fathers for the blessing of spiritual rest.

—JOSEPH CONRAD, *Under Western Eyes*

Orphans is what I say we are.

—VIRGINIA WOOLF to Janet Case, 21 May 1922

Despite *Nostromo*'s deficiencies of proportion, it remains Conrad's most ambitious and most challenging work; in Virginia Woolf's fine phrase, it is one of literature's "magnificent wrecks," a failure of astonishing solidity ("Mr. Conrad's Crisis" 126). The novel is afflicted by flaws in its structure, by shifts in perspective and imbalances in plot and character development that often seem more accidental than purposeful, more the product of haste or confusion than deliberate technique. It nevertheless succeeds as a prescient rendering of the turbulent political experience of many postcolonial nations in the twentieth century, turbulence resulting in part from a transplanting of European political institutions and ideologies to alien settings. The novel constitutes, furthermore, Conrad's most detailed, complex, and nuanced meditation on modernity, and this accomplishment is what I shall focus on here, with a double purpose. First, I hope to show that *Nostromo* extends Conrad's concern with the implications of reoccupation. Like his earlier work, this one confronts the moral challenge of redemption, but it also moves beyond its predecessors by examining the effects of reoccupation on political institutions, and on the state in particular. In the process of describing this expanded ambition and accomplishment, I hope, secondly, to supplement earlier critical assessments of Conrad's politics by showing that the dynamite threatening and protecting the silver mine is not only an important plot detail and a brilliant stratagem on the part of Charles Gould, but also a symbolic condensation of Conrad's thoughts on the foundations of the modern state.[1]

Historicizing *Nostromo* Criticism

Many readers have perceived *Nostromo*'s uniqueness in Conrad's oeuvre and in the history of the novel. Whereas earlier the sea or an isolated primitive locale served to simplify and intensify Conrad's fictional meditations on the individual and society, here the setting encourages a complex expansiveness. This complexity has helped secure Conrad's unique historical position between nineteenth-century realism and high modernism. Edward Said describes this "exceptional status" as a moment of greater self-consciousness about the problem of beginnings, especially the beginning premises of novels (*Beginnings* 137); Fredric Jameson sees "the peculiar heterogeneity of the moment of Conrad" as a rare surfacing of unconscious political content in the form of the novel (*Political Unconscious* 280). In psychoanalytic terms, we might say that the novel goes beyond its predecessors in exposing the uncanny as something domestic; its uncomfortable truths are only lightly disguised, barely repressed.

With Conrad's most influential postcolonial and Marxist critics both singling it out for special attention, *Nostromo* provides an opportunity to revisit briefly two of the critical perspectives I considered in chapter 2 of this book, two perspectives which strive admirably to historicize the novel. ("Always historicize!" are Jameson's first words in *The Political Unconscious* [9], although agreement on the need to historicize often leads to competing historicizations rather than interpretive consensus.) In different ways, both Said and Jameson respond to the novel's uncanny dynamic, its projection of European concerns onto a distant landscape. One of the strengths of Said's reading is that he treats the novel as colonial realism, much as Achebe reads Africa in *Heart of Darkness*. Despite his earlier comments on Conrad's exceptional self-consciousness about the premises of the novel, Said comments in *Culture and Imperialism* on Conrad's "limitations of vision." He concludes a brief discussion of *Nostromo* as follows:

---

1. In addition to Said and Jameson, others to examine the ways in which *Nostromo* is and is not a political novel include Howe, Tillyard, Hay (*Political Novels*), Fleishman (*Conrad's Politics*), Williams (*English Novel*), Parry, Conroy (*Modernism and Authority*), Armstrong, Visser, and Reilly.

It is not paradox . . . that Conrad was both anti-imperialist and imperialist, progressive when it came to rendering fearlessly and pessimistically the self-confirming, self-deluding corruption of overseas domination, deeply reactionary when it came to conceding that Africa or South America could ever have had an independent history or culture, which the imperialists violently disturbed but by which they were ultimately defeated. (xviii)

I do not wish to contest any part of this description, which provides a useful point of departure for a reading of *Nostromo*, but I think something more remains to be said—and is said in the novel—about the self-confirming, self-deluding dynamic of imperial culture. To discover it, we need to supplement Said's comment with an understanding of the ways in which the novel is also *not* about South America and the West's involvement there, but about problems immanent in European culture. Such an expanded perspective, by exploring the historical roots of some of the drives behind colonialism, can eventually serve to carry the postcolonial critique to a deeper level.[2]

Jameson similarly acknowledges Conrad's reactionary impulses, but he reads *Nostromo* as the representation of a phenomenon originating and fully present within Europe: reification. His interpretation begins by identifying instances of "ideological interference" on three semantic levels: in the representation of a shiftless Latin race unable to govern itself, in the identification of positive figures with the aristocratic Blanco party and of evil Monterist figures with the mestizos, and in the use of the theory of *ressentiment* in descriptions of the Montero brothers (270). Passage through these three semantic levels of ideological interference already initiates a movement in Jameson's analysis from Latin America to Europe, a movement soon reinforced by the transition from a realist to a symbolic approach to the text; his interest in the "political unconscious" results in a method for deciphering uncomfortable truths buried—or, in the case of Conrad, half-buried—in the text.

One of the defining characteristics of capitalism for Jameson (via Marx and Engels) is the fact that it dissolved older forms of social relations, and any attempt to return a text to "concrete" history, his critical touchstone, must expose this historical rupture and the attempts of capitalist culture to smooth it over. The concept Jameson foregrounds for his reading of Con-

---

2. Said's brief comments on *Nostromo* in *Culture and Imperialism* serve as a postscript to his work in *Beginnings*, where he offers a detailed and useful reading of *Nostromo*. I offer an interpretation of the novel here that is in a sense an elaboration of his earlier analysis of the novel's mimetic function in relation to "man's overambitious intention to author his own world" (118), although my focus on theories of the state leads me away from his suggestion that the novel reduces political history "to a condition of mind, an inner state" (110). See also his *Joseph Conrad and the Fiction of Autobiography*.

rad, "reification," names the historical process that has produced this rupture and thus identifies the deepest semantic level he finds in Conrad's work. The disappearance of genuine community and value is in his view the true unconscious content of Conrad's flirtations with romance and *ressentiment* in *Nostromo*. His identification of this semantic level follows the general pattern of the secularization thesis. One strength of Jameson's Marxism, though it is a strength that brings the process of historicizing to a halt, is that it embraces its secularization openly and eagerly, exploiting it for maximum rhetorical effect. The notion of community is not merely the basis for nostalgia in his work, but a utopian image he uses to reoccupy religious positions such as faith, the intention toward the totality of society, and eschatology. His discussion of *Nostromo* links the idea of community directly to religion when he talks about the loss of both under capitalism and places Conrad's pessimism in the context of "aesthetic religion":

> Religion, to the henceforth "religiously unmusical" [Max Weber's self-description] subjects of the market system, is the unity of the older social life perceived from the outside: hence its structural affinity with the image as such and hallucination. Religion is the superstructural projection of a mode of production, the latter's only surviving trace in the form of linguistic and visual artifacts, thought systems, myths and narratives, which look as though they had something to do with the forms in which our own consciousness is at home, and yet which remain rigorously closed [to] it. Because we can no longer think the figures of the sacred from within, we transform their external forms into aesthetic objects. (252)

Since "religion has the symbolic value of wholeness" (252), it has an affinity with Marxism's own ideals, with the "genuine community" of which Jameson dreams and the imagination of the whole that he inherited from Lukács and others. And thus Jameson quite effectively uses the surviving "aesthetic objects" of the sacred in the service of a Marxist image of wholeness.

An example of such usage in his *Nostromo* critique ties his historicizing impulses to a particular metaphysical position:

> That life is meaningless is not a proposition that need be inconsistent with Marxism, whose affirmation is the quite different one that History is meaningful, however absurd organic life may happen to be. The real issue is not the propositions of existentialism, but rather their charge of affect: in future societies people will still grow old and die, but the Pascalian wager of Marxism lies elsewhere, namely in the idea that death in a fragmented and individualized society is far more frightening and anxiety-laden than

in a genuine community, in which dying is something that happens to the group more intensely than it happens to the individual subject. (261)

The utopian impulse in this passage is an instance of self-conscious secularization, as Jameson's own references to death and Pascal's wager suggest. In fact the rhetoric of secularization is precisely what makes "History" meaningful in this passage. But in the process of imagining history meaningful, however tentatively or speculatively, the rhetoric brings the historicizing process to an end by providing a "concreteness," a final semantic level, that obstructs further inquiry.

In this instance further inquiry—further historicizing—might question the underlying aspiration toward the totality of society that utopian Marxism shares with religion. This further inquiry could begin by noting that the need to imagine some future, collective negation of death, or some compensatory meaning for it, finds a substantially different response in utopian Marxism than in Christian eschatology: the compensation imagined by the former is immanent in history rather than dependent on the intervention of a suprahistorical agent. Conrad is, in his own way, acutely aware of this difference, of the added burden for the community of creating immanent meaning. Jameson's reoccupations sometimes make him less aware of the way the totalizing impulse functions in *Nostromo*—the way, for example, the futile drive for total solidarity is not merely a response to, but the cause of much of the novel's pervasive weariness. His rhetoric of secularization, his unquestioned desire for the totality of society, his self-imposed limits on historicization all prevent Jameson from recognizing that Conrad is reflecting on the cost involved in using only human means to make history totally meaningful.

Occidental Weariness, A Father's Unnatural Error

In *The Epic Strain in the English Novel*, E. M. W. Tillyard speaks of his "experience of constantly thinking of Homer when reading *Nostromo*":

> Conrad's union of colour and romance and fairy-lore with irony and the most accurate eye for the living detail recalls Homer's union of the fabulous with the actual in the *Odyssey*. And they are alike in the span of life they cover and in the sense of teeming life within that span. (167)

Nostromo is in many respects Conrad's closest approach to epic. But in the context of the present study it must be acknowledged that, despite its uncanny structure, *Nostromo* conforms less to the odyssey pattern than much of his earlier work. There are certainly plenty of individual journeys within the novel—numerous flights and pursuits into the *campo*, across the mountains, or along the coast, and excursions from the States or Europe to Sulaco (and *vice versa*)—but none of these journeys takes on the symbolic or structural importance of an odyssey. The novel seems in fact to evoke a world in which colonial odysseys are no longer possible. While Jim, Kurtz, and Marlow are able to journey to the periphery of empire in search of a measure of independence or isolation, in *Nostromo* such remote regions no longer exist. The narrative may begin by emphasizing the remoteness of Costaguana's Occidental province, insulated as it is from the capital Santa Marta by mountains and from the sea by the placid gulf, unnavigable for sailing ships; but by the time of the novel's major events, the isolation has been compromised by the steam ships of the O.S.N. Company, by the telegraph, and by the construction of a railway. These products of modernization help link Sulaco not only to its capital but also, more importantly, to the United States and Europe. Thus bound to the metropolitan world, Sulaco does not serve as the destination for a colonial odyssey in the way that the Congo Inner Station or Jim's Patusan do.

This global integration through technology is only one sign that the supposed exotic nature of Sulaco is at heart an extension or projection of Europe. As if to emphasize the Europeanness of events, Conrad names the province "Occidental" and later, after it secedes, preserves the name for the republic even though the region's independence makes its geographical position in relation to the former capital less relevant. The town's history also follows a decidedly European pattern. The chairman of the railway board, recently arrived from London, responds to Emilia Gould's proud assertion of Sulaco's historical importance with the claim that,

> We can't give you your ecclesiastical court back again; but you shall have more steamers, a railway, a telegraph-cable—a future in the great world which is worth infinitely more than any amount of ecclesiastical past. You shall be brought in touch with something greater than two viceroyalties. (36)

His statement embodies nicely (because crudely) a celebration of modernity as an age of enlightenment (represented in this case by technology); enlightenment more than compensates for, and is made possible by, liberation from divine and monarchial authority. If the irony of Emilia Gould's response to him is characteristically muted, the novel itself is more openly scornful of this view of progress.

Conrad's skepticism about the effects of modernization is captured in an image adapted from *Lord Jim*. In the earlier novel Marlow comments on Patusan by asking,

> Do you notice how, three hundred miles beyond the end of telegraph ca-
> bles and mail-boat lines, the haggard utilitarian lies of our civilisation
> wither and die, to be replaced by pure exercises of imagination, that have
> the futility, often the charm, and sometimes the deep hidden truthfulness,
> of works of art? (282)

In *Nostromo* Conrad confronts modernity and modernization more deliberately, and more readily foregoes any thought of escape through exercises of imagination; Sulaco is more developed, less isolated, less open to
romance than Patusan. In *Nostromo* the narrator observes that a

> sparse row of telegraph poles strode obliquely clear of the town, bearing a
> single, almost invisible wire far into the great campo—like a slender, vi-
> brating feeler of that progress waiting outside for a moment of peace to
> enter and twine itself about the weary heart of the land. (166)

The weariness is in part the result of frequent revolutions and civil strife,
the political and economic turmoil that regularly sweeps across
Costaguana and through Sulaco. In this passage and elsewhere in the
novel, the town of Sulaco is placed on the side of the metropolitan world
in opposition to the less developed rural regions; progress lurks in the
town awaiting its opportunity to bind the weary countryside. But Conrad's irony quickly undermines the opposition, infecting the forces of
progress, Sulaco, and Europe with weariness. Most of the characters of
European descent have this weariness attributed to them: both of the
Goulds, Dr. Monygham, Martin Decoud, and, perhaps most surprisingly,
Nostromo. The final confirmation that the weariness pervasive in *Nostromo*, like that encountered in Conrad's earlier works, derives from a late-
modern sense of belatedness comes when Conrad ties the weariness *topos*
to imagination and to his own writing of the novel, a link anticipated by
the opposition between telegraph cables and works of art in *Lord Jim*.

The narrator hints at the late-modern impotence of imagination in describing the novel's most prolific author, Decoud, as he speaks with his
beloved, Antonia Avellanos: "Nothing new can be said by man or
woman" (181). It remains ambiguous whether the thought here belongs to
Decoud or to the omniscient narrator, but the comment anticipates Conrad's own about the novel, offered retrospectively in the 1917 "Author's
Note." Prior to his discovery of the idea for *Nostromo*, he observed "a subtle change in the nature of the inspiration; a phenomenon for which I cannot in any way be held responsible," and he grew concerned that "after

finishing the last story of the 'Typhoon' volume it seemed somehow that there was nothing more in the world to write about" (vii).[3] But a reminder of words heard in "early youth" about the historical model for *Nostromo* took him back to "that distant time when everything was so fresh, so surprising, so venturesome, so interesting. . . . Perhaps, perhaps, there still was in the world something to write about" (ix). As he had in *Lord Jim* and "Youth," Conrad here identifies the romance of adventure as a desperate attempt at rejuvenation, an attempt to overcome the sense of belatedness that he shares with Decoud, though now he applies the description to himself rather than to his characters. In the movement from nothing-new-can-be-said to perhaps-still-something-to-write-about, Conrad accordingly finds one way to apply the odyssey motif to *Nostromo*: he describes his own creative labors as an odyssey of the imagination. In the "Author's Note," he says of his decision to begin writing: "I hesitated, as if warned by the instinct of self-preservation from venturing on a distant and toilsome journey into a land full of intrigues and revolutions. But it had to be done" (x). One must be cautious, once again, about weighing too ponderously the pronouncements in his late author's notes, but his association of writing with fatigue is spread over an extended period, and it hints at his perception of the underlying purpose of his fiction. For all his efforts to create and maintain distance from his fiction through narrative framing and exotic settings, it is here, in the character of Decoud and in the theme of the weariness-inspired odyssey, that Conrad comes into closest psychological contact with this novel.

Especially revealing in relation to this underlying purpose is the case of the Goulds, who are as important a focus for the novel as its title character. For the Goulds, weariness is not merely the consequence of their audacious endeavors but the initial motivation, for they are responding to the weariness of their predecessor, Gould's father, whose spirit was broken by his involuntary ownership of the mine. The beginning of Charles' love for Emilia coincides with the death of Charles' father, and subsequently

> a vague idea of rehabilitation had entered the plan of their life. That it was so vague as to elude the support of argument made it only the stronger. . . . It was as if they had been morally bound to make good their vigorous view of life against the [father's] unnatural error of weariness and despair. (74)

That such ideas remain "so vague as to elude the support of argument" is in keeping with the unconscious or preconscious status of the inherited

---

3. Conrad completed "To-morrow," the final story in *Typhoon and Other Stories*, early in 1902; he began writing *Nostromo* in December 1902.

obligation to redeem. Through the Goulds Conrad has incorporated into the novel reflection on the claims in his nonfiction about fiction as a means of rehabilitation, and his representation of the Goulds' moral enterprise shows he remains as pessimistic as ever about the prospects of success and the consequences of failure.

Much of *Nostromo* can indeed be understood as a dramatization of the solidarity and solitude described in the *Narcissus* preface. The drive for solidarity is evident not only in the Goulds' desire to rehabilitate his father's work, but also in Emilia Gould's benevolence toward most of Sulaco's residents, natives and foreigners alike, in Decoud's solicitous behavior toward Antonia and his sister in Paris, in Nostromo's relation to the people, and so on. The burden of such solidarity is evident in the paradoxical fact that those who feel it most profoundly are often those most afflicted by solitude. Conrad connects Emilia's weariness directly to the aims of the artist spelled out in the preface, where he spoke of a solidarity that "binds together all humanity—the dead to the living and the living to the unborn." Emilia

> resembled a good fairy, weary with a long career of well-doing, touched by the withering suspicion of the uselessness of her labours, the powerlessness of her magic. . . .
>
> It had come into her mind that for life to be large and full, it must contain the care of the past and of the future in every passing moment of the present. Our daily work must be done to the glory of the dead, and for the good of those who come after. (520–21)

This description begins the novel's most revealing look into her mind, a passage in which she meditates on loneliness, desolation, and dread, on the "moral degradation of the idea" inherent in successful action, on her own childlessness and the material interests that have taken her husband from her. Her weariness indicates that despite political and economic success, the Goulds have not escaped the unnatural error of the father.

Reoccupation via Dynamite

Through the founding of the Occidental Republic and through the figure of *"el rey de Sulaco"* (as Charles Gould is called), *Nostromo* carries Conrad's meditations on modernity beyond the largely psychological and moral problem of rehabilitation-through-solidarity to the political realm. The novel investigates the problem of political legitimacy in a secular age.

The narrative of the inception of the independent Republic of Sulaco exposes the roots of state power, roots extending beyond the reach of any particular party or ideology.

Although many of the characters play important roles in the secession of Sulaco, Conrad seems to go out of his way to undermine the supposition that a state can be founded upon individual heroism, rational argument, and republican ideals. Not only does mere chance play a critical role in the unfolding of events, but the rationale for an independent state suffers a double blow through Decoud, the political journalist who first conceives the idea of secession. The first blow is Decoud's skeptical insistence that he is no patriot or ideologue and is motivated solely by his love for Antonia, a confession that has the effect of making his political activity merely an effect of private passions. The second blow is his suicide following his heroic but ill-fated escape with the silver; the suicide reveals again the hollowness of his convictions, and Conrad's irony undermines Decoud's apparent heroism, since Sulaco's secession does not depend for its success on the preservation of the silver.

If the example of Decoud suggests that individual intelligence and action have little to do with the foundations of the modern state, one man nevertheless plays a central role in the founding of the Occidental Republic, and that is Charles Gould, through his management of the mine, his "Imperium in Imperio." While Conrad earlier examined, in the character of Jim, a failed attempt to secure a "sovereign power" over the self, in the character of Gould he more clearly links this attempt to questions of political sovereignty; the result is equally disconcerting. Despite Gould's commitment to "material interests" as the means to a stable society (a position lauded by Robert Penn Warren), his greatest influence comes not in any constructive form but in the threat of violence, in his arrangement to have the mine dynamited if his control or his safety is compromised by any political force. The threat serves to keep Pedro Montero at bay until Decoud's idea of independence is posthumously realized. In the absence of viceroyalties and ecclesiastical courts, Conrad seems to suggest, state power is based on the rather illegitimate foundation of the threat of violence, or terror. By means of that threat, Gould reoccupies the position of an absolute monarch, earning his title *el rey de Sulaco*.

By the time he embraces the plan for secession, Gould himself would not disagree with this rather critical assessment of his position. In a fine dramatic scene, Conrad has him encounter an emissary of Hernández, the feared bandit who becomes a Ribierist General as the Ribierist government is crumbling, and then provides safe refuge for those like the Avellanos family who are fleeing the approaching Monterists. When the emissary of this bandit-turned-general asks Gould, "has not the master of the mine any message to send to Hernández, the master of the Campo?" the narrator explains that

> the truth of the comparison struck Charles Gould heavily. In his deter-
> mined purpose he held the mine, and the indomitable bandit held the
> Campo by the same precarious tenure. They were equals before the law-
> lessness of the land. It was impossible to disentangle one's activity from its
> debasing contacts. A close-meshed net of crime and corruption lay upon
> the whole country. An immense and weary discouragement sealed his lips
> for a time. (360–61)

While staring down at the dying Don José Avellanos, the idealistic republican author of "Fifty Years of Misrule" who has been "vanquished in a
lifelong struggle with the powers of moral darkness" (362), Gould unseals
his lips and enters into a pact with the bandits. Conrad leaves Gould and
the reader with little doubt about the nature of Gould's accomplishment,
founded not on any rational principle or ideal of political and economic
justice, not on heroic action or the will of the people, not even in the end
on the progress of material interests, but on Gould's "determined purpose," tainted by its debasing contacts with crime, corruption, lawless-
ness, and terror.

Before Gould encounters Hernández's emissary, he is brought into contact with the bandits by an intermediary responsible for securing Hernández his appointment as General: Father Corbelán. Corbelán serves not
only this dramatic function, but also a more important thematic one. It is
he who connects the problem of political legitimacy most explicitly to the
problems of modernity, and specifically to secularization. For Father Corbelán, we are told, "the idea of political honour, justice, and honesty . . .
consists in the restitution of the confiscated Church property. Nothing else
could have drawn that fierce converter of savage Indians out of the wilds
to work for the Ribierist cause!" (188–89). That this is not merely a case of
single-issue politics becomes evident if we remember that the concept of
secularization originally referred quite specifically to the appropriation of
church lands by the state. Thus Father Corbelán's campaign for the restitution of church property can be understood as a general indictment of
the modern age and its attempts to legitimize state power in the absence
of divine authority. From such a perspective, autocratic tyrants, representatives of material interests, and republican idealists are all thieves, and
this helps explain Corbelán's readiness to broker the rapprochement between the robber Hernández and the Ribierists. If his objection to secularization (conceived narrowly as the appropriation of church property) is

taken as a sign of his rejection of secular modernity, then his idea of "political honor, justice, and honesty" has an old and broad base. Or at least *had* one. In the novel, his conception of justice does not attract a single adherent other than himself. What makes him so eccentric is his belief that a society can restore an abandoned belief, recover an elusive sense of community, redeem a lost legitimacy. At the opposite end of the spectrum from the chairman of the railway, who knows the ecclesiastical court cannot be brought back again and prefers modernization anyway, Father Corbelán fights for just such a restitution. As Decoud says, Corbelán's conviction is like a self-destructive madness. The dream of return is not an alternative endorsed by Conrad.

To corroborate this internal evidence of Conrad's political reflections, we have one of his more interesting nonfictional political statements, written shortly after *Nostromo*. "Autocracy and War" (1905) contains a sentence often cited by critics of *Nostromo* to establish what our examination of Charles Gould has shown, namely that "the true peace of the world will be . . . built on less perishable foundations than those of material interests" (*Notes on Life and Letters* 107). But the essay also provides Conrad's description of what the "true greatness of a State" would entail: "Its inspiration springs from the constructive instinct of the people, governed by the strong hand of a collective conscience and voiced in the wisdom and counsel of men who seldom reap the reward of gratitude" (91). Admittedly, this is not a very precise political theory—it leaves plenty of room for speculation about what "instinct," a "strong hand," a "collective conscience," and the voiced "counsel of men" may mean in practice. It possesses the contradictions of a utopian vision, preserving a profound ambiguity on the proper relation between egalitarian and authoritarian impulses, between popular inspiration and strong-handed governance. The ambiguity allows him to distinguish this ideal legitimacy, based on the instinct of the people, from the historical phenomenon of modern European egalitarianism, for in the same essay he calls the French Revolution "in essentials a mediocre phenomenon." Its mediocrity apparently derives from the fact that the constructive spirit of the people could not have inspired such a violent, destructive revolution, whose "parentage" Conrad nevertheless acknowledges as "intellectual" and "elevated." He uses a revealing and paradoxical political metaphor to describe the fate of this parentage:

> It is the bitter fate of any idea to lose its royal form and power, to lose its "virtue" the moment it descends from its solitary throne to work its will among the people. It is a king whose destiny is never to know the obedience of his subjects except at the cost of degradation. (86)

Dressing egalitarian ideals in royal metaphors, Conrad betrays his ideological ambivalence, his perplexity, his confusion. At one moment in the
essay, egalitarian movements are seen to fail because they do not truly
originate in the spirit of the people; in the next, they fail because they
must involve the people.

Given the recurrence of Conrad's old skepticism about the fate of ideas
translated into action, it is not surprising to find him more fatalistic than
utopian in this essay, as he is in the novel. "Perhaps this earth shared out
amongst our clashing ambitions by the anxious arrangements of states-
men will come to an end before we attain the felicity of greeting with
unanimous applause the perfect fruition of a great State" (91). The problem, I would argue, is that his criteria for state legitimacy are shaped by
the phenomenon of reoccupation, by modernity's underground inheritance from Christianity of a habit of absolutist thought. He identifies not
merely a particular political problem but the challenge faced by modernity generally when he observes that "it is impossible to initiate a rational
scheme of reform upon a phase of blind absolutism" ("Autocracy and
War" 96).[4] In the case of political institutions, theological absolutism
leaves its mark on ideas about political absolutism and its alternatives.
While the criteria for legitimacy are excessive, his pessimism implicitly acknowledges their excessiveness.

Among political theorists, Carl Schmitt provides the most interesting
foil for Conrad's reflections in the years 1903–05 on political legitimacy
and the foundations of the modern state. In *Political Theology* (1922),
Schmitt embraces the process of reoccupation without reservation in the
belief that to guarantee order, political authority in the modern age must
match the divine authority that it replaces and from which it derives historically. He emphasizes the need for a strong sovereign by focusing on a
situation in which chaos most threatens the state: the "exception" (*Ausnahmezustand*), a state of emergency in which the constitution, or the
norm, is suspended. "Sovereign is he who decides on the exception," declares the opening sentence of *Political Theology* (5). This "decisionism"—
the observation that the highest power resides in one who "decides
whether there is an extreme emergency as well as what must be done to
eliminate it" (7)—presents a serious challenge to constitutional liberalism
and any theory of the state that focuses on the norm, the periods of politi-

---

4. This statement, like other passages in "Autocracy and War" and the epigraph for this
chapter from *Under Western Eyes*, applies specifically to Russia, and Conrad sometimes
strives to insulate Europe from such observations. But their easy applicability to *Nostromo*
and Europe suggests that they provide another example of Conradian projection. One
might see this projection as a form of retaliation by the man whose family and country
were victims of Russian imperialism.

cal order and calm. Schmitt observes that "all tendencies of modern constitutional development point toward eliminating the sovereign" (7), and he raises doubts about such a development by also observing that "there exists no norm that is applicable to chaos" (13). In an attempt to restore a strong notion of sovereignty, he declares that "all significant concepts of the modern theory of the state are secularized theological concepts" (36), leading Blumenberg to attack his work as "the strongest version of the secularization theorem" (*Legitimacy* 92).[5] Observing a "mirror-image correspondence of political to theological absolutism" (90), Blumenberg is critical of Schmitt for taking theological terminology literally in political contexts. But taking it literally—insisting on the structural homology of theology and political thought and on the historical derivation of the latter from the former—is precisely what Schmitt wishes to do. "The decision frees itself from all normative ties and becomes in the true sense absolute," he declares, for he is convinced the state must match the authority of God (12).

Schmitt's decisionism has a strong affinity with Thomas Hobbes' view of the state. Strictly speaking Schmitt is no monarchist and no reactionary; like Hobbes, he is motivated by a profound sense of the need for order, and guaranteeing order is for him the *raison d'être* of the state. Slavoj Žižek rightly observes that Schmitt's decisionism involves

> not a decision for some concrete order, but primarily the decision for the formal principle of order as such. The concrete order of the imposed order is arbitrary. . . . This is the main feature of modern conservatism which sharply distinguishes it from every kind of traditionalism: modern conservatism, even more than liberalism, assumes the lesson of the dissolution of the traditional set of values and/or authorities—there is no longer any positive content which could be presupposed as the universally accepted frame of reference. (18–19)

Thus Schmitt adopts an antithesis from *Leviathan* (and *Nostromo* can be read as a skeptical dramatization of this phrase): *autoritas, non veritas facit legem* (authority, not truth, makes the law). Schmitt is no Father Corbelán, hoping for a return to ecclesiastical authority, but he desires a sovereign

5. The original edition of *The Legitimacy of the Modern Age* appeared in 1966. Schmitt included a response to Blumenberg in *Politische Theologie II* (109–26), which appeared in 1970, and then Blumenberg responded by revising his book; the revision appeared in three volumes, with the volume containing the response to Schmitt appearing in 1974. The English translation of *Legitimacy* is based on this revised German edition, and thus its discussion of Schmitt incorporates Blumenberg's response to Schmitt's response (see pt. 1, chap. 8, "Political Theology I and II").

with comparable authority, a sovereign who can create an order, any order, to replace the lost sense of traditional community.

Nostromo shows a republic founded in a state of emergency, founded more along the lines of Schmitt's decisionism than on principles of constitutional liberalism. The novel's republican authors and politicians have in the end little to do with the success of Sulaco's secession, and those who work hardest to preserve parliamentary institutions in Sulaco, like Juste Lopez, the President of Provincial Assembly, are dismissed by Gould and Conrad alike for their "strange impotence" (406). In contrast to the republican idealists and parliamentarians, Gould acts "from the conviction of practical necessity, stronger than any abstract political doctrine" (142), and the action is effective. *El rey de Sulaco* conforms more closely than any other character in the novel to Schmitt's description of the sovereign, who "produces and guarantees the situation in its totality. . . . The exception reveals most clearly the essence of the state's authority. The decision parts here from the legal norm, and (to formulate it paradoxically) authority proves that to produce law it need not be based on law" (*Political Theology* 13). Conrad and Žižek present this paradox in a more critical fashion, emphasizing the violence inherent in such an extra-legal production of law. Žižek's paraphrase of the paradox could apply to Gould's strategic use of dynamite: "The rule of law ultimately hinges on an abyssal act of violence (violent imposition) which is grounded in itself" (18). Even Conrad does not push the paradox as far as Walter Benjamin later would when, in the shadow of the Third Reich and as if in direct response to Schmitt, he wrote of the "state of emergency" (*Ausnahmezustand*) that "is not the exception but the rule" (257), thus declaring that history (fascism in particular) is a perpetual state of emergency, that the world lacks a sovereign to decide on its interminable exception.[6] But Conrad is much closer than Schmitt to Benjamin's despair over the barbarism of civilization. *Nostromo* is daring in representing so openly, with Gould's dynamite, the abyssal violence at the foundation of the republic.

While Conrad juxtaposes modern politics and theology, the state and religion, it is his weary recognition of the failure of secular culture to become absolute that distinguishes him from Schmitt and, in the end, from

6. Gourgouris comments on Schmitt's claim that "the exception in jurisprudence is analogous to the miracle in theology" (*Political Theology* 36) in ways especially useful for the present discussion: "By this analogy, Schmitt affirms that sovereignty ('the state of exception') is as such miraculous, insofar as it occupies the space of the absolutely redemptive moment in the face of social annihilation, in the face of death. . . . Walter Benjamin . . . strips away from Schmitt this redemptive moment. . . . The difference is simple: the point of view that comes with the tradition of the oppressed always eluded Schmitt" (22). On Schmitt's complex relation to Hobbes, see Meier.

Hobbes. The acute awareness he shares with them of the need for political order is moderated by his recognition that an autocratic state appropriates and perpetuates the violence it is meant to prevent. His despair about the vacuum of power in Costaguana (which he represents as a god-shaped vacuum) is the clearest sign that he does not embrace political absolutism, as Schmitt later would under Hitler. Thus in the novel as in "Autocracy and War," Conrad's sense of the elusiveness of appealing alternatives does not soften his critique of the autocratic state. This critique is apparent in Gould's most revealing discussion of the source of his power to found the new republic, a discussion commencing when the Engineer-in-chief of the railway learns that Gould has "enough dynamite stored up at the mountain to send it down crashing into the valley . . . to send half Sulaco into the air." They agree that Gould's policy is "radical" in the sense of "going to the roots." As if to emphasize Gould's decisionism, Conrad sets him apart from the political figures who have been deliberating in the Casa Gould: he stands in "the empty sala, whence the political tide had ebbed out to the last insignificant drop," and he declares of the dynamite stratagem, "It's my choice. It's my last card to play." When the Engineer-in-chief calls the dynamite a weapon, Gould says no, "you may call it rather an argument" (204–6). Such is the rhetoric radical and powerful enough to found the Occidental State.[7]

Gould associates the need and opportunity for such an expedient with the absence of divine authority when he imagines the startled response to this policy of his San Francisco financier: "But then, he [Holroyd] is very far away, you know, and, as they say in this country, God is very high above." Behind the material and spiritual authorities that supposedly lend Gould his legitimacy, in other words, lies the rhetorical power of terror, the very real threat of total destruction. The engineer laughs at Gould's comment as he descends the stairs of the Casa, "where the Madonna with the Child on her arm seemed to look after his shaking broad back from her shallow niche" (206). Critics have often seen this Madonna as mute ironic commentary on Emilia Gould's childlessness and the sterility of material interests, but here the irony is also directed at the Madonna herself and the religious authority she represents. The shallowness of her niche, contrasted with the technocrat's broad back, explains much about the need for such "radical" policies of administration. In the absence of theological absolutism, a terrifying political absolutism takes its place. When no adequate democratic legitimation of the state is avail-

---

7. On transfers of power as rhetorical acts, see Blumenberg: "Not accidentally, the act by which the subject of history is determined and legitimized has borne the name of a fundamental rhetorical figure, as *translatio imperii*" ("Anthropological Approach" 451).

able to replace earlier forms of authority, as Conrad believes is the case, then the resulting vacuum leads to a state of terror.

The Body Politic as *Corpus Dei;* or, The Death of the Father

A passage from Edmund Burke's *Reflections on the Revolution in France* offers a metaphorically rich statement of Hobbesian political realism, the rage for order and fear of chaos, that I have been associating with Schmitt and, in a far more restrained way, with Conrad:

> To avoid therefore the evils of inconstancy and versatility, ten thousand times worse than those of obstinacy and the blindest prejudice, we have consecrated the state, that no man should approach to look into its defects or corruptions but with due caution; that he should never dream of beginning its reformation by its subversion; that he should approach to the faults of the state as to the wounds of a father, with pious awe and trembling solicitude. By this wise prejudice we are taught to look with horror on those children of their country, who are prompt rashly to hack that aged parent in pieces, and put him into the kettle of magicians, in hopes that by their poisonous weeds, and wild incantations, they may regenerate the paternal constitution, and renovate their father's life.

Burke participates in the rhetorical act of secularization that generally accompanies Hobbesian realism when he views the state as "consecrated" and worthy of "pious awe." Central to this consecration is the paternal metaphor, and in this passage he fully exploits its anthropological and theological resonance. He wishes to protect the state with the full force of taboo, to make it into the totem that divides civilization from barbarism. Thus he gives the theological rhetoric its fullest possible political force by likening attacks on the state to a patricidal cannibalistic feast. One need not share Burke's political views to marvel at the brilliance of his rhetoric. His conjuring of a scene of "wild incantations" around a kettle full of the dismembered father and poisonous weeds is analogous to Gould's stockpiling of dynamite at the silver mine: to protect the state at all costs, absolutely, they argue that horror is the only alternative.

Conrad, however, is not persuaded by such rhetoric. He presents Gould's accomplishment with profound skepticism. The dynamite stratagem suggests that Gould's rule depends on terror as much as or more than it suppresses terror. He is repeatedly replacing, displacing, and defying fathers—his own father, Father Corbelán, Holroyd the father-figure, God the father—attempting to clear the way for the Occidental state to be an absolute power. Such symbolic patricides do not, however, allow him ever to become a father, either literally or symbolically: his marriage is infertile, and at the end of the novel the new republic remains under threat of renewed revolt and anarchy. By showing the elusiveness of political order, and especially by having the passing period of calm derive from Gould's dynamite, Conrad refuses to consecrate the newly founded republic, to treat it with piety, to let *it* become the father. He rejects what Schmitt would later call political theology; he never accepts the state as an effective totemic defense against barbarism. Thus he shares Burke's disapproval of the French Revolution in practice but not in principle, leading him into the oxymoronic formulation in "Autocracy and War" that the idea of democratic revolution is a king with royal parentage and power. The formulation constitutes a strained attempt to transfer the authority of the father from the sovereign to the people. The oxymoron comes to embody Conrad's political pessimism when he insists on the impossibility of being obedient to this king, on this monarch's inevitable dethronement as soon as he attempts to rule. Thus Conrad acknowledges the impossible pressures of reoccupation on political arrangements in the modern age.

While he refuses to turn to the state for a secularized absolutism, Conrad pays the price of weary pessimism for this refusal. Given a choice of nightmares, he prefers the unnatural error of the ineffectual father over the terror of an autocratic one. He sees no other way to fill the father-shaped power vacuum, no way merely to live with it, and no way to walk away from it. In the spirit of his claim that in writing about imaginary people a novelist "is only writing about himself . . . , a figure behind a veil" (*Personal Record* xxi), we might recall here his biographical link to Gould. Like the character, the novelist remembers his father suffering from fatigue and defeat. In both cases, father and son shared a vocation: the Goulds their silver mine, the Korzeniowskis their writing. Conrad remembers his father superintending the "burning of his manuscripts a fortnight or so before his death. . . . His aspect was to me not so much that of a man desperately ill, as mortally weary—a vanquished man. That act of destruction affected me profoundly by its air of surrender" (*Personal Record* viii). If the analogy to Gould holds, it suggests viewing Conrad's literary endeavors as attempts at rehabilitation in response to the father's "unnatural error of weariness and despair" (*Nostromo* 58).[8] In fact we have reason to doubt the veracity of the manuscript-burning story (Najder, *Joseph Conrad* 28), but even—or especially—if it is invented, it serves to

8. By no means do I wish to reduce Conrad's long and persistent reflections on remorse and power to biography, to the Korzeniowski family romance. But Burke, among others, has made vividly clear the potential for parallels between family and political "romances" that do not reduce one to the other. This is an instance where two critical approaches can reinforce rather than compete with each other.

suggest the importance for Conrad of the pattern we have observed in his other writings. The father has abdicated; the resulting vacancy and the effort to reoccupy it make the unnatural error of weariness the son's own.

Conrad's status as literary orphan is partly what makes him a sympathetic figure for Virginia Woolf. When she attacks his contemporaries for their failings as literary fathers, she exempts him; he serves her more as a brother than as a father. But the paternal metaphor introduces the question of sex: can weariness pass from fathers to daughters?[9] Has the vacuum once occupied by God the Father exerted a stronger pull on sons than on daughters? Do the will to power and the will to death afflict women as much as men? Does the autocratic state appear any more necessary or foreboding to the modern age's orphaned daughters than it does to its orphaned sons? On this last question, judging from the case of Woolf, sex makes all the difference: she is much quicker than Conrad to abandon the pieties of patriarchy. She is not the least tempted by any political arrangement that might serve as a substitute for theological absolutism. Her engagement with authoritarian politics, most notably in *Three Guineas* (1938), elicits from her a swift and sweeping rejection of the symbiosis between statehood and fatherhood. Her daring equation of "the tyranny of the patriarchal state" with "the tyranny of the Fascist state" makes clear she is concerned only with the illegitimacy of the state from the perspective of an "outsider" and not with ways to secure its legitimacy (102). In other words, she does not share the concern for order that would lead Conrad to understand the appeal and danger of political absolutism. Her political reflections are one arena where, in identifying political and religious leaders alike as representatives of patriarchy, she manages to dispense with the father without feeling the need to reoccupy his position.

Woolf's attack on the patriarchal state in *Three Guineas* comes relatively late in her career. In other categories of thought and earlier, she can indeed be found stepping in to take over the abandoned helm, and then she ends up sounding more like Conrad. This happens especially in response to the problem of redemption, when art is enlisted in the task of remembering and rescuing. In her sensitive obituary composed on short notice for the *TLS*, she sees in Conrad less a weary adventurer than one who succeeded

9. Woolf, like Conrad (to continue for a moment in a biographical mode), shared an occupation with her father. A famous diary entry implicitly places the daughter in the position of the father, but the memory of her father's death provokes in her feelings of liberation rather than thoughts of rehabilitation: "1928 Wednesday 28 November Father's birthday. He would have been 1928 1832 96 96, yes, today; & could have been 96, like other people one has known; but mercifully was not. His life would have entirely ended mine" (3: 208).

in snatching "exalted moments" from the "dark background" (*Common Reader* 227). But in fact his futile aspiration to illuminate all regions of darkness helped prepare the way for her to focus more intensively on such exalted moments, to go farther in working through the losses and desires associated with reoccupation. Conrad explores and critiques the multiple forms in which the totalizing impulse manifests itself in the modern age: geographically (through empire), epistemologically (through the Enlightenment), morally (through redemptive art), and politically (through the autocratic state). But he does not devise a way to dispense with the underlying impulse, and thus he remains afflicted by pessimism and despair until later in his career he chooses simply to look away from the dark background. His analysis and display of weariness demonstrate the need to escape from the late-modern bind of failed reoccupation. Woolf responds to this need by exploring ways to weaken the totalizing impulse in the odyssey of the self. This shift is not an easy or fully conscious one; it is radical in the sense of going to the roots, and for that very reason it is unlikely to be abrupt or complete. It is a shift that effects not only modernist writers but readers of modernism: for critics too, the challenge is to sever critical and utopian impulses from the habit of thinking in terms of totality in order better to perceive the modernists' own struggles to leave the dark background dark.

4

Shadows of a "Silver Globe": Woolf's Reconfiguration of the Darkness

Darkness drops like a knife over Greece.
　　　　　　　　—VIRGINIA WOOLF, *Jacob's Room*

No doubt the human vessel is so limited that it can only contain a few exalted detached and impersonal feelings at one time.
　　　　—VIRGINIA WOOLF to Vita Sackville-West, 29 June 1936

In *Mrs. Dalloway*, Woolf echoes Conrad's comments in the *Narcissus* preface on the function of art. The echo, largely overlooked, comes midway between two widely recognized borrowings from *Heart of Darkness*, in the Regent's Park scene where we are first introduced to shell-shocked Septimus Smith and his wife Lucrezia. Lucrezia's expression of despair draws on Marlow's observation that we live as we dream, alone, and on his reflection that England was once, as a Roman colony, one of the dark places on the earth: "I am alone; I am alone! she cried . . . as perhaps at midnight, when all boundaries are lost, the country reverts to its ancient shape, as the Romans saw it, lying cloudy, when they landed, and the hills had no names and rivers wound they knew not where—such was her darkness" (*Mrs. Dalloway* 24). Moments later a young Maisie Johnson, newly arrived in London, is upset at the site of disturbed Septimus and distraught Rezia sitting in the park: "Horror! horror! she wanted to cry" (27). These borrowings build on Conrad's association of England with darkness and barbarism, and thus they provide an important frame for the echo of Conrad's preface buried midway between them. When his wife tells him "look," Septimus reacts like an artist resisting his calling:

> Look the unseen bade him, the voice which now communicated with him who was the greatest of mankind, Septimus, lately taken from life to death, the Lord who had come to renew society, who lay like a coverlet, a snow blanket smitten only by the sun, for ever unwasted, suffering for ever, the scapegoat, the eternal sufferer, but he did not want it, he moaned, putting from him with a wave of his hand that eternal suffering, that eternal loneliness. (25)

The central concepts are from Conrad's preface: redemption, through vision, of all suffering and solitude. The sanity in Septimus's insanity is that he recognizes the weight of this burden, the impossibility of the task; this recognition informs his self-presentation as a Christ-like scapegoat.

The fictional context makes it difficult to tell what Woolf's attitude is toward Conrad's manifesto. Her association of his views with insanity suggests a sharp irony, and yet much of the novel's most serious comment on the function of art is attached to Septimus. At the moment when Rezia implores him to look, heeding Dr. Holmes's advice to make him "notice real things," most Londoners have their attention riveted to the airplane writing letters in the sky, "curving up and up, straight up, like something mounting in ecstasy, in pure delight" (28–29). This description is in keeping with the mood of Septimus's earlier response when he first perceived the skywriting:

> Tears filled his eyes as he looked at the smoke words languishing and melting in the sky and bestowing upon him in their inexhaustible charity and laughing goodness one shape after another of unimaginable beauty and signalling their intention to provide him, for nothing, for ever, for looking merely, with beauty, more beauty! (21–22)

Woolf moderates this image of the liberating, redemptive beauty of writing in a number of ways, most noticeably by associating it comically with a particularly ephemeral form of commercial advertising.[1] Despite such moments of deflation, however, the novel treats Septimus's visionary power seriously, and his vision is always focused on the dead. Narrative whimsy often leavens his tragic vision, but he remains a "giant mourner," "like some colossal figure who has lamented the fate of man for ages in

---

1. North's *Reading 1922* discusses *Mrs. Dalloway* in relation to the origins and early press coverage of skywriting (81–86).

the desert alone with his hands pressed to his forehead, furrows of despair on his cheeks" (70). Given the importance of descents to hell for communicating with the dead, it should come as no surprise that Septimus is closely associated with Dante's *Inferno*, more so than any other character in Woolf's oeuvre.[2]

Maria DiBattista's discussion of Woolf's "memento mori" is one of the more compelling interpretations of the relation between art and death in *Mrs. Dalloway*.[3] While acknowledging the disturbing proximity of Septimus and the narrator—each is a "transcriber of voices issuing from the land of the living and the dead" (50)—she also observes that the narrative eventually dissociates itself from Septimus in order to embrace the affirming social vision of Clarissa: "This crucial dissociation of the creative will from the corrupting impulse for mastery is the triumph of feminine art, of Clarissa's 'exquisite sense of comedy'" (61). DiBattista's formulation demonstrates how profoundly the novel engages the visionary aims spelled out in Conrad's preface. Through Septimus and Clarissa, Woolf reflects on the redemptive power of memory, on the usefulness of art for transmuting suffering into affirmation. Whether or not feminine art experiences greater success, as DiBattista suggests, in dissociating the will to create from the will to power, the depth and breadth of the pressures of reoccupation make such dissociation a formidable challenge for any art. Easier to demonstrate than the success of such dissociation is that when the impulse for redemptive mastery does appear in feminine art, the object of the impulse is often different.

Woolf's interest in Conrad's redemptive mission and her ultimate indifference about his concern for fatherly order are both evident in a single passage from *A Room of One's Own*, where the obscure lives that the artist must see and redeem are women. The passage suggests that even a rejection of patriarchy does not necessarily free the creative will from the desire for a redemptive mastery of the past. Reflecting on appropriate material for the contemporary woman novelist, Woolf—or her persona, Mary Beton—imagines in her "mind's eye" an elderly woman walking in London, close to eighty, who remembers some significant political events of the Victorian era but little of her own lifelong domestic labors:

> Nothing remains of it all. All has vanished. No biography or history has a word to say about it. . . .

2. Most notably, this is the work Septimus is reading: " 'Septimus, do put down your book,' said Rezia, gently shutting the *Inferno*" (88). Schlack has traced his many other connections to the *Inferno* (*Continuing Presences* 69–72).

3. Also relevant in this context is Miller's reading of the novel as a raising of the dead (*Fiction and Repetition* 176–202).

> All these infinitely obscure lives remain to be recorded, I said . . . ; and
> went on in thought through the streets of London feeling in imagination
> the pressure of dumbness, the accumulation of unrecorded life. (89)

Conrad's *Narcissus* preface also declared the "obscure lives" of the voiceless to be the appropriate subject matter of art, and Woolf's repetition of
"all" in this passage is an important indication that she too intends for the
recuperation to be total. Her description of accumulated pressure is reminiscent of the narrator's explanation of English sadness in *Jacob's Room*:
"All history backs our pane of glass. To escape is vain" (49). ("No doubt if
this were Italy, Greece, or even the shores of Spain," the narrator notes
with wistful irony, reflecting Jacob's philhellenism, "sadness would be
routed by strangeness and excitement and the nudge of a classical education.") The pane of glass recurs in Woolf's writing as a metaphor for a protective but lamentable separation from other people and their suffering.[4]
The "pressure of dumbness" described in *A Room of One's Own* is the
moral equivalent of what Blumenberg refers to as a *Problemdruck*—the
pressure of an inherited epistemological problem that cannot be readily
solved (*Legitimacy* 67). The frustrated drive to rescue the voiceless multitude clearly remains strong in Woolf, and yet it is redirected by her consciousness of sexual difference. When Conrad feminizes the voiceless
multitude, they threaten emasculation; Woolf, by contrast, does not blame
the pressure of dumbness on women even when it emanates from them.

While Woolf's consciousness of sexual difference plays an important
role in her redirection of the redemptive impulse in art, this redirection is
only one component of a shift in her thought that occurs early in her career. The shift involves an attempt not merely to critique the effects of reoccupation, as Conrad did, but also to resist the underlying impulse, to renounce what we have identified by way of Lukács and Blumenberg as an
aspiration toward the totality of reality. Her experience as a woman was
neither a necessary precondition nor a guarantee that she would try to
weaken this aspiration. Indeed, the experience of social marginalization is
by no means incompatible with the habit of thinking in terms of totality, a
habit that is exhibited in the work of both Conrad and Forster despite the
exile experience of one and the sexual orientation of the other. Yet sexual
politics did contribute to Woolf's motive, method, and limited success in
resisting the habit of imagining the whole. In order to highlight this gradual shift in her thought, my narrative of her career will emphasize evi-

4. Note in particular Woolf's reaction, recorded in her diary, when her niece Angelica
Bell was hit by a car and Woolf accompanied Angelica's mother Vanessa to the hospital,
fearing Angelica had died: "My feeling was 'a pane of glass shelters me. I'm only allowed
to look on at this.' at which I was half envious, half grieved" (5 April 1924; 2: 299).

dence of her success, but inevitably such a shift is incremental. Woolf does not solve the problem of modernity; she does not answer conclusively the questions posed by Conrad. To claim that she does would be to embrace a teleological argument in keeping with neither the spirit of Woolf's work nor the premises of the anthropological approach to culture I have adopted under the influence of Blumenberg. But if Blumenberg's anthropology eschews teleology, it also recognizes that fundamental questions, like answers, are not constant. Questions and answers come into and go out of phase throughout history, and as the gap between them varies so can the resulting discontent. The argument that Woolf responds differently than Conrad to totalizing impulses and redemptive solidarity merely assumes that, in the absence of final answers, Woolf begins reading the questions a little differently on "this progress through life" (*Diary* 2: 311). For Woolf, the "eternal suffering" persists, but her expectations for its representation in art shift.

While the shift is gradual and, as I have been arguing, never complete, for heuristic purposes I suggest that it becomes most apparent shortly after her first novel, *The Voyage Out* (1915). The novel follows Rachel Vinrace on a four-week voyage aboard her father's ship from London to South America, where, following an expedition upriver into the wilderness, she dies. In other words, the story conforms to the pattern of the modernist colonial odyssey, though the subsequent shift in Woolf's thought will carry her away from this subgenre. Criticism on Woolf has tended to emphasize the thematic and formal continuity between *The Voyage Out* and her subsequent work, perhaps on the assumption that her later innovations in technique and form are self-evident.[5] I wish to emphasize the ways in which her first effort is anomalous for her. I do not intend, therefore, to offer a systematic reading of the novel, but rather to place it in the context of this early shift in her thought, which necessitates embedding it in a narrative that encompasses her earlier juvenilia and later publications. I will tell several condensed, parallel versions of this narrative, each focusing on a different fundamental trope or motif. Woolf herself claimed that as soon as thought commences, so does metaphor (Silver, *Virginia Woolf's Reading Notebooks* 109). Thus the changing contours of her fundamental modes of expression provide the best indication of the evolution of her thought. Her references to Greece, her metaphorical uses of "avenue," "globe," "sea journey," and "tunnelling," and her interest in

5. For example, Richter claims that "there is not a single mode of subjectivity used in her later novels which is not present in *The Voyage Out*" (93). Others who have observed links between Woolf's first novel and her mature work include Marder, Naremore, Fleishman (*Virginia Woolf*), Leaska, Bishop ("Toward the Far Side"), Poresky, Harper, Hussey, and Froula.

"moments of being" all provide glimpses, in their evolution, of her attempt to weaken the inclination to think in terms of totality; thus they also help illuminate her turn away from the colonial odyssey as a literary form. I begin in the next two sections by examining Woolf's use of Greece. The first provides an overview of her evolving view of Greece, in part by focusing on her use of "avenue" as a metaphor for the history of civilization; the second focuses on her tentative equation of Greece with Africa, a move that links her philhellenism to imperialism.

Avenues to Greece

In the discussion of Hellenism above, I argued that the "battered" statue of Ulysses appearing near the end of *Jacob's Room* serves as commentary on the fate of ancient Greece in modern Britain, but less immediately evident is the extent to which Fanny Elmer, who seeks out the statue in an attempt to experience its fading effect, serves in this scene as a stand-in for her author. Woolf too returned repeatedly to the Greeks despite her awareness that their effect, like that of the British-Museum Ulysses, was "wearing thin." No modernist was more persistently fascinated by the Greeks than she, and yet it is also true that none surpassed her skepticism about their continuing relevance. While the Victorians—in particular the Cambridge of her brother Thoby and Forster—initiated and shaped her fascination early in her life, the skepticism, though weaker at first, began almost as early. Woolf's colonial odyssey, *The Voyage Out*, is much closer to Forster's than to Conrad's in its use of Greece, because she was struggling with but still not free of this inherited Hellenism. Like *A Passage to India*, *The Voyage Out* is shaped by Hellenism in ways that have not been fully recognized.

Rowena Fowler has provided a reevaluation of Woolf's "complicated" relationship to Greece as a modern nation, as an ancient culture, and as a language (or linguistic realm). This reevaluation corrects her earlier view of Woolf as someone excluded from a formal classical education whose appropriation of the classics is to be understood in terms of subversion, compensation, and revenge. Now she observes that while Woolf was dismissive of dry scholarship and sometimes weak in her knowledge of Greek grammar, she nevertheless sustained an interest in studying Greek throughout her life, for such study was "a precondition of her intellectual and creative life, of her self-respect as a woman and of her fulfillment as a writer" (218). Fowler's overview of Woolf's career leads her to conclude that Woolf's relation to Greece and Greek was "pervasive and complex"; that Woolf's "own experience of the connection between Greece and England was unsystematic, intermittent, unbiddable: by turns dazzling and puzzling" (219). Building on Fowler's work, I wish to add two elements to the discussion of Woolf's Greece. First, in response to Fowler's synthesis drawing on evidence from throughout Woolf's life, I would like to consider the way Woolf grows increasingly skeptical about the relation between England and Greece even as her handling of the classical models becomes more assured. Second, I would like to consider the ways in which her view of Greece is intertwined with her view of the British empire. Of course, the two elements I am foregrounding here are not unrelated. Woolf's growing skepticism about England's ties to Greece coincided with her increasingly critical view of England's right to rule in other regions of the world.

To appreciate the distance she traveled in her relationship to Greece, one must understand the extent of her early attachment to late-Victorian Hellenism. Thoby provided her with an early, direct link to the Cambridge Hellenism in which Forster too was immersed. Long before the Bloomsbury gatherings that provided her with access to Thoby's Cambridge friends, she was soliciting study tips from him and reading the work of his professors (borrowed from her father's bookshelves), while he was still a student in the 1890s ("it was through him that I first heard about the Greeks" [*Moments* 125]). Beginning in 1899, while still a teenager, she arranged tutoring for herself, a rare experience for a woman so acutely aware of her lack of formal education. Her chosen subjects were Greek and Latin, and at this early stage she established the routine of setting aside a part of each day for reading and translating Greek authors, a routine to which she returned at various periods later in her life (a survey of her reading notebooks reveals both the extent and the frequency of her engagement with the Greeks). Her Greek tutors—first Clara Pater, sister of Walter, and later Janet Case—secured places of importance in Woolf's emotional life. Pater served as a model for Woolf's characters, Case as confidante for Woolf's account of the sexual abuse she had suffered at the hands of George Duckworth.[6] In 1906, after years of Greek study, she trav-

6. Pater served as the model for Julia Craye in the story "Moments of Being: 'Slater's Pins Have No Points' " and perhaps for Lucy Craddock in *The Years*. Woolf wrote an admiring "rough sketch" of Case in her diary on 22 July 1903: "She showed herself possessed of clear strong views, & more than this she had the rare gift of seeing the other side; she had too, I think, a fine human sympathy which I had reason, once or twice to test" (*Passionate Apprentice* 184). Years later, Woolf would call on this sympathy to describe George Duckworth's abuse. In a letter written in July 1911 to her sister Vanessa, Woolf describes having revealed to Case "all Georges malefactions. To my surprise, she has always had an intense dislike of him; and used to say 'Whew—you nasty creature', when he came in and began fondling me over my Greek. When I got to the bedroom scenes, she . . . gasped like a benevolent gudgeon. By bedtime she said she was feeling quite sick, and did go to the W.C." (*Letters* 1: 472).

eled to Greece with three siblings and a friend, an act of philhellenism that proved fatal for Thoby, who died of typhoid shortly after his return (and thus provided a model of sorts for Woolf's first protagonist, Rachel, as well as for Jacob). One ambiguous symptom of the importance for her of Greek and the Greeks surfaced shortly after her father died, during one of her breakdowns, when she thought "the birds were singing Greek choruses" (*Moments* 184).

During these years of preoccupation with things Greek, Woolf entertained the Hellenist idea of a direct mental link between the ancients and the English, between those at the beginning of civilization and those at its culmination. She composed at least three passages imagining such a direct lineage. They appear in (1) a 1903 diary entry in which she reflects on her reading habits, (2) the odd, posthumously published "Dialogue upon Mount Pentelicus," most likely written immediately after she returned from her first visit to Greece in 1906, and (3) a scene from *The Voyage Out* in which Rachel sits alone under a tree reading Gibbon. None of these assertions of common ground with the Greeks appears in an unambiguous context, but their recurrence suggests the extent to which Woolf was drawn to the idea of the continuity of tradition. Only with these early passages as points of reference can one recognize the distance Woolf needed to travel in her view of the Greeks in order to arrive at the opening assertion in the landmark 1925 essay "On Not Knowing Greek": "Between this foreign people and ourselves there is not only difference of race and tongue but a tremendous breach of tradition" (23).

The earliest of the three passages is perhaps her boldest declaration of the continuity. "I think I see for a moment how our minds are all threaded together—how any live mind today is of the very same stuff as Plato's & Euripides. It is only a continuation & development of the same thing. It is this common mind that binds the whole world together; & all the world is mind" (*Passionate Apprentice* 178–79). Fowler follows S. P. Rosenbaum in emphasizing the similarity between this "common mind" and the notion of the "common reader" Woolf would develop in the 1920s (Rosenbaum 143; Fowler 219). But if her Greek studies provided the seed for her later understanding of readers' reception of texts from the past, it is important not to overlook the dramatic shift in her use of the word "common." The move from Hellenism to modernism involved, for Woolf, shifting the meaning of "common" from "shared" to "unassuming." The change reflects a reversal of attitude, from the Hellenist presumption of England's privileged relation to Greece to a humble embrace of her position as a reader who, neither critic nor scholar, makes do without refinement or learning and thus readily acknowledges the impossibility of "knowing"

Greek. In 1903, the assertion of a common mind is preceded by a gnawing doubt about whether she can share in this mind, a doubt based on her sex. She is planning her summer reading and reflects:

> Learning seems natural to the country. I think I could go on browsing & munching steadily through all kinds of books as long as I lived at Salisbury say. The London atmosphere is too hot—too fretful. I read—then I lay down the book & say—what right have I, a woman to read all these things that men have done? They would laugh if they saw me. But I am going to forget all that in the country. (178)

Planning to shed her feminine embarrassment in the country, Woolf eagerly anticipates discovering the mind she shares with Plato.

The second passage comes at the end of "A Dialogue upon Mount Pentelicus." During her 1906 visit to Greece, Woolf and her companions climbed Pentelicus, site of the marble quarry that supplied the Parthenon (figure 4). The climb, recorded at the time in her Greek diary (*Passionate Apprentice* 326–27), helped inspire the dialogue and a rather different climbing scene in *The Voyage Out*. In the dialogue, English tourists resting in the shade beside a stream debate the relation of Englishmen and of modern Greeks to the ancient Greeks. The discussion is interrupted by the arrival of a local monk:

> The light in the brown monk's eye . . . pierced through much, and went like an arrow drawing a golden chain through ages and races till the shapes of men and women and the sky and the trees rose up on either side of its passage and stretched in a solid and continuous avenue from one end of time to the other.
>
> And the English could not have told at the moment at which point they stood, for the avenue was as smooth as a ring of gold. But the Greeks, that is Plato and Sophocles and the rest[,] were close to them, as close to them as any friend or lover, and breathed the same air as that which kissed the cheek and stirred the vine. (*Complete Shorter Fiction* 68)

This story proves especially slippery if one tries to determine its position on Hellenism or to divine from it something unequivocal about Woolf's attitude toward Greece. The narrator maintains an ironic distance from the two interlocutors, one of whom argues sentimentally for the perfection of the ancients, while the other, guilty (like Thoby Stephen) of the "heresy" of voting to eliminate Greek as a compulsory subject at Cambridge, responds skeptically; the monk then appears as a conclusive "reply" to such skepticism. In *Topographies of Hellenism*, Artemis Leontis

Figure 4. The Stephens ascending Mount Pentelicus in 1906. Mounted, left to right: Vanessa, Thoby, Virginia.

has analyzed Anglo-Hellenist views on what Woolf's narrator calls "the tough old riddle of the modern Greek and his position in the world today," and her analysis includes a reading of Woolf's dialogue as an ironic, modernist distancing of Hellenism. Leontis does not, however, consider the diary Woolf kept on her visit to Greece, and the diary helps one recognize what unresolved tensions hide in the irony of the dialogue and thus how difficult it is to determine Woolf's position.

Her sharp disappointment with modern Greeks is the most striking feature of the Greek diary. The disappointment leads her to elaborate a strident claim that was common in late-Victorian Hellenism—namely, that the English are more Greek than modern Greeks. Her primary criterion for considering a person Greek is knowledge of the ancient language, and the criterion itself is borrowed from the ancient Greeks, who considered knowledge of their language synonymous with civilization. Hence the word "barbarians," derived from the Greek name for those who spoke foreign tongues, mimics a meaningless *bar-bar-bar*. Woolf plays with this etymology in "A Dialogue upon Mount Pentelicus" in describing the reaction of the English tourists when the modern Greeks do not understand their attempts to speak the tongue of Plato: "one word came aptly to their lips; a word that Sophocles might have spoken, and that Plato would have sanctioned; they were 'barbarians' " (64). In the diary, she implicitly makes a claim for her own Greek lineage when she reports that while visiting Mycenae "the taste of Homer was in my mouth. Indeed, this is the pearl of seeing things here; the words of the poets begin to sing & embody themselves. . . . If statues & marble are solid to the touch, so, simply, are words resonant to the ear" (*Passionate Apprentice* 331). The modern Greeks she encounters are clearly deaf to this resonance, for, as she claims elsewhere in the diary,

> the people of Athens are, of course, no more Athenians than I am. They do not understand Greek of the age of Pericles—when I speak it. Nor are their features more classic than their speech: the Turk & the Albanian & the French—it seems—have produced a common type enough. It is dark & dusky, small of stature, & not well grown. (328)

Her strategy, in other words, involves a splitting of her ambivalence about Greece: the ancients are mysterious, the moderns barbarous.

If Woolf's primary criterion for aligning herself with the ancients and not the moderns is linguistic, another criterion, as this last passage demonstrates, is racial: the kind of Greek that flows off of one's tongue has something to do with the color of one's skin. Here is another passage from Woolf's Greek diary where language and race are linked:

> Like a shifting layer of sand these loosely composed tribes of many different peoples lie across Greece; calling themselves Greek indeed, but bearing the same kind of relation to the old Greek that their tongue does to his. For the language they talk is divided from the language that some few of them can write as widely as that again is divided from the speech of Plato. The spoken language because it has not been fixed by grammar or spelling, twists itself afresh on each tongue. . . . So you must look upon Modern Greek as the impure dialect of a nation of peasants, just as you must look upon the modern Greeks as a nation of mongrel element & a rustic beside the classic speech of pure bred races. (340)

Woolf's images here of fluid, ungrammatical speech are telling, given the fluid, sometimes ungrammatical nature of her own Greek, characteristics that Fowler emphasizes. Clearly Woolf had not yet embraced such qualities at the time of her first visit to Greece. Judging from her diary, she is still writing under the influence of Cambridge. This passage continues with one of her many reverential references to the Acropolis, an infatuation associated with Hellenism, as Leontis has shown. The Acropolis provokes Woolf once again to contrast ancient and modern Greece in the starkest terms, counterintuitively associating "the quick" with "the old" and "the dead" with "the new":

> Athens means many more things than the Acropolis, & the sanest plan is to separate the quick from the dead, the old from the new, so that the two images shall not vex each other. It is amusing to be able to abuse entirely, just as it is far better to praise enthusiastically.
>
> So I take some pains to put old Greece on my right hand and new Greece on my left & nothing that I say of the one shall apply to the other. The justice of that division has been proved etymologically, & ethnologically,—*indeed* & I daresay I could go on proving it through all the arts & sciences, but these shall be sufficient. (340)

A few pages later, describing her parting view of Athens, she again makes an invidious comparison of ancient and modern Greece by celebrating the Acropolis, which stands silently "alone & apart from all the modern world" and succeeds in canceling her impression of Athens as "a modern town, speaking a barbarous language, peopled by liars & cheats" (346).

The Pentelicus dialogue shows her satirizing some of the most unpleasant racial and historical assumptions from Cambridge, possibly as expiation for what she had written in the diary. Notably, she chooses a modern Greek to serve as catalyst for the climactic moment in which "a golden chain [draws] through ages and races," opening for the English a "solid and continuous avenue" to antiquity. The monk's delivery of a single Greek word of greeting triggers this moment, and when the English tourist responds in kind, they are speaking, we are told, "as a Greek to a Greek and if Cambridge disavowed the relationship the slopes of Pentelicus and the olive groves of Mendeli confirmed it" (68). Leontis correctly observes that the experience of the English is epiphanic, having the quality, as Woolf says, of "a miracle" (67), but this mysterious revelation and the ironic comments about Cambridge do not fully sever this work from Hellenist ideals and prejudices. Woolf persists in emphasizing the darkness of the monk's complexion, and the brief triviality of the verbal exchange leaves some doubt about whether she is really rehabilitating modern Greece in her portrayal of the monk. At best, she compensates for her dismissal of modern Greece while a tourist there by drawing the modern monk into the charmed circle of the English, but she does not abandon her claim of proximity to the ancients. Although the light, fanciful touch of this piece shows her reexamining her relationship to all things Greek and beginning to create some distance from the arrogance of her Greek diary, the irony does not destroy her dream of "the first days and the un-obliterated type" when there was "such a thing as Man" (67). The monk interrupts the skepticism of the second English interlocutor as much as the slavish Hellenism of the first; to the extent we can position Woolf among them, she still seems to cling to the idea of a common mind, an avenue like a ring of gold linking the moderns and the ancients.

The third passage in which Woolf imagines a direct link to antiquity appears in *The Voyage Out,* and it too employs the image of an avenue. She began writing the novel possibly as early as the year she visited Greece, but she added most of the passage in question to one of the later drafts, sometime after 1910 (*Melymbrosia* 131–32). Like the Pentelicus dialogue, this third passage depends on an epiphany—Rachel's—to link the English to "barbarians." (I describe this epiphany in detail below, in the discussion of Woolf's moments of being.) While still under the spell of the revelation she experienced moments earlier, Rachel reads a passage from Gibbon that produces the following reaction:

> Never had any words been so vivid and so beautiful—Arabia Felix— Aethiopia. But those were not more noble than the others, hardy barbarians, forests, and morasses. They seemed to drive roads back to the very beginning of the world, on either side of which the populations of all times and countries stood in avenues, and by passing down them all knowledge would be hers, and the book of the world turned back to the very first page. (175)

Reading serves again, as in the 1903 diary entry, as a way to access a common mind. Even in the absence of an explicit reference to Greece, the collective knowledge she dreams of here carries echoes of Hellenism. She draws implicitly on a Hellenist idea she makes explicit elsewhere, namely, the popular equation of Africa and Greece, allowing one—Aethiopia, for example—to represent the other. This geographical conflation also involves a telescoping of temporal perspective, so that Greece can mark not only the beginning of history but also "the very beginning of the world." Thus, like much popular Hellenism, Woolf's early musings on Greece often fail to distinguish between the different historical layers of antiquity, between Homer's Greece and Plato's, between democratic Athens and imperial Rome. This spatial and temporal leveling is evident in Rachel's response to Gibbon in *The Voyage Out.*

The subsequent development of anthropology and the concept of the primitive, a heightened sensitivity in the 1930s to fascist appropriations of Greece, and a growing awareness that we sometimes project onto Greece "all that we dream and desire" (as one Pentelicus character suggests [66]) lead Woolf over time, as they have led us, to a far more complex and layered sense of the historical Greece. This complexity brought to an end the dream of a wide avenue leading to antiquity, of a mind common to England and Greece. The Hellenism evident in Woolf's preoccupation with Greece in the first decade of the century has vanished by the early 1920s when she writes "On Not Knowing Greek" and *Jacob's Room*. In its place we find a liberating laughter. She laughs at her own early earnestness— the earnestness of the Hellenists—and sometimes she laughs at the perceived earnestness of the ancients. An example of the latter is buried in an obscure reference in "On Not Knowing Greek," first published in *The Common Reader* (1925). Based on meticulous research and extensive reading, the essay constitutes an intensive reevaluation of the Greeks and her relationship to them; no essay in the remarkable *Common Reader* volume cost her as much effort as this one. Her research extended over nearly three years and included readings of the *Odyssey* of Homer, the dialogues of Plato, the plays of Aeschylus, Sophocles, Euripides, and Aristophanes, and biographies of Hellenists Richard Bentley and Sir Richard Jebb; during her reading of *Agamemnon* she made "a complete edition, text, translation, & notes of my own" (3 December 1922; *Diary* 2: 215). Thus she fulfills her intention during this period to "read Greek now steadily" (4 October 1922; *Diary* 2: 205), and yet the conclusion reached through this effort is that it is not really possible to know Greek.

She notes one example of the distance of the Greeks near the conclusion of the essay when she refers enigmatically to a humor in Homer that Homer did not intend:

> Where are we to laugh in reading Greek? There is a passage in the *Odyssey* where laughter begins to steal upon us, but if Homer were looking we should probably think it better to control our merriment. To laugh instantly it is almost necessary (though Aristophanes may supply us with an exception) to laugh in English. Humour, after all, is closely bound up with a sense of the body. . . . We pause in reading Homer, to make sure that [we] are laughing in the right place, and the pause is fatal. (36)

Her comment on the humor of Homer is tantalizing in being both specific and uninformative—she refers to a single passage and then fails to identify or describe it. The reading notebook she kept while preparing this essay helps solve the mystery of this passage and offers a clue to her sense of humor. In the notebook she records her amusement, and her uncertainty about whether the humor is Greek, in response to Homer's description of Odysseus before his departure from Calypso in the fifth book of the *Odyssey*. Through what appears to be Woolf's impromptu translation, copied into her notebook, Homer tells us that Odysseus "did not love the nymph. And he slept beside her in the cave, without desire for her who desired him." Woolf's comment on the line reads, in part: "Would the Greeks have seen the humour of this wh[ich] we can't help seeing?"[7] Humor is indeed, as she says, closely bound up with a sense of the body. Her notes here suggest that sex plays a role in her recognition that a breach of tradition separates her from Homer, and they suggest moreover that she now desires such distance, that her laughter is liberating. Her decision in the essay to suppress this sexual example of bodily humor is perhaps not all that surprising given the audience she imagined for *The Common Reader*. But the suppression makes clear that her long struggle to distance and transform the Greek models was also a sexual and political struggle.

The sexual politics of this struggle become clear also from *Jacob's Room* (1922), which can be read usefully in conjunction with *The Voyage Out* and "On Not Knowing Greek."[8] The novel presents a female narrator's meditation on not knowing Jacob, who is an amalgam of Woolf's brother Thoby and the multitude of young men who died in the Great War. While thinking back on ancient Greece, Jacob and his friend Timmy Durrant experience an elation not unlike Rachel's when she reads Gibbon: "Civilizations stood round them like flowers ready for picking. Ages lapped at their feet like waves fit for sailing" (76). But Woolf now mocks Jacob, and she mockingly exaggerates her own earlier presumption when she has him tell Durrant, "we are the only people in the world who know what the Greeks meant." She then subtly extends the irony to encompass her earlier metaphor of a road or avenue to Greece when she has her narrator announce that "Jacob knew no more Greek than served him to stumble through a play. Of ancient history he knew nothing. However, as he tramped into London it seemed to him that they were making the flagstones ring on the road to the Acropolis" (76). What this "boastful, triumphant" young man imagines as an avenue to Greece merely leads him,

7. Woolf's next comment in this reading notebook addresses lines in which Calypso asks Odysseus to remain with her voluntarily, insisting anxiously that she must be as attractive as Penelope. Woolf's response: "What they call a feminine touch. . . . Yet this is done through a glass: softened: made dignified." It provokes in Woolf the curiosity "one has in old books like Homer & D. Quixote—whether the authors knew what they were saying: whether they didn't say things as children do." A more complex, polished version of this intuition appears at the end of "On Not Knowing Greek," where she concludes that in the *Odyssey* there is "nothing immature; here are full-grown people, crafty, subtle, and passionate" but they "have been born to their possessions, are no more self-conscious than children" (*Common Reader* 37–38).

Quotations from Woolf's reading notes on Homer are transcribed from *Holograph Reading Notes*, vol. 25 (Berg Collection), reproduced in *Virginia Woolf Manuscripts*, reel 13.

8. On the representation of Greece in *Jacob's Room*, see Koutsoudaki and Bishop ("The Subject").

in fact, into modern London. The road to the Acropolis appears later in the novel when Sandra, the woman he meets in Greece, writes Jacob a letter while remembering "something said or attempted, some moment in the dark on the road to the Acropolis which (such was her creed) mattered for ever" (169). Woolf thus reinforces her irony by reducing the romance of Greece to a lustful encounter. She has learned how "vain and foolish" it was to talk of knowing Greek with the ancient Greeks trapped on the far side of a "tremendous breach of tradition" (*Common Reader* 23). Jacob, associated by Fanny with Ulysses, represents not only Thoby Stephen and the dead young men of the Great War, but also, ironically, the Greeks, and in *Jacob's Room* Woolf bids farewell to all three.

The adulation of Greece which slackened in *The Voyage Out* and is relinquished in the two later works does not of course lead her to abandon Greek models and metaphors altogether. Her preoccupation with them persists, but she handles them from a greater distance and with more control. Even in the 1920s, when she is acutely aware of their irreducible foreignness, the Greeks provide Woolf some relief from late-modern weariness. The remarkable conclusion of "On Not Knowing Greek" focuses in particular on the *Odyssey*, which "remains the triumph of narrative" (37). Homer's characters

> know all that is to be known. With the sound of the sea in their ears, vines, meadows, rivulets about them, they are even more aware than we are of a ruthless fate. There is a sadness at the back of life which they do not attempt to mitigate. Entirely aware of their own standing in the shadow, and yet alive to every tremor and gleam of existence, there they endure, and it is to the Greeks that we turn when we are sick of the vagueness, of the confusion, of the Christianity and its consolations, of our own age. (38)

Death is no longer the *telos* of Woolf's odyssey, for death now informs every moment along the way. In their mature lack of self-consciousness, the ancients confront their mortality more directly than the moderns. As John Mepham has observed, Woolf admires the Greeks because communal forms of mourning made it possible for them "to directly express intense emotion" (152). Woolf's conclusion retains some elements, in broad outline, of Hellenism, in particular the return to Greece as a rejection of Christianity and modernity. But now the return is free of any illusion of a "common mind," of the ancients' proximity to the English. She claims that even "the unlearned" can recognize "Greek is the impersonal literature" as well as "the literature of masterpieces" which "surpass the limits of small triumphs and tentative experiments"; this contrasts with the literature of her own generation, which she describes in other essays from the same period as experimental explorations of the ego. The return to Greece now serves less as a return to a certain ideal of civilization than as a return to reality—in particular, the reality of death. Death for the ancients—and for this modernist essayist—is neither a fate to be softened in the context of the total meaning of history nor a destination to be desired in the absence of this elusive totality. Instead, the ever-present shadow of death now serves to throw into sharper relief "every tremor and gleam of existence."

"I Think of the Greeks as Naked Black Men"

While Rachel uses the image of ancient roads earnestly in imagining her ties to the past, elsewhere *The Voyage Out* speaks of roads for comic and ironic effect. Upon departure from London on board the *Euphrosyne*, William Pepper inflicts on his traveling companions "a disquisition upon the proper method of making roads." Passing from Greek to Roman and English methods, he winds up with "a fury of denunciation directed against the road-makers of the present day" (26). The other characters then notice they are out at sea and feel "exhilaration" because "they were free of roads, free of mankind" (27)—thus the voyage becomes a flight from civilization (represented by an ancient tradition of road building and Pepper's scholarly study thereof). This helps set up a far more somber use of the image at the other end of the journey. While Rachel lies dying, Terence and St. John "quarrelled about a road, the Portsmouth Road. St. John said that it is macadamised where it passes Hindhead, and Terence knew as well as he knew his own name that it is not macadamised at that point" (342). The context—amid the pathos of Rachel's death—heightens the absurd triviality of the dispute. Quentin Bell suggests that Woolf's brothers Thoby and Adrian carried on the exact same argument "for some days" while in Athens with Virginia in 1906 (1: 109). By having Rachel extend her voyage out beyond South America unto death and in having her leave the road-making and other concerns of empire-building to her male compatriots, Woolf figuratively dismisses these concerns.

In such scenes, Woolf's relationship to the avenue metaphor is far more distant than in the scene of Rachel reading Gibbon, for in these scenes she is, to borrow the metaphor, no longer on the road of civilization. Their presence in *The Voyage Out* suggests that, in relation to the shift in Woolf's thought, the novel exhibits what Ernst Bloch calls nonsimultaneity, a concept indicating that in a complex cultural process one will find multiple stages of development present at any one moment. She consolidates the shift away from Hellenism after this first novel, but such fundamental shifts, encompassing and complex, are never instantaneous, and thus the novel already contains abundant evidence of her growing skepticism. Positioning *The Voyage Out* in relation to her development is further complicated by the novel's notoriously long and tortured genesis. The text, as Louise DeSalvo and Elizabeth Heine have shown, derives from the incomplete merging of many drafts over many years. Woolf herself would later judge the novel "such a harlequinade as it is—such an assortment of patches" (4 February 1920; *Diary* 2: 17); DeSalvo similarly declares it a "curious amalgam" of "feverishly but imperfectly fused" stages (158).[9] The phenomenon of nonsimultaneity, Woolf's youthful confusion, and the protracted, imperfect revision process result in a novel that is confused in its handling of the central, interrelated themes of Greece, sex, and empire.

The confusion is evident, to return to the example of William Pepper, in the way the opening chapters of the novel place Rachel's *Euphrosyne* voyage in the odyssey tradition. Pepper is one of the most ridiculous and most ridiculed characters, and yet he often sets the tone for the novel's serious appropriations of the Greeks. On the voyage out Rachel pronounces him a "piece of old shoe leather" (19) and we learn that he has never married because "he had never met a woman who commanded his respect. . . . His ideal was a woman who could read Greek" (25). He is rumored to be on the voyage "to write upon the probable course of Odysseus, for Greek after all was his hobby" (19), and this prepares us for the voyage of the *Euphrosyne*, which enlists the Greek model for a female protagonist in an imperial context. But the novel does not simply try to update the Greek story; it also betrays a Hellenist nostalgia, a desire to recover "the taste of Homer." Pepper's eccentricity sets a precedent for such nostalgia when we learn that he has translated "English prose into Greek iambics" (19). And it is Pepper who recites, while the novel cites, in Greek, the opening lines of the "Hymn to Man" from *Antigone*, a tragedy that would remain a touchstone for Woolf throughout her life. In these lines the chorus proclaims man's wondrousness and offers the first example: he is able to cross the sea surrounded by wind and tossing surf. This won-

---

9. In the later drafts, Woolf strove to identify less immediately with Rachel, making her less autobiographical, more naïve, less well read, and less sexually aware. This adds yet another complicating element to any attempt to divine through Rachel the course of Woolf's development. My reasons for not detecting more irony, or distance, in Woolf's handling of Rachel's reading of Gibbon will become clearer below when I discuss the moment of being Rachel experiences in the same scene. Whatever Woolf may have thought of Gibbon by the time she finished revising this scene, she had not abandoned the impulse to totalize that emerges in Rachel's response. In addition to DeSalvo and Heine, critics who discuss the way Rachel changes in successive drafts of the novel include Tvordi on the suppression of Sapphist references and Schlack on the thinning out of Rachel's reading list ("Novelist's Voyage").

drousness assumes for Rachel a frightening sexual aspect, for the wind and tossing surf land her in the arms of Mr. Dalloway, whose kiss launches her on a voyage of sexual discovery that will be cut short in images of drowning. The incorporation of *Antigone* into the journey of the *Euphrosyne* anticipates both the wonder located in the South American interior and the death of the heroine.

The novel's concern with and confusion about Greece infects its exploration of sexual identity, as Pepper's use of *Antigone* suggests. Rachel, as an Odyssean voyager, sometimes adopts a male subject position, refusing the feminine roles awaiting her; at the same time, she tries to feminize the story of male adventure, making of the novel a female *Bildungsroman*. In *Penelope Voyages*, Karen Lawrence has shown how women's travel in the British literary tradition serves as a way for women both to seek social freedom and to explore cultural constraints, and she nicely demonstrates how Rachel, in her fatal illness, tests the limits of the self. In such travel narratives, Lawrence explains, women often occupy a dual position as "traveller and signatory of discourse" (27), the latter position belonging traditionally to Penelope, who waits with her loom at the conclusion of the journey. I wish to enlist Lawrence's conceptual framework to demonstrate briefly the extent to which Rachel's sexual roles remain confused. As an exploring, traveling woman, she never assumes the position of Penelope, never becomes a signatory of discourse. Helen Ambrose assumes this role instead. While her husband, Ridley, spends all of his time on the ship (and later in South America) working "at his Greek," Helen sits on deck embroidering the scene of Rachel's future fatal journey:

> She chose a thread from the vari-coloured tangle that lay in her lap, and sewed red into the bark of a tree, or yellow into the river torrent. She was working at a great design of a tropical river running through a tropical forest, where spotted deer would eventually browse upon masses of fruit, bananas, oranges, and giant pomegranates, while a troop of naked natives whirled darts into the air. (33)

A description of Helen sewing her embroidery later, in Santa Marina, suggests something of Woolf's ambivalence about this traditional role for women. The narrator observes:

> With one foot raised on the rung of a chair, and her elbow out in the attitude for sewing, her own figure possessed the sublimity of a woman's of the early world, spinning the thread of fate—the sublimity possessed by many women of the present day who fall into the attitude required by scrubbing or sewing. (208)

Woolf seems drawn to the sublimity—and then decides to distance it. While insisting on the continuity of femininity from the early world to the present day, this passage also calls attention to the limits of the continuity, found only in a certain type of woman (domestic), while Rachel's generation, which is Woolf's, falls into a different attitude. Thus the analogy is not particularly useful for describing the voyage Rachel is on—*Rachel* is no Penelope. Her inability to act as signatory of her own travel discourse assures the failure of the novel as a *Bildungsroman*, for Rachel cannot ever make the texts she reads her own; she cannot achieve independence from her various mentors, including Helen.

Rachel's detachment from traditional female roles is reflected sexually in her inability to consummate the relationship with Terence and in her ambiguous relationship with Helen. But this detachment and ambiguity do not translate into an effective response to patriarchy; her death calls into question her ability to resist patriarchal sex roles rather than representing, as some critics suggest, the culmination of her resistance. In later drafts of the novel, Woolf narrowed Rachel's options, while making her sexuality more enigmatic. As Jessica Tvordi has shown, Woolf's revisions diluted the lesbian allusions, closing off a possible liberating path for her voyaging heroine, and Rachel's baffling hallucination of a three-way sexual encounter with Helen and Terence does little to clarify her sexual preferences or roles (*Voyage Out* 283–84). What Shirley Neumann has observed about Rachel—that she exhibits "an unresolved ambiguity about her sexual choice" (63)—reflects a more general ambiguity in the novel's treatment of sex roles and sexuality.

Similarly complex, if not confused, is the novel's treatment of imperial themes, especially as they relate to a fading Hellenism. Rachel's reading of Gibbon and the scene on Helen's embroidery (tropical river with naked natives) have already introduced imperial motifs into the analysis of Hellenism and sex roles. The entanglement of these themes produces complexities hinted at in a quotation from *The Voyage Out* that equates ancient Greece and modern Africa. During a discussion among guests at the hotel in Santa Marina, Miss Allan comments, "When I think of the Greeks I think of them as naked black men" (114). In the phrase "naked black," Allan identifies the twin anxieties, sexual and racial, which the novel expresses and tries to contain—and, remarkably, she links both to Greece. The fictional and historical contexts make it difficult to determine precisely what Woolf's attitude is toward Allan's conceit. Allan is responding to Mrs. Thornbury's exclamation, "I would give so much to realise the ancient world! . . . After all we are *founded* on the past. . . . One never does think enough about the ancients and all they've done for us" (114). Miss

Allan's emphasis on the exoticism of the Greeks corrects Mrs. Thornbury's egocentric identification with them. But Allan is uneasy also with her own pronouncement and therefore qualifies it by quickly adding that her mental image of the Greeks "is quite incorrect, I'm sure." Thus between the two of them the women manage to identify the Greeks with both civilization and barbarism, both the English and Africans; yet both positions are qualified, and the reader receives little guidance in finding any middle ground.[10]

With an understanding of Woolf shaped by her later sophistication in treating classical allusions and imperial motifs, one can easily read this passage (as I used to read it) as a parody of the sentiment common in popular adventure fiction, where ancient Greece, compared to contemporary Africa, becomes a paradoxical embodiment of both civilization and barbarism. Allan and Thornbury divide between them two views of Greece the Hellenists held simultaneously: Greece as a source of *logos*, a rationality that helps contain the uncertainties stirred up by encounters with the non-Western world, and Greece as a source of mystery, an antidote to modern disenchantment. One can imagine Woolf working to expose the tension this produces within popular Hellenism, which ends up identifying Greece both with civilized England and with England's racial and cultural Others. However, our review of Woolf's attitude toward Greece before writing *The Voyage Out* and of her allusions to Greece elsewhere in the novel suggests that the ambiguity in this scene is less an instrument of Woolfian irony than an indication of her own lingering Hellenism and youthful confusion. By the time of her work on *The Voyage Out*, she had certainly grown skeptical about the more extreme views of Greece—the Greeks as noble black savages and the Greeks as purebred Englishmen—but she still had not fully worked through the impulses behind these contradictory views and still was unable to articulate an alternative. Her handling of Miss Allan's comment contributes to the impression that her first novel, in contrast to her mature work, deploys irony sporadically and in ways seemingly in conflict with its more earnest passages. While her desire for the steadying influence and authority of Greece is still evident, the imperial context seems to reveal to Woolf the deficiencies of Hellenist strategies.

Indeed, Woolf's first novel, like Forster's last, often blames the disinte-

---

10. An early draft of the novel has Terence responding to Miss Allan: " 'I am afraid I don't think of them [the Greeks] very much' Hewet confessed. 'Except as people lying under trees talking perpetually' " (*Melymbrosia* 90). This image is reminiscent of the setting for "A Dialogue upon Mount Pentelicus."

gration of a Mediterranean ideal on the attempt to extend it to encompass the empire. She hints at this over-extension in a symbolically weathered image: on board the *Euphrosyne* Rachel sits in a room with a print, "The Coliseum"—but the tropical sun has faded it to "a faint yellow colour" (19). As the narrator explains, English visitors to tropical South America have found that "the country itself taxed all their powers of description, for they said it was much bigger than Italy, and really nobler than Greece. Again, they declared that the natives were strangely beautiful, very big in stature, dark, passionate, and quick to seize the knife" (90). Here, to borrow the phrase Wyndham Lewis appropriated from W. E. B. DuBois, "the Congo is flooding the Acropolis," and such racial panic surfaces periodically throughout the novel. While they desire the nobility and beauty, the English find their powers sapped by South America's resistance to appropriate form; while they yearn for the wondrous and new, they fear the threat to their identity.

Rachel's fate is unsettling, because it epitomizes this loss of power and identity. Her early death appears senseless, and this has contributed to the perception that the novel is intractable. When viewed as a *Bildungsroman*, a social comedy, or a social critique, it seems to promise something very different than the demise of its heroine. Woolf herself acknowledged the form "was too loose in *The Voyage Out*" (*Letters* 2: 400), and critics have noticed its distance from traditional genres, as when Avrom Fleishman suggests that it "is no more an exotic novel of the colonies than it is a traditional social novel" (*Virginia Woolf* 2). I have spoken of inconsistencies in Woolf's handling of major themes, but much of the confusion is structural and arises from Rachel's death. If the sexual theme by itself cannot adequately account for the centrifugal voyage to death, neither can the imperial theme—unless one discovers in them manifestations of Rachel's desire for an all-encompassing unity. In discussing *A Passage to India*, I suggested that although Forster attributes the demise of his Mediterranean ideal to imperial experience in India, in fact the discontents of modernity—including in particular the phenomenon of reoccupation—lie behind the novel's handling of both Hellenism and imperialism. A similar dynamic is at work in *The Voyage Out*. Woolf distinguishes herself from Forster, however, by pursuing the implications of reoccupation farther than he managed to. She indulges the totalizing impulse more energetically than he does and explores more fully the associated death drive. The manifestation of this drive is the most important aspect of Rachel's life. The aspiration for total comprehension arising from the process of reoccupation determines the trajectory—and ultimate failure—of Rachel's voyage out.

"What's the Truth of It All?"; or, Spheres of Being

Rachel sums up her wonder and perplexity by asking, "What is the truth? What's the truth of it *all*?" (123; emphasis added) and, on another occasion, "Would there ever be a time when the world was one and indivisible?" (296).[11] These questions, which motivate Woolf's novel as well, express a curiosity shaped fundamentally by Christian theology; they are questions that have pressed themselves on the modern age, provoking the process of reoccupation. The theological influence is evident in Rachel's use of the word "all," a word Allen Mandelbaum has labeled the "bootleg sublime" in reference to its appearances in the English poetic tradition. Mandelbaum's term suggests that modern poets, no longer able to realize the totality of experience in their work, have been forced to invoke transcendent sources covertly, for example, in their use of the word "all." Mandelbaum's term implies, and Rachel's life demonstrates, that the process of reoccupation is difficult to resist and equally difficult to complete successfully. Rachel's association of "truth" with "all" implies that truth must be grasped not piecemeal but in its entirety, and not as *a* truth but as *the* truth. Her questions reveal an intention toward the world in its totality, an aspiration to imagine the whole.

Rachel's grand questions shape her response to Gibbon. When she reads him, she is transported, as we have seen, by the hope for access to "all times and countries," "all knowledge." The combination of temporal and geographical completeness that she perceives momentarily while reading informs also her attempts to answer these questions by traversing the globe. Like *Heart of Darkness*, *The Voyage Out* becomes a voyage in and a voyage back in time: having crossed the seas, the characters journey upriver to the interior.[12] In other words, in order to explore the meaning of it all, Woolf turns to the global totality brought within reach of the English after the blank "white spaces" on maps—the white spaces to which Conrad and Marlow refer—had become filled in. "Conquer a territory?" says one of her characters, "they're all conquered already, aren't they?" (136). Like Conrad, she represents this new global extent to show its deficiency as a compensatory totality; she demonstrates the failure of geographical

11. With a substitution of "meaning" for "truth," Woolf attributes the first of these questions to another character later in the novel, one minor indication that the question is not merely the protagonist's but Woolf's own. After fending off a marriage proposal from Alfred Perrott, Evelyn Murgatroyd wonders, "What was the meaning of it all?" (367).

12. For comparisons of *The Voyage Out* and *Heart of Darkness*, see Brewster, Naremore, Fleishman, Lee, Pitt, Apter, Zwerdling, DeKoven (*Rich and Strange*), and Phillips.

occupation as a means of epistemological reoccupation. Despite this failure, the habit and unhappy consequences of thinking in terms of totality, and of doing so through the empire, persist.[13] When she explores the opportunity offered by empire for imagining the individual's relation to the absolute, her pessimistic conclusion emerges both in her representation of South America and through her transformation of the odyssey plot by placing death in the position of the homecoming.

The expansive vistas of the continent are one means by which Woolf demonstrates the excessive demands placed on the modern subject. The characters' discomfort surveying these vistas contrasts with scenes Mary Louise Pratt has found to be common in Victorian explorer narratives, scenes in which the discoverer becomes monarch of all he surveys (*Imperial Eyes* 204–5). When South America opens up views of an "infinite" earth, Rachel and Terence become uncomfortable, and in one scene they turn away from the land toward the sea. They consider that this same sea "flowed up to the mouth of the Thames; and the Thames washed the roots of the city of London," but any hope that command of this ubiquitous sea might provide these Britons with access to a world one and indivisible is quickly dashed when they lament that London cannot be in South America (210). On another occasion when the novel associates "wonder" with "the infinite distances of South America," the narrator describes the characters standing on a mountain top: "Mr. Perrott was standing in the attitude of a statesman in Parliament Square, stretching an arm of stone towards the view. A little to the left of them was a low ruined wall, the stump of an Elizabethan watch-tower" (131). But even with the reminder of the historical precedent for a British presence on the continent, such attempts to reconcile the familiar and the mysterious fail.[14] London and Santa Marina are juxtaposed not to bring out what unites them, but to demonstrate that they are mutually exclusive. Coming to see the blue of

13. *The Voyage Out* has often served as a focus for discussions of Woolf's relationship to British imperialism, and it has provoked a striking variety of conclusions. One not unusual assessment is that Woolf, through her heroine Rachel, rejects imperialism along with patriarchy: Rachel's subjection to patriarchal authority—and her passive resistance through sickness and death—place her in a position analogous to that of the colonized subject. Another view is that a critique of patriarchy does not necessarily lead one into a critique of empire, and that Rachel's encounter with South America and its inhabitants reveals that being patriarchy's outsider does not prevent one from being an imperial insider. I am concerned to show that Woolf's earliest work, like Conrad's fiction, can be simultaneously critical of and complicit in imperial culture. The rhetorical reconfigurations I trace in this chapter serve to make her work less complicit. For a very different reading of the novel's relation to imperial ideology, see Phillips; see also A. Lewis and Tratner (84–96).

14. Fox, tracing the pattern of Woolf's allusions to the Elizabethan age, argues that Woolf wanted to make *The Voyage Out* an Elizabethan voyage. See also Lawrence's use of Fox's analysis.

sky and sea as a curtain cutting her off from the rest of the world, Rachel impatiently expresses the desire to have London in South America (302). The globe that includes both hemispheres remains inaccessible in its totality to the individual, and South America comes to embody the individual's failure to understand "the truth of it all."

If Rachel's journey explores a global or spatial expanse, it also entails a search for temporal comprehensiveness. The narrator explains that the wonder and mystery of the continent for the British derive from its promise of something new: there was "a kind of dissatisfaction among the English with the older countries and the enormous accumulations of carved stone, stained glass, and rich brown painting which they offered to the tourist," resulting in a "movement in search of something new. . . . The place [Santa Marina] seemed new and full of new forms of beauty" (90). In short, they seek *nova terra*, like Dante's and Tennyson's Ulysses. Hughling Elliot and Mrs. Thornbury later "prove that South America was the country of the future" while Mr. Perrott comments "that a country with a future was a very fine thing" (136). Yet what Rachel finds there, especially on the journey up the river and in her illness, is a path back to the earliest ages and the uncanniness of an archaic world. She travels back, as we have seen, to "the very beginning of the world," to "the very first page" of "the book of the world" (175). This temporal range overwhelms her as much as the spatial expanse.

This critique of modern subjectivity follows in Conrad's footsteps, but Woolf goes a step beyond him in responding to the process of reoccupation: she not only exemplifies this failed process but also resists it more actively. In fact, her work displays a tension between the desire to discover the meaning of it all and the desire to dismiss the question, between the pressure to reoccupy the epistemological position and the need to excise it from the body of human knowledge. The desire to dispense with the inherited great questions surfaces in "The Mark on the Wall" (1917), the short story in which her innovations in narrative technique first emerged. The narrator asks,

> And what is knowledge? What are our learned men save the descendants of witches and hermits who crouched in caves and in woods brewing herbs, interrogating shrew-mice and writing down the language of the stars? And the less we honour them as our superstitions dwindle and our respect for beauty and health of mind increases . . . Yes, one could imagine a very pleasant world. (*Complete Shorter Fiction* 87)

This is a bold attempt to renounce certain forms of "knowledge," an attempt that faces enormous obstacles. Foucault's archaeology and Blumenberg's anthropology have demonstrated, in quite different ways, that the "epistemological field" or *episteme* (Foucault), the "budget of man's needs in the area of knowledge" (Blumenberg), shapes knowledge by providing a preconscious framework determining what must be known and what cannot be known in each age. An attempt to renounce certain forms of knowledge is an attempt to contract this "field" or "budget," to narrow the range of questions asked and answered. Blumenberg has observed that the transition from one age to another is a rhetorical act, a *translatio imperii*, and a diminished *episteme* risks losing the rhetorical battle. Such an *episteme* offers the individual the dubious attraction of inhabiting a less rich, less capacious world, and reoccupation in the modern age is an attempt to deny or to compensate for such a loss. We have already encountered Charles Gould's deployment of dynamite in *Nostromo* as an example of the attempt to summon maximum rhetorical as well as political authority in a secular age. Resisting reoccupation requires one to confront and accept the loss of authority in a way that Gould does not. The resulting sense of loss explains the difficulty of excising positions from the body of human knowledge. Like all mourning, this may be an interminable process (whatever its various stages), and thus we should not expect it to be achieved in the lifetime of any one author.

The rhetorical nature of reoccupation also helps account for the persistence of fundamental figures of speech across epochal thresholds. The new epoch, the new system of knowledge, must draw on the rhetorical power of the old tropes and myths even if it deploys them in a new configuration; the old instinct brings back the old names, though they are applied in a new context. Woolf's use of the globe provides a miniature example of this phenomenon, and it shows her tackling the ambitious task of reducing the epistemological claims of an "absolute metaphor" so that it represents something less than the "totality of reality."[15] *The Voyage Out* establishes the precedent of searching for an answer of global proportions by drawing on an empire that encompasses, in the words of conservative imperialist Richard Dalloway, "enormous chunks of the habitable globe" (51); subsequently, however, she finds a way to shrink the "globe," disengaging it from imperial geography. She seems to have found the inspiration for this maneuver while reading Thomas Browne and reflecting on an early phase of English exploration, long before the end of expansion brought about by the New Imperialism. "The Elizabethan Lumber Room," an essay first appearing in *The Common Reader* (1925), concludes with Woolf's tribute to Browne's sublimely idiosyncratic genius. She de-

---

15. "Absolute metaphor" is Blumenberg's term for metaphors used to represent the "totality of reality," which cannot be represented in any other way. He first introduced the concept in "Paradigmen"; see also my "Unbegrifflichkeit."

scribes him as "brooding in solitude over the mysteries of the soul" and suggests this "immense egotism has paved the way for all psychological novelists" (45). Then she quotes these lines from *Religio Medici*: "The world that I regard is myself; it is the microcosm of my own frame that I cast mine eye on; for the other I use it but like my globe, and turn it round sometimes for my recreation."[16] And: "We carry with us the wonders we seek without us; there is all Africa and her prodigies in us" (qtd. in *Common Reader* 45–46).[17] These lines are not unambiguous; in them one might read the suggestion that for Browne, as for Rachel, the self and the globe are coextensive, and arguably this constitutes an expansion of the domain of the subject as much as a shrinking of the globe. But the passages Woolf cites from Browne have a different emphasis than *The Voyage Out*: while Rachel attempts to discover the self by traversing the globe, Browne discovers the globe within.

Woolf's reading of Browne marks a turning point in her use of "globe," for he seems to have suggested to her the possibility of making the term increasingly metaphorical. Her subsequent echoes of his phrasing exploit this possibility, stripping "globe" of all geographical references so that it becomes strictly an ontological term and thereby helps distance the self from empire. In the same diary entry where she famously declares that her father's survival would have ended her life, she suggests that she is hypnotized by life like a child by a "silver globe": "I should like to take the globe in my hands & feel it quietly, round, smooth, heavy. & so hold it, day after day" (28 November 1928; 3: 209). She passes the conceit on to Bernard in *The Waves*: "Let us again pretend that life is a solid substance, shaped like a globe, which we turn about in our fingers" (251). Now the experience of wonder and mystery is no longer structured by colonial travel. She has found a new frontier to replace the mysterious white patches of undiscovered territory that had appeared on maps of the world prior to the Scramble for Africa.

Like "globe," "drops" and "beads" provide Woolf with spherical metaphors for life, and they too undergo a shift in usage after *The Voyage Out*. Rachel's dream and hallucinatory vision are both set in subterranean enclosures in which "drops" collect and run down damp walls (77, 331).

16. Four sentences later in the same section of *Religio Medici*, Browne comments that he who does not see in himself the image of God "hath not his introduction or first lesson, and is yet to begin the Alphabet of man," possibly suggesting to Woolf the idea for characterizing Mr. Ramsay as someone working his way through the alphabet but unable to complete lesson R (Browne 1: 87).

17. Woolf used "globe" as a metaphor for the soul as early as 1907, when she was working on *The Voyage Out*. In a playful letter to Violet Dickinson she wrote: "Your soul was floating like a captive balloon last time I saw you; a white globe, transparent and ethereal, veined with fire. O isn't that pretty?" (15 February 1907; *Letters* 1: 284).

Though the setting is womblike, these drops form in a space Rachel associates more with death than with fertility. In the Sapphist short story "Moments of Being: Slater's Pins Have no Points" (1928), silver drops, like the "silver globe" of Woolf's diary entry, become an affirmation of life in an image now more ejaculatory than womblike: "All seemed transparent for a moment to the gaze of Fanny Wilmot, as if looking through Miss Craye, she saw the very fountain of her being spurt up in pure, silver drops. She saw back and back into the past behind her" (*Complete Shorter Fiction* 220). "The Death of the Moth" twice uses "bead" as an image for the life force embodied in the moth, which is invigorated at first but then opposed by the energy in the fields outside the window: the moth is "a tiny bead of pure life" (360) but not even the writer's pencil can save this "life, a pure bead" from death (361). In each of these instances the spherical object—globe, drop, or bead—represents not simply the individual life, but a life force or essence, *Sein* or Being.

Woolf offers another twist on the globe metaphor in her treatment of Lily Briscoe, who suggests that handling and shaping the globe is the work of the artist. Near the end of *To the Lighthouse*, while working on her painting, she thinks back on the dinner orchestrated by Mrs. Ramsay:

> Love had a thousand shapes. There might be lovers whose gift it was to choose out the elements of things and place them together and so, giving them a wholeness not theirs in life, make of some scene, or meeting of people (all now gone and separate), one of those globed compacted things over which thought lingers, and love plays. (192)

Like Joyce's Bloom, Lily recognizes that love is what life really is. The image of a globe represents the wholeness and community that Lily and Bloom both desire. For Bloom, however, love is up against "all" force, hatred, history. One of the shapes of love Lily recognizes is a globe compacted, not extended; it represents a wholeness without totality, a wholeness specific to a scene, a few people, a moment of being. Even with this modest scope, however, the silver globe of life does not escape the shadow of death or the burden of recuperation. Lily's struggles with grief and with her elegiac painting demonstrate that her love of wholeness does not lead her to deny the core of darkness.

Sea Voyages and Shipwrecks

With Woolf's shrinking of the globe—or, more precisely, with her shifting of its meaning from "earth" to "sphere"—her idea of sea voyages and odysseys undergoes a corresponding contraction, becoming liberated from the fatal shipwreck that interrupts Rachel's voyage. "To be flung into the sea, to be washed hither and thither, and driven about the roots of the world—the idea was incoherently delightful," Rachel thinks (298). This expression of Thanatos prefigures her death, which she experiences as if "curled up at the bottom of the sea," a symbolic drowning. Although Rachel dies in bed on solid ground, Woolf presents her death figuratively as a sea voyage ending in shipwreck. In contrast, *Mrs. Dalloway*, like *Ulysses*, confines the journey to a single city and a single day, and in the process it transfers the death from the female adventurer to her male foil, Septimus.[18] Detached from the intention toward the world in its totality, the odyssey motif remains part of Woolf's rhetorical repertoire, employed now to different ends: namely, to trace the circumference of the "silver globe" of life, the experience of life that is accessible to the individual.

We find such use of the sea-voyage motif applied not only to Clarissa Dalloway but also, in *To the Lighthouse*, to Mr. and Mrs. Ramsay. References to Mr. Ramsay as a voyager initially serve the purpose of parodying him. The description of his intellectual journey from A to Z ("if thought . . . like the alphabet is ranged in twenty-six letters all in order" [33]), a journey on which he gets stuck at Q, one letter short of his own initial, is intertwined with an extended metaphor of global exploration:

> Qualities that would have saved a ship's company exposed on a broiling sea with six biscuits and a flask of water—endurance and justice, foresight, devotion, skill, came to his help. R is then—what is R? . . .
>
> Qualities that in a desolate expedition across the icy solitudes of the Polar region would have made him the leader, the guide, the counsellor, whose temper, neither sanguine nor despondent, surveys with equanimity what is to be and faces it, came to his help again. R— (34)

As the chapter progresses, the alphabet metaphor gives way increasingly to this expedition fantasy. The references to polar exploration—a form of adventure that fascinated Conrad and Marlow in their youth—help place Mr. Ramsay as a late-Victorian figure. The expedition becomes a "forlorn hope" under the leadership of the "dying hero," Mr. Ramsay, who is permitted "to think before he dies how men will speak of him hereafter" (35). In a final ironic twist, he is denied this heroic death—the leader of the "doomed expedition" discovers "by some pricking in his toes that he lives" and "requires sympathy" (36). Geographical exploration has been

---

18. In her analysis of *Mrs. Dalloway*'s relation to Homer and Joyce, Hoff includes an overview of other critical works on this topic.

reduced here to a humorous conceit satirizing Mr. Ramsay's emotional and intellectual limitations.

The satire is softened somewhat in "The Lighthouse," the third part of the novel, when he resumes his role, in the view of Cam, as leader of an "expedition," this time to the lighthouse. Here the expedition is no longer polar or global, and its metaphorical use is not applied merely to Mr. Ramsay's thought, stuck at Q; rather it has now become a metaphor for existence. Cam links the expedition motif to the shipwreck metaphor, which has long served as a fundamental metaphor for human life, and her use of the metaphor makes clear that this life is intricately bound to the family romance.[19] "So we took a little boat, she thought, beginning to tell herself a story of adventure about escaping from a sinking ship" (188); and later, as she realizes they are gliding above actual shipwrecks, "she went on telling herself a story about escaping from a sinking ship, for she was safe, while he sat there" (190). As a further indication of a growing distance from and control over the odyssey/shipwreck metaphor, Cam remains half outside of it, playing with it consciously as a not-quite-supreme fiction:

> It seemed as if they were doing two things at once; they were eating their lunch here in the sun and they were also making for safety in a great storm after a shipwreck. Would the water last? Would the provisions last? she asked herself, telling herself a story but knowing at the same time what was the truth. (205)

The double consciousness, tied to the reconfiguration of the odyssey motif in Woolf's fiction, permits Cam a rapprochement with her father. As leader of the expedition he is no longer a tyrant; their common fate, their common susceptibility to shipwreck, allows her a double vision of him as both a pitiable man, "shabby, and simple," and as one "leading them on a great expedition where, for all she knew, they would be drowned" (205). Woolf grants Cam what Conrad could not devise for Jim: an escape from the shipwreck of history.

The shipwreck metaphor as a reminder of life's perils also helps shape the famous dinner scene. At the beginning of the meal Mrs. Ramsay finds herself sunk in separateness, outside the eddy of life, and she begins to will herself out of the melancholy by extending pity to her neighbor, "as a sailor not without weariness sees the wind fill his sail and yet hardly

19. See Blumenberg's history of this *Daseinsmetapher* in *Schiffbruch mit Zuschauer*. For a reading of *To the Lighthouse* that emphasizes how the family romance continues to constrain Cam on the trip to the lighthouse, see Abel, who contrasts Cam's and James's "Oedipal fictions" with Lily's "recuperative matricentric story" (47).

wants to be off again and thinks how, had the ship sunk, he would have whirled round and round and found rest on the floor of the sea" (like Dante's and Tennyson's Ulysses as well as Eliot's Phoenician Sailor in *The Waste Land*). Lily Briscoe observes Mrs. Ramsay's melancholy "as one follows a fading ship until the sails have sunk beneath the horizon," and her revival "was as if the ship had turned and the sun had struck its sails again." In a train of thought that could serve as a critique of Conradian redemptive solidarity, Lily comments that Mrs. Ramsay's show of pity seemed "as if her own weariness had been partly pitying people, and the life in her, her resolve to live again, had been stirred by pity," though the pity was based, Lily feels, on a misjudgment and seemed "to arise from some need of her own rather than of other people's" (84). Transformed from moral imperative to some need of one's own, the obligation to others potentially becomes less oppressive; it becomes a means not of rescuing others, but, as in the case of Mrs. Ramsay, of rescuing oneself from weariness. Remembering Mrs. Ramsay's example years later while completing her elegiac painting, Lily manages, with difficulty, to navigate the sea of memory:

> One glided, one shook one's sails . . . between things, beyond things. Empty [life] was not, but full to the brim. She seemed to be standing up to the lips in some substance, to move and float and sink in it, yes, for these waters were unfathomably deep. Into them had spilled so many lives. (192)

Conrad's Jim is once again an instructive foil: Lily, with Mrs. Ramsay as a model, learns better than Jim, mentored by Stein, how to navigate while immersed in the destructive element.

While Rachel's sea journey leads her to death, Mrs. Ramsay and Lily sail only metaphorically, as a way of staving off death. Woolf's writings in the 1920s break more dramatically from the odyssey models and use "sailing" and "shipwreck" metaphors to record a subtle, precarious, yet unmistakable shift from Thanatos to Eros. The shift is evident even when Woolf does once again represent foreign travel in her fiction. In *Orlando* (1928), the adventurer not only returns home but becomes the signatory of her own discourse; Orlando finds love and completes her poem, "The Oak Tree." Karen Lawrence begins her analysis by noting that "the centrifugal impulse in the narrative is reminiscent of Rachel Vinrace's voyage out for new models of desire," but unlike Rachel, "Orlando, the woman, makes a round-trip journey. The dual trajectories of the narrative—centrifugal and liberating, centripetal and domesticating—create a complex cultural politics and poetics" (*Penelope Voyages* 182–83). Lawrence's useful exploration of this complexity leads her to conclude that "Orlando's repatriation illustrates more than the hostile climate encountered by a woman writer; it represents a revisionary Romanticism": "Culture is not elided in the round-trip journey of the narrative; rather, the voyage out enables a return to the scene of the home in which home itself is transformed by the return of Shakespeare's sister, the survivor" (205–6). Orlando's revision contrasts with Rachel's rejection, her longevity with Rachel's early demise.

A parallel shift occurs in the fundamental trope I propose examining next: the tunnel. While tunnels, caves, and corridors are dark regions of sexual repression and death in *The Voyage Out*, in subsequent work they funnel light onto the complex intermingling of past and present, onto the "extreme obscurity of human relationships" (*To the Lighthouse* 171).

Tunnels, Corridors, Caves

Mrs. Ramsay contains her yearning for peaceful rest on the floor of the sea, counterbalancing it with a commitment to leave a lasting memory in the hearts of her family and friends. Woolf's diary comment, "I meant to write about death, only life came breaking in as usual" (17 February 1922; 2: 167), could apply nicely to much of her mature work, including *To the Lighthouse*. She made a similar but less convincing claim about *The Voyage Out*. Writing to Lytton Strachey a year after the novel's publication, she explained that her intention had been "to give the feeling of a vast tumult of life, as various and disorderly as possible, which should be cut short for a moment by the death, and go on again—and the whole was to have a sort of pattern, and be somehow controlled" (*Letters* 2: 82). It is true that at the end of the novel even the least sympathetic characters thread themselves into the social fabric that mends itself after being rent by Rachel's death, and this coda suggests that just as Woolf does not, the reader should not merely follow the heroine imaginatively into death. This is one way Woolf tried to contain the Thanatos that emerges in Rachel. Louise DeSalvo's study of the numerous drafts has shown that Woolf's revisions diluted the impulse for self-annihilation. Yet it remains the case that Thanatos dominates Rachel, and that Rachel dominates the story. For Woolf's first novel, we might reverse her later formulation: she meant to write about life, only death came breaking in.

The most revealing image of Rachel's Thanatos appears in the pair of dreams about tunnels and vaults. The dreams frame Rachel's journey; the first occurs on the voyage out in her father's ship and the second comes in her fatal delirium, following her trip upriver and engagement with Terence. When Mr. Dalloway forces a kiss on her during the journey from England, she responds with indignation and excitement. That night, she dreamt that she was walking down a long tunnel, which grew so narrow by degrees that she could touch the damp bricks on either side. At length the tunnel opened and became a vault; she found herself trapped in it, bricks meeting her wherever she turned, alone with a little deformed man who squatted on the floor gibbering, with long nails. His face was pitted and like the face of an animal. The wall behind him oozed with damp, which collected into drops and slid down. Still and cold as death she lay, not daring to move. (77)

At the other end of her journey, she has a similar, delirious vision:

Rachel . . . shut her eyes, and found herself walking through a tunnel under the Thames, where there were little deformed women sitting in archways playing cards, while the bricks of which the wall was made oozed with damp, which collected into drops and slid down the wall. (331)

Rachel's dreams bind together three uncanny phenomena: sex, empire, and death. The site of the tunnel—"under the Thames"—reveals that the foreignness Rachel encounters abroad actually stems from a domestic repression: imperial experience possesses an uncanny structure. And the womb imagery here is not particularly subtle, anticipating Freud's analysis of the uncanny a few years later: each time Rachel is tempted to succumb to the homesickness of love, she is haunted by the *unheimlich* image of a damp, oppressive, womb-like cavern.

In *Rich and Strange*, Marianne DeKoven explores *The Voyage Out* (like *Heart of Darkness*) as a "vaginal passage," a passage from masculine to feminine that represents a return to the womb. Her inspired reading of Rachel's second dream describes it as Woolf's reinstatement of a "patriarchal maternal" represented by the "deformed women" occupying the womb (137–38). But the scene says less about Rachel's impotence as a result of her subjection to patriarchy than it does about the impotence of patriarchy itself and the paradoxical emasculation of a woman, Rachel, who has adopted a patriarchal position. The uncanniness of her visions has not only the specific sexual significance Freud attributed to the uncanny in his essay, it also points to the death drive of *Beyond the Pleasure Principle*, a drive shaped by reoccupation.[20] Rachel's Thanatos represents the failure of reoccupation—her death is a final attempt to recover "the meaning of it all" and make the world "one and indivisible." As Mrs. Dalloway ac-

---

20. Boone discusses the importance of Woolf's subterranean images and Abel offers a useful analysis of Woolf's relation to Freud and Klein, though both critics focus on later stages of Woolf's career. Dick's history of Woolf's narrative technique from *The Voyage Out* through *To the Lighthouse* focuses on the tunneling motif.

knowledges in response to Septimus's suicide, "death was an attempt to communicate. . . . There was an embrace in death" (184).[21]

While Rachel's tunneling in *The Voyage Out* leads her to archaic depths and death, Woolf soon reconsiders the social and psychological significance of tunnels and caves; she eventually ties them to a past that is not oppressive and does not lead directly to nonexistence. Given Rachel's experience with tunnels, it is striking that Woolf later chooses the same term to describe her distinctive approach to narrative. Streams of consciousness and moments of being help reveal the temporal and psychological depths of her characters, a method she calls "tunnelling." The tunnels not only link a character to the past, they link characters to each other and to Woolf—and they link the various stages of Woolf's career. In a letter to Ethel Smyth recollecting her discovery, in "A Mark on the Wall" (1917) and "An Unwritten Novel" (1920), of a way to "embody all my deposit of experience in a shape that fitted it," Woolf refers to this discovery as a tunnel leading to her novels of the 1920s: "I saw, branching out of the tunnel I made, when I discovered that method of approach, *Jacobs Room, Mrs Dalloway* etc—How I trembled with excitement" (16 October 1930; *Letters* 4: 231). Diary entries place the discovery a few years later but show she identified her method as a tunneling process over a long period. On August 30, 1923, while writing *Mrs. Dalloway* (which she was planning to title *The Hours*), she noted: "I should say a good deal about The Hours, & my discovery; how I dig out beautiful caves behind my characters; I think that gives exactly what I want; humanity, humour, depth. The idea is that the caves shall connect, & each comes to daylight at the present moment" (*Diary* 2: 263). While Rachel becomes "trapped" in her dark cave, Woolf imagines her subsequent characters emerging from caves into the light of day; while Rachel and Terence find union only in death, their successors "connect" to each other with "humanity, humour, depth." A diary entry on October 15 of the same year adds: "it took me a year's groping to discover what I call my tunnelling process, by which I tell the past by instalments as I have need of it. This is my prime discovery so far" (*Diary* 2: 272). In her *Lighthouse* notebook she applies the term once again to her own progress toward new creation rather than to the past; she describes a series of stories she writes upon completing *Mrs. Dalloway* as a "corridor" leading to her next novel (*To the Lighthouse: Original Holograph* 44).

Woolf passes on her "prime discovery" as an artist to Lily Briscoe in *To*

21. Noting that Rachel's symbolic drowning figures her "deepest impulses," Stewart punningly calls it a "communicable decease" (260–62), because Terence's identification with her helps transform the death into a moment of "complete union and happiness" (*Voyage Out* 353). DeKoven (*Rich and Strange* 136–38) and Lawrence (*Penelope Voyages*) elaborate on Stewart's discussion of the drowning motif.

the Lighthouse: "She went on tunnelling her way into her picture, into the past" (173) until she sees Mrs. Ramsay at the other end of "the corridor of years" (174). This corridor shapes not only Lily's painting but Woolf's novel, which Woolf diagrammed in her notebook by drawing the outline of a wide "H," the long crossbar of which represents the central "Time Passes" section of the novel. "Two blocks joined by a corridor" is Woolf's description of the diagram and the novel (*To the Lighthouse: Original Holograph* 48). Although Mrs. Ramsay and others die in this corridor, death is no longer the *telos*, as it was in Rachel's tunnel; Mrs. Ramsay's death is suspended in the corridor of years between the two blocks of the diagram, two days on which people affirm the bonds of love across time. Working on her painting, Lily reaches back through the tunnel to an "extraordinarily fertile" moment of intimacy she shared with Mrs. Ramsay on the beach. The memory ushers her into "a high cathedral-like place, very dark, very solemn," where "the perfection of the moment . . . was like a drop of silver in which one dipped and illumined the darkness of the past" (171–72). The "drop of silver" accessible through the corridor anticipates Woolf's enchanting "silver globe" of life.

The transformation from Rachel's experience of tunneling as Thanatos to Woolf's and Lily's creative tunneling is striking. In these later uses the caves and tunnels are no longer figures for the uncanny, however great may be the shock of revelation. The tunnels now lead to lived experience, individual and communal, not to an archaic origin and nonexistence; they are places of light, not darkness.[22] But it is worth remembering once again that in accomplishing this rhetorical reconfiguration, Woolf does not solve the problem of the darkness. In detaching her fundamental tropes from the desire to represent the totality of reality, she does not necessarily eradicate the desire. This is evident in her use of the tunnel metaphor in her first diary entry following Conrad's death in 1924. The passage is commenting on the "sheer beauty—beauty abounding & superabounding" that she has encountered on a journey from Charleston. With "one" opposed to "all" and three iterations of "all," Woolf shows she still shares Rachel's desire to grasp the totality of experience, but the tunneling now refers to the progress through life, not the rush to its end:

> One almost resents it, not being capable of catching it all, & holding it all at
> the moment. This progress through life is made immensely interesting by

22. In a lighter vein, the narrator of "The Mark on the Wall" associates life with another kind of tunnel, with God as *telos*: "Why, if one wants to compare life to anything, one must liken it to being blown through the Tube at fifty miles an hour—landing at the other end without a single hairpin in one's hair! Shot out at the feet of God entirely naked!" (*Complete Shorter Fiction* 84).

trying to grasp all these developments as one passes. I feel as if I were put-
ting out my fingers tentatively on . . . either side as I grope down a tunnel,
rough with odds & ends. (15 August 1924; 2: 311)

Reality without Totality?

The pattern emerging repeatedly in the evolution of Woolf's absolute
metaphors has been that she increasingly distances them from any pressure to refer to "the totality of reality" and narrows their scope to a range of
experience appropriate for the individual, and in the process she seems to
mitigate the intention toward death. Now avenues lead not through all civilization to and from Greece, but all roads lead home, to London; the new
and mysterious is sought not on the margins of the terrestrial globe, but in
the silver globe of life; expeditions explore not the interior of South America, but a philosopher's family romance; tunnels lead not to an uncanny
darkness and death, but to veins of love and the light of day. Employing
much the same rhetoric, the new framework resulting from this shift attempts to replace the comprehensive authority claimed by imperial culture
and the transcendent authority claimed by theology. Woolf names and explores this new framework most directly in her moments of being, which
constitute a secular form of mysticism, a direct engagement with reality
that explores the limits of the self without the need to travel to the end of
the world and the end of time. But before her moments of being could
serve this function, they too needed to undergo a narrowing of scope.

The Voyage Out offers a fully developed example of a moment of being
even though Woolf's distinctive narrative techniques for representing
such moments are still undeveloped. In this early example, the moment is
tied to an imperial and temporal totality. Rachel is walking alone down a
path the day after an exhilarating evening of dance at the hotel, and she is
"filled with one of those unreasonable exaltations which start generally
from an unknown cause, and sweep whole countries and skies into their
embrace" (173). The colonial setting, if not the immediate cause of such
exaltation, appears to be at least an essential element: not only does she
walk where she can "lose sight of civilisation," but the moment is triggered by one of "those trees which Helen had said it was worth the voyage out merely to see" (173). The tree

stopped her as effectively as if the branches had struck her in the face. It
was an ordinary tree, but to her it appeared so strange that it might have
been the only tree in the world. Dark was the trunk in the middle, and the
branches sprang here and there, leaving jagged intervals of light between

them as distinctly as if it had but that second risen from the ground. Having seen a sight that would last her for a lifetime, and for a lifetime would preserve that second, the tree once more sank into the ordinary ranks of trees, and she was able to seat herself in its shade. (174)

While the moment seems ephemeral, surviving primarily in the memory of the participant ("would last her a lifetime"), in fact it is embedded in the imperial motifs that shape other scenes and the novel as a whole. She has been carrying books by Balzac and Gibbon with her, and in the afterglow of this moment, seated under the tree, she chooses Gibbon and begins reading about the conquest of "Aethiopia and Arabia Felix" and the "hardy race of barbarians" in Germany. Generally Gibbon leaves her unimpressed, but, following this moment of being, his prose inspires her and opens roads "back to the very beginning of the world" (as we have seen in the discussion above of Woolf's Hellenism). The strangeness and ordinariness, the darkness and light of this tree are thus tied to the total temporal and spatial structures of imperialism, with its claim to write the book of the world.

The tree as a symbol (and thus the moment of being it triggers) is tied furthermore to Rachel's sexual confusion and death.[23] At least this was the case for Woolf herself, and her autobiographical "A Sketch of the Past" provides the background for readers to make the same connection:

> I go back then to the year that Stella died—1897.
> I could sum it all up in one scene. I always see when I think of the months that followed her death a leafless bush, a skeleton bush, in the dark of a summer's night. This rather finely drawn many twigged tree stands outside a garden house. Inside I am sitting with Jack Hills [Stella's widower]. He grips my hand in his. He wrings my hand. He groans: "It tears one asunder . . ." He gripped my hand to make his agony endurable; as women in childbirth grip a sheet. "But you can't understand", he broke off. "Yes I can", I murmured. Subconsciously, I knew that he meant his sexual desires tore him asunder; I knew that he felt that at the same time as his agony at Stella's death. Both tortured him. And the tree outside in the August summer half light was giving me, as he groaned, a symbol of his agony; of our sterile agony; was summing it all up. Still the leafless tree is to me the emblem, the symbol, of those summer months. (*Moments* 140–41)

---

23. Richter observes the frequency with which trees appear as important symbols of life in Woolf's work. "A Sketch of the Past" provides the counterexample of one of Woolf's childhood memories: "It seemed to me that the apple tree was connected with the horror of Mr Valpy's suicide. I could not pass it" (71). *Jacob's Room* offers another exception: in a study of the "black hole" of desire in *Jacob's Room*, Knowles has commented on the pervasiveness of trees associated with Jacob's death (105).

Thus the tree is a symbol simultaneously of death and of frustrated sexual desire. The sexual agony is as relevant to Rachel's experience as the death. After reading the passage in Gibbon she traces the origin of her confused exaltation to her interest in Hirst and Hewet. She finds "her body trying to outrun her mind" and, wondering what it means to be in love, she is "awed by the discovery of a terrible possibility in life" (175–76). Later, in her delirium, some of the hallucinated scenes are among "trees and savages" reminiscent of her fatal journey inland (341). When the moment's revelation is temporally and spatially total, the self suffers; when Eros must embrace all the world, failure is marked by its reversal into Thanatos, by its embrace of death.

There is some danger in generalizing about the moments of being appearing in Woolf's later work, for their genesis and content vary widely. But across this wide variety they tend to be dissociated, unlike Rachel's moment, from the intention toward reality in its totality. They preserve the ephemeral by freezing the moment in the minds of participants, but transhistorical structures such as those invoked in *The Voyage Out* are lacking. The narrowed scope is suggested, for example, in Lily Briscoe's speculation that "the great revelation perhaps never did come. Instead there were little daily miracles, illuminations, matches struck unexpectedly in the dark" (*To the Lighthouse* 161).[24] Rather than making us see "all the truth of life," as Conrad desired, the moments in Woolf's fiction show the truth fragmented. They show the truth from various perspectives amid reminders that too many perspectives are needed for someone ever to capture all of it: "One wanted fifty pairs of eyes to see with," Lily reflects in *To the Lighthouse* (198).

In "The Sacred," Georges Bataille, borrowing from Emile Dermenghem's discussion of Sufi conceptions, speaks of the "privileged instant" in a way that helps explain how Woolf's moments of being can remain detached from totalizing impulses (*Visions of Excess* 241). Bataille suggests that

> the development of knowledge touching on the history of religions has shown that the essential religious activity was not directed toward a personal and transcendent being (or beings), but toward an impersonal reality. Christianity has made the sacred *substantial*, but the nature of the sacred . . . is perhaps the most ungraspable thing that has been produced between men: the sacred is only a privileged moment of communal unity, a moment of the convulsive communication of what is ordinarily stifled. (242)

---

24. In a chapter titled "Matches Struck in the Dark," Beja calls attention to the "everyday character" of Woolf's moments of vision (*Epiphany* 112). He also comments throughout on Woolf's relation to Conrad.

This description serves as a useful gloss on the Woolfian moment of being: a privileged instant of convulsive communication. The conception of such moments evolves from a tradition of religious mysticism, certainly, but Bataille makes clear that this modern experience is fundamentally different in its content, in its substance.[25] Without needing to achieve transcendence to imagine the whole, Woolf's mature art communicates a convulsive, communal, momentary unity. Thus while Rachel and Septimus yearn for death in an attempt to communicate, the moments of being represented in Woolf's mature fiction are attempts to communicate that may flirt with death but stop short of it.

Bataille emphasizes the potential for violence created by the "disjunction between the sacred and transcendental substance" (242), a potential that Woolf recognizes as well. Her famous discussion in "A Sketch of the Past" refers to the "sledge-hammer force of the blow" she receives from "exceptional moments" (*Moments* 72), and for her, too, the "sudden shocks" and "revelation of some order" are not tied to a transcendental substance. She associates them with the idea that "the whole world is a work of art":

> *Hamlet* or a Beethoven quartet is the truth about this vast mass that we call the world. But there is no Shakespeare, there is no Beethoven; certainly and emphatically there is no God; we are the words; we are the music; we are the thing itself. And I see this when I have a shock. (72)

At first glance this may appear to be an example of reoccupation, placing humankind in the position of God. But in fact Woolf is careful not to make such a substitution.[26] "We" are not the creator in her formulation; we are the text, the work of art with no artist. This is a rhetorical move that accomplishes what Hellenism could not: it shifts the locus of meaning from a transcendental substance to worldly immanence. Her moments of being

---

25. On elements of mysticism in Woolf's fiction, see Corner, Gough, Henke, Hussey, Kane, Minow-Pinkney, and Moore.

26. One fundamental element of Bataille's analysis of the sacred does not apply to Woolf. He sees in the modern privileged instant an opportunity for Nietzschean affirmation and, I would argue, a reoccupation of the position of God: "God represented the only obstacle to the human will, and freed from God this will surrenders, nude, to the passion of giving the world an intoxicating meaning. Whoever creates, whoever paints or writes, can no longer concede any limitations on painting or writing; *alone*, he suddenly has at his disposal all possible human convulsions, and he cannot flee from this heritage of divine power—which belongs to him" (245). This heritage of divine power is not inherent in the definition I have cited of the sacred privileged instant. I have been demonstrating that Woolf honed her skepticism while developing her notion of moments of being; by conceding the limitations to her power to give the world an intoxicating meaning, she refined and indulged her passion to do so.

define a deposit of experience detached from imperial as well as from transcendental structures of meaning. It is not merely a new form that she finds; equally important is that the experience she wishes to fit into the form falls within a narrower scope. She directs her attention, in the words of Bataille, not toward a "transcendent being" but toward an "impersonal reality."

Woolf uses her trope of life as a sphere or "vessel" to describe this encounter with an impersonal reality. Her diary entry for 10 September 1928 reads: "So afraid one is of loneliness: of seeing to the bottom of the vessel." When she sees to the bottom of the vessel, she gains "a consciousness of what I call 'reality,' " and she calls this her "gift" (3: 196). "A Sketch of the Past" introduces a more violent account of this process. She speaks of her "instinctive notion . . . that we are sealed vessels afloat on what it is convenient to call reality; and at some moments, the sealing matter cracks; in floods reality," leaving behind vivid impressions or "scenes" that "survive undamaged year after year" (*Moments* 122). Such encounters with reality are as pleasurable as they are traumatic. Woolf seems to turn the tenets of Kabbalah on their head by welcoming the breaking of vessels as much as their mending. Thus Mrs. Ramsay, gazing at the lighthouse in a moment of solitude, is "hypnotised, as if it were stroking with its silver fingers some sealed vessel in her brain whose bursting would flood her with delight" (65). Val Gough, locating Woolf in a tradition of literary mysticism, highlights Woolf's use of negation, irony, and apophasis ("That Razor Edge"). Employing a psychoanalytic approach to produce analogous insights, Charles Bernheimer foregrounds the masochistic element in Woolf's moments of being. "Her writing," he concludes, "is simultaneously a search for re-membered union and a means of perpetuating traumatic disunion" (206). In practicing such a conflicted art, Woolf no longer aims to understand the meaning of it all, no longer strives to make art totally redemptive. Instead, her moments of being show reality rupturing the vessel of the self, and thus they repeatedly demonstrate human limits.

Vision Liberated from Redemption?

In *To the Lighthouse*, Lily Briscoe employs many of Woolf's reconfigured metaphors, as we have seen. Inspired by drops of silver, compacted globes, the corridor of years, and matches struck in the dark, her painting distinguishes itself from Woolf's vision in *The Voyage Out*. But Lily also demonstrates, through her relationship with Carmichael, that even with such perceptual and rhetorical tools, such reconfigured metaphors, it is difficult to leave certain epistemological positions unoccupied and certain moral questions unanswered.

As Lily composes her picture, she struggles to represent a space on the drawing-room steps left empty by Mrs. Ramsay and thus to work through the "pain of the want." In the process, she uses Carmichael as an object of transference. Their relationship remains one-sided: Lily feels that he shares her thoughts but we never hear his thoughts and are told repeatedly that the two of them do not speak. The novel's brief final chapter, when they stand side-by-side surveying the sea, recalls the scene in *The Voyage Out* where Rachel and Terence are overwhelmed by the immensity of the ocean view. Although the view has "stretched her mind and body to the utmost," Lily is saved from the need to grasp the meaning of it all, in part by Carmichael. They stand on the edge of the lawn together sensing that the Ramsay family has arrived at the lighthouse. Lily perceives that Carmichael, "looking like an old pagan god, . . . stood there as if he were spreading his hands over all the weakness and suffering of mankind; she thought he was surveying, tolerantly and compassionately, their final destiny" (208). Enigmatic Mr. Carmichael is not a Christian redeemer, not a scapegoat. Nor is he exactly a father figure: immune to the charms of Mrs. Ramsay and the authority of Mr. Ramsay, he remains safely outside the family romance that leaves its mark on every other character in the novel. Without understanding a great deal about him, Lily nevertheless uses him to fill a place, to serve a function that is evident when he spreads his hands over (she believes) the totality of human weakness and suffering. As soon as she sees him in this pose—as soon as she transfers to him the obligation to redeem all—she has her moment of vision.

Mr. Carmichael thus plays a function analogous to Septimus' in *Mrs. Dalloway*: both are associated with the need to redeem all human suffering, and both become objects of displacement enabling heroines to have creative moments of vision. The presence of Mr. Carmichael indicates that Woolf does not, perhaps cannot, dispense entirely with the totalizing drive for redemptive solidarity.[27] But perhaps this drive begins to slacken in her work. Psychically she invested much less in Carmichael than in

---

27. Hence Miller's fanciful speculation that Carmichael is the novel's narrator. Enigmatic Carmichael has invited a variety of projections from critics as well as from Lily. Note in particular Moore's formulation: "Gone is the priesthood of the father. . . . In his place is Mr Carmichael" (90). And Minow-Pinkney emphasizes his blankness: "Apart from chanting the poem at dinner he never speaks; moreover, his consciousness is never rendered from the inside. I suggest that this is because he embodies an impossibility, representing both the endless deferral involved in the practice of art *and* the present, full possession of the phallus. Each one of these aspects cancels the other, yet the novel insists Carmichael has both. It therefore gives him an inflated external grandeur to compensate for its inability to flesh out his inner life. He is a blank or absence in the text" (115).

Septimus, and perhaps she is more invested in Lily than in Clarissa; in *To the Lighthouse* she identifies less with the redeemer, more with the female artist, and this development implies a growing distance from the need to make art totally redemptive. We know what role Lily projects onto Carmichael in far more detail than we know any of Carmichael's mental activity as a poet. In her moment of vision, with Carmichael standing near her, Lily sees the steps are empty and leaves Mrs. Ramsay's place unoccupied. "An odd-shaped triangular shadow" on the drawing-room step facilitates her moment of vision (201), and this phrase recalls Mrs. Ramsay's introspective reflection that she is most herself and yet not herself when she becomes "a wedge-shaped core of darkness" invisible to others (62–63). Without imaginatively resurrecting Mrs. Ramsay, Lily's painting apparently evokes this invisible core of darkness as a shadow. The core remains unilluminated, but the darkness has been circumscribed; it remains at the center of life, but does not engulf all of life. It infects Lily with neither Septimus' mad belatedness nor the mortal weariness of Conrad's survivors; rather, having served Mrs. Ramsay as a place of rest and a "platform of stability" for life (63), it now helps center and structure Lily's vision, successfully represented in her painting. She finds a way, paradoxically, to "express that emptiness there" (178) without filling it in.

Epilogue: Circling Home

[Odysseus's] return to his native place is a movement of the restoration of meaning, presented according to the pattern of the closing of a circle, which guarantees the tenor of the world and of life as order.

—HANS BLUMENBERG, *Work on Myth*

This promise of where they were going lay back of all their minds or feelings, common to all of them.

—HENRY GREEN, *Party Going*

Returning home from an odyssey is a way of closing a circle and securing meaning, but forcing the circle closed in a world deficient in meaning runs the risk of triviality, solipsism, or madness. The modernists, burdened with questions about the absolute for which they had no viable answers, wisely left the circle open. They did not seek an answer by returning to ancient Greece; rejecting Hellenism, they relegated to "yesterday the belief in the absolute value of Greek," as W. H. Auden says in "Spain." And they told stories of centrifugal colonial odysseys in which the absence of homecoming indicated the inadequacy of answers provided by imperial culture.

In contrasting the epic and the novel, Lukács describes ancient Greece as a culture that possessed only answers, no questions. The Greek, he argues, "drew the creative circle of forms this side of paradox, and everything which, in our time of paradox, is bound to lead to triviality, led him to perfection" (31). The meaningful sense of closure (*Vollendung* is Lukács's German word for "perfection") captured in the "creative circle" of Greek form is precisely what the modernists find elusive when they confront questions about transcendence that are inherited, according to

Blumenberg, from theology. Forster yearned for "spirit in a reasonable form" (*Passage to India* 314), but because this yearning was inseparable from the desire that "infinity have a form" (234), his colonial odyssey could only lament the elusiveness of both spirit and reasonable form. The open circles of modernist colonial odysseys represent this transcendental homelessness, this sense of defeat in the face of questions about the meaning of human experience in its totality. When these novelists represent in one fashion or another attempts to close the circle, to create a form that can serve as answer and home, they share Lukács's conviction that the result is not perfection but triviality (*Flachheit*, "insipidity"; literally "flatness").

Stevie's incessant drawing of circles in Conrad's *The Secret Agent* (1907) provides the purest, most extreme symbol I know of the flatness of modern attempts to close the creative circle of form in order to secure a literal and figurative home. (In *Mrs. Dalloway*, mad Septimus similarly draws meaningless "circles traced round shillings and sixpences" [147].) Conrad connects the story of the Verlocs to earlier odysseys, including his own, by comparing Adolf Verloc to Odysseus, his wife Winnie to Penelope (139), but here the action remains resolutely focused on the home rather than the journey, for both Verlocs die before realizing the aim of fleeing "far from England" at the end of the story (189). The novel is a study of the bourgeois home, the home of the Verlocs, "nestling in a shady street behind a shop where the sun never shone" (194), but the narrator reminds us repeatedly that the events unfold "at the very centre of the Empire on which the sun never sets" (162). So even though the setting and structure provide a stark contrast to Conrad's colonial odysseys, we find again in this work an imperial paradox: darkness resides at the heart of imperial enlightenment. Mr. Verloc perceives in his wife "the sacredness of domestic peace" (137) before she murders him; and she has entered into the marriage to provide a domestic refuge for her insipid brother Stevie, whom her husband drags into a fatal attempt to bomb Greenwich Observatory. Thus the novel demonstrates the futility of insularity, the failure of attempts to circumscribe a domestic refuge—and nothing symbolizes this theme better than Stevie's mad circles.

Stevie sits at the center of Verloc domestic life both literally and figuratively. He provides its *raison d'être* (unknowingly for Mr. Verloc), and he often seats himself at the kitchen table to trace the vacuity of home life and, by extension, of imperial life:

> He helped his sister with blind love and docility in her household duties. Mr. Verloc thought that some occupation would be good for him. His spare time he occupied by drawing circles with compass and pencil on a piece of paper. He applied himself to that pastime with great industry, with his elbows spread out and bowed low over the kitchen table. (14)

This passage, from the first chapter of the novel, ironically foreshadows the fatal "occupation" Mr. Verloc will find to take Stevie away from his domestic circles. Subsequent descriptions of Stevie's creations indicate that their triviality reaches beyond bourgeois domesticity and imperial politics to evoke humankind's troubled relation to the absolute: "Poor Stevie usually established himself of an evening with paper and pencil for the pastime of drawing those coruscations of innumerable circles suggesting chaos and eternity" (179). The novel, in other words, locates a transcendental homelessness in the Verloc household at the center of the empire. *A Passage to India* suggests that when people desire a reasonable form for infinity, "India fails to accommodate them" (234), but *The Secret Agent* shows that the deficient accommodations are in fact located in London.

In their trivial, chaotic evocation of eternity, Stevie and his circles serve as Conrad's boldest blast against the romantic ideal of the artist as a redeeming hero. Like Jim and Kurtz early in their careers, Stevie exhibits a "tenderness to all pain and all misery" (129) and "universal charity" (130), and like them, though with greater absurdity, his desire to act on such charity is frustrated. He has a "bizarre longing" to take an abused horse to bed with him, because experience has taught him that "to be taken into a bed of compassion was the supreme remedy, with only the one disadvantage of being difficult of application on a large scale" (129). His circles come to represent the inaccessible ideal of redemptive art, difficult of application on a large scale. Calling him "the artist," Conrad's narrator speaks of

> the innocent Stevie, seated very good and quiet at a deal table, drawing circles, circles, circles; innumerable circles, concentric, eccentric; a coruscating whirl of circles that by their tangled multitude of repeated curves, uniformity of form, and confusion of intersecting lines suggested a rendering of cosmic chaos, the symbolism of a mad art attempting the inconceivable. (40)

Like Jim, this mad ambitious artist is "difficult to dispose of" (13). The method of his disposal is accordingly radical. Although Conrad is generally scornful of his anarchists, he is genuinely sympathetic to anarchy to the extent that he wishes to destroy an unfulfillable totalizing intention that underlies his own art and, having failed to accomplish such a destruction, he seems prepared to resort to any method. Paradoxically, Conrad's art struggles against its own deepest impulses to imagine the whole; paradoxically, insipid Stevie is the deepest reflection in *The Secret Agent* of Conrad's own desire to circumscribe the inconceivable.

The Secret Agent epitomizes the age of paradox—epitomizes it so unflinchingly that Conrad no longer needs to project the discontents onto distant colonies. The modernist colonial odyssey proved itself, in fact, to be a relatively short-lived form; announcing its own failure from the beginning, it did not take long to implode. It emerged during the brief period in which consciousness of the extent and dangers of an empire that encircled the globe coincided with the tortured working through of a failed reoccupation—the failure of the modern subject to replace God as the subject of history. Remnants of the odyssey tradition served as vehicles to transfer this tortured working-through to foreign territory where Europeans could still entertain fleeting dreams of omnipotence and where the failure would at least appear distant. But with the decline of British imperial influence, the colonial scene lent itself less readily to such projection. And with growing acceptance of the failure of reoccupation, authors could locate modernity's transcendental homelessness closer to home, as in *The Secret Agent*, or could begin to move beyond the compulsion to become the subject of history, as in Woolf's mature work.

I have suggested that Woolf's use of "globe" as a metaphor for the self shifted over time, shedding its geographical and imperial associations so that the form would fit a more modest conception of the subject. As an image of the self, "globe" also hints at her desire to avoid what Lukács calls the triviality of forms in the age of paradox. By detaching the creative circle of form from its transcendental aspirations, she works to create a sphere of subjectivity no longer suffering from *Flachheit*. Perhaps a desire to leave behind the transcendentally "flat" forms of the modern age also lay behind her dream of finding a genre more appropriate for her experience than the novel, that epic of a godforsaken world. If we accept Lukács's description of the genre's defining features, the fact that the novel continues to thrive in the next century may be one indication that the habit of thinking in terms of totality is not as easy to dismiss as some champions of postmodern pluralism would like to think. However, the novel's health may also indicate that the form is more versatile and less tied to transcendental questions than Lukács supposed. But both of these speculations about the subsequent fate of the novel are too complex for detailed treatment here. Instead I shall conclude with another example of the imploded modernist colonial odyssey which, in terms of the logic of literary history, may be seen to open the way for the voyages of (post)colonial subjects *in* to the center of the (former) empire, voyages that reverse the pattern of the colonial odyssey.[1]

Party Going (1939) by Henry Green (the pseudonym of Henry Yorke)

---

1. I speak of the logic of literary history fully aware of the numerous anachronisms such a construction produces when, in fact, narratives of voyages to Europe taken by colonial subjects were often contemporaneous with imperialist narratives of voyages out. The narratives of voyages in have attracted attention from postcolonial criticism; see, for example, Said, *Culture and Imperialism*.

provides a less ghastly example than *The Secret Agent* of the imploded colonial odyssey. Green tells the story of a planned trip abroad with no departure—the English travellers never make it out of the London train terminal. Over a period of four hours a party of rich young Londoners gather to catch a channel train, accompanied by various servants, a suitor, and an aunt to see them off. A dense fog prevents the trains from running, though the subways continue to funnel commuters into the station at the rate of nine hundred and sixty-five each minute (according to the station master). To escape the throng, the partygoers, hosted by the wealthy and handsome Max Adey, retreat into the attached hotel, where they drink, care for the ill aunt, pursue their social and erotic intrigues, gaze out the windows onto the suffering crowd in the station below, and wait. One of many critiques of class difference in the novel comes in a description of a picture hanging in one of their hotel rooms, an image of "Nero fiddling while Rome burned, on a marble terrace. He stood to his violin and eight fat women reclined on mattresses in front while behind was what was evidently a great conflagration" (432). Irritatingly snobbish and foolish as they are, however, these characters never entirely lose Green's compassion. Conrad's Stevie, once again saying more than he knows, judges it a "bad world for poor people" (132); Green would not disagree, but he does not focus on the poor in *Party Going*, which shows instead that the world contains perils for the rich, too.

Party Going shares with *The Secret Agent* its confinement in a dark, damp, grimy London, but it also shares some characteristics with *Heart of Darkness*. Like the Congo Inner Station, the London train station is marked by dark, dense fog (a realistic detail) and dense vegetation (a metaphor describing the crowd). Green describes the approach to the terminal as if it were both a journey to Africa and a descent to the underworld of the dead (or in some cases an ironic reversal of such journeys). As Alexander rides to the rendezvous in a taxi,

> He likened what he saw to being dead and thought of himself as a ghost driving through streets of the living, this darkness or that veil between him and what he saw a difference between being alive and death. Streets he went through were wet as though that fog twenty foot up had deposited water, and reflections which lights slapped over the roadways suggested to him he might be a Zulu, in the Zulu's hell of ice, seated in his taxi in the part of Umslopogaas with his axe, skin beating over the hole in his temple, on his way to see She, or better still Leo. (401)

The humorous borrowing from Haggard is accompanied by repeated comparisons of the terminal to the land of the dead: it is "like an exaggerated grave yard" (402); "it would be like that when they were all dead and waiting at the gates" (414); "I wondered whether we weren't all dead really" (414); a row in the bar "might have been an argument with death" (452); and so on. However, despite specific similarities to Conrad's work, Green's fictional world creates a very different atmosphere, a difference not explainable entirely by reference to Green's contrasting, idiosyncratic prose style. In his work elements of romance and mystery survive less scathed, on a different footing. Although conditions in the terminal at their worst become "so weary, so desolate" (496), the novel draws back from this desolation. The Hades atmosphere does not deprive Green's world of a future, as it does Conrad's. Although Aunt May's illness and comical attachment to a dead pigeon seem likely to end in death through much of the story, she recovers in the end and the spoiled partygoers anticipate an imminent departure. As the trains begin to run, the oppressive masses break up into individuals as they are released through gates onto the departure platforms, like shades who have drunk of Lethe returning to the world.

The partygoers' intended destination is never a colony—they were hoping to find sunshine in the south of France—but Green introduces the imperial context into the novel through a series of exotic images, most notably the recurring image of dense patches of bamboo. Its first appearance transforms the crowded terminal into a colonial setting when Robert, searching for others in the party, passes a crowded bar and decides to stop for a drink. "Forcing his way through, meeting half resistance everywhere," he is reminded of a childhood fantasy: "When small he had found patches of bamboo in his parents' garden and it was his romance at that time to force through them; they grew so thick you could not see what temple might lie in ruins just beyond. It was so now" (406–7). Julia grew up with Robert "pretending they were explorers in jungles" and remembers the same bamboo patches, though their secret charm for her was not a ruined temple but the wooden pistol she buried in the middle of them, a charm she rescued and still carries with her. She also suggests that "probably they had been overgrown artichokes" (442). Finally, in a move characteristic of Green, the image of bamboo, which has been rooted in the private childhood fantasies of Robert and Julia, is transferred to a stranger who has only incidental contact with them. For him, like Robert, "to push through this crowd was like trying to get through bamboo or artichokes grown thick together" (483).

The image of dense bamboo remains a cliché in the novel, befitting childhood romance. And it is not always clear how well the romance suits the adults—Julia's wooden-gun charm does not seem to serve her well in her interaction with the philanderer Max, as she persists in hoping "she could take him back into her life from where it had started and show it to him for them to share," including its "artichokes" (528). But Green's exotic images, like his use of the Hades motif, are not motivated by a transcendental aspiration, as Conrad's were. They make no claim of or appeal to British imperial dominance, nor, conversely, do they associate the colonies with death. The pervasiveness of death in the terminal serves as a reminder, at times ominous, of a common fate, but it does not constitute a burdensome claim of the past on the living. No compulsion to perform rescue work lies behind either the colonial images or the odyssey allusions. While he condemns his characters' lack of charity, Green struggles less than Conrad with the pressure to encircle the world with universal charity. When he has Julia say that "one must not hear too many cries for help in this world" (438), he blasts the characters' upper-class insularity, and yet at the same time he marks his own distance from Conrad.

Through simile and repetition of detail, Green slowly builds his characters' subjective impressions into intersubjective experience. Individual and realistic phenomena slowly, mysteriously evolve into something emblematic; mundane descriptions of unremarkable characters gradually acquire ontological weight. The subject assumes a relatively modest form, foregoing the attempt to comprehend the totality of reality; at the same time, this subject remains porous, open to the alien, recognizing the alien within itself. With full, critical consciousness that the romance on which it draws is both a naïve childhood fantasy and a specifically English imperial dream, the novel turns away from desolation and despair. In the heart of London, from an underworld terminal that could mark either end or beginning of a metaphorical, metaphysical journey, it asks: What next?

Works Cited

Abel, Elizabeth. *Virginia Woolf and the Fictions of Psychoanalysis.* Chicago: U of Chicago P, 1989.

Abrams, M. H. *Natural Supernaturalism: Tradition and Revolution in Romantic Literature.* New York: Norton, 1971.

Achebe, Chinua. "An Image of Africa." *Joseph Conrad: Third World Perspectives.* Ed. Robert D. Hamner. Washington: Three Continents P, 1990. 119–29.

Adams, David. "Metaphors for Mankind: The Development of Hans Blumenberg's Anthropological Metaphorology." *Journal of the History of Ideas* 52 (1991): 152–66.

——. "Ökonomie der Rezeption: Die Vorwegnahme eines Nachlasses." Trans. Michael Bischoff. *Die Kunst des Überlebens: Nachdenken über Hans Blumenberg.* Ed. Franz Josef Wetz and Hermann Timm. Frankfurt: Suhrkamp, 1999. 369–86.

——. "Unbegrifflichkeit." *Historisches Wörterbuch der Philosophie.* Ed. Joachim Ritter, Karlfried Gründer, and Gottfried Gabriel. 13 vols. Basel: Schwabe, 1971–.

Ambrosini, Richard. *Conrad's Fiction as Critical Discourse.* Cambridge: Cambridge UP, 1991.

Anderson, Benedict. *Imagined Communities: Reflections on the Origin and Spread of Nationalism.* Rev. ed. London: Verso, 1991.

Anderson, Perry. "Components of the National Culture." *New Left Review* 50 (1968): 3–57.

Andreas, Osborn. *Joseph Conrad: A Study in Non-conformity.* [Hamden]: Archon, 1969.

Ansell-Pearson, Keith, Benita Parry, and Judith Squires, eds. *Cultural Readings of Imperialism: Edward Said and the Gravity of History.* New York: St. Martin's, 1997.

Anspaugh, Kelly. "Dante on His Head: *Heart of Darkness.*" *Conradiana* 27 (1995): 135–48.

Apter, T. E. *Virginia Woolf: A Study of Her Novels.* New York: New York UP, 1979.

Armstrong, Paul B. *The Challenge of Bewilderment: Understanding and Representation in James, Conrad, and Ford.* Ithaca: Cornell UP, 1987.

——. "Conrad's Contradictory Politics: The Ontology of Society in *Nostromo.*" *Twentieth Century Literature* 31 (1985): 1–21.

Arnold, Matthew. *Culture and Anarchy*. Ed. Samuel Lipman. New Haven: Yale UP, 1994.

——. "The Scholar Gypsy." *The Norton Anthology of English Literature*. Ed. M. H. Abrams, Stephen Greenblatt, et al. 7th ed. Vol. 2. New York: Norton, 1999. 1486–91.

Auden, W. H. *The Enchafèd Flood; or, The Romantic Iconography of the Sea*. New York: Random, 1950.

——. "Spain." *W. H. Auden: Selected Poems*. New ed. Ed. Edward Mendelson. New York: Vintage, 1979. 51–55.

Bakhtin, M. M. *The Dialogic Imagination: Four Essays*. Trans. Caryl Emerson and Michael Holquist. Ed. Michael Holquist. Austin: U of Texas P, 1981.

Baldick, Chris. *The Social Mission of English Criticism, 1848–1932*. Oxford English Monographs. Oxford: Oxford UP, 1983.

Bataille, Georges. *Visions of Excess*. Trans. Allan Stoekl. Theory and History of Literature 14. Minneapolis: U of Minnesota P, 1985.

Batchelor, John. *The Life of Joseph Conrad: A Critical Biography*. Oxford: Blackwell, 1994.

Beckett, Samuel. *Three Novels: Molloy, Malone Dies, The Unnamable*. New York: Grove, 1991.

Behrenberg, Peter and David Adams. "Bibliographie Hans Blumenberg." *Die Kunst des Überlebens: Nachdenken über Hans Blumenberg*. Ed. Franz Josef Wetz and Hermann Timm. Frankfurt: Suhrkamp, 1999. 426–70.

Beja, Morris. *Epiphany in the Modern Novel*. Seattle: U of Washington P, 1971.

——. "James Joyce and the Taxonomy of Modernism." *A Collideorscape of Joyce: Festschrift for Fritz Senn*. Ed. Ruth Frehner and Ursula Zeller. Dublin: Lilliput P, 1998. 353–67.

Bell, Michael. "The Metaphysics of Modernism." *The Cambridge Companion to Modernism*. Ed. Michael Levenson. Cambridge: Cambridge UP, 1999. 9–32.

Bell, Quentin. *Virginia Woolf: A Biography*. 2 vols. London: Hogarth, 1972.

Bendz, Ernst. *Joseph Conrad: An Appreciation*. Gothenburg: Gumpert, 1923.

Benjamin, Walter. *Illuminations*. Trans. Harry Zohn. Ed. Hannah Arendt. New York: Schocken, 1969.

Bergren, Ann L. T. "Odyssean Temporality: Many (Re)Turns." *Approaches to Homer*. Ed. Carl A. Rubino and Cynthia W. Shelmerdine. Austin: U of Texas P, 1983. 38–73.

Bernheimer, Charles. "A Shattered Globe: Narcissism and Masochism in Virginia Woolf's Life-Writing." *Psychoanalysis and. . . .* Ed. Richard Feldstein and Henry Sussman. New York: Routledge, 1990. 187–206.

Bersani, Leo. *The Culture of Redemption*. Cambridge: Harvard UP, 1990.

Billy, Ted. *A Wilderness of Words: Closure and Disclosure in Conrad's Short Fiction*. Lubbock: Texas Tech UP, 1997.

Bishop, Edward L. "The Subject in *Jacob's Room*." *MFS: Modern Fiction Studies* 38 (1992): 147–75.

——. "Toward the Far Side of Language: Virginia Woolf's *The Voyage Out*." *Twentieth Century Literature* 27 (1981): 343–61.

Bloch, Ernst. *Erbschaft dieser Zeit*. Frankfurt: Suhrkamp, 1962.

Bloom, Harold. *The Anxiety of Influence: A Theory of Poetry*. New York: Oxford UP, 1973.

Blumenberg, Hans. "An Anthropological Approach to the Contemporary Significance of Rhetoric." Trans. Robert M. Wallace. *After Philosophy: End or Transformation?* Ed. Kenneth Baynes, James Bohman, and Thomas McCarthy. Cambridge: MIT P, 1987. 429–58.

——. "The Concept of Reality and the Possibility of the Novel." *New Perspectives in German Literary Criticism: A Collection of Essays*. Ed. Richard E. Amacher and Victor Lange. Princeton: Princeton UP, 1979. 29–48.

——. "Eschatologische Ironie: Über die Romane Evelyn Waughs." *Hochland* 46 (1953–54): 241–51.

——. *The Genesis of the Copernican World*. Trans. Robert M. Wallace. Cambridge: MIT P, 1987.

——. *Höhlenausgänge*. Frankfurt: Suhrkamp, 1989.

——. *The Legitimacy of the Modern Age*. Trans. Robert M. Wallace. Cambridge: MIT P, 1983.

——. "Paradigmen zu einer Metaphorologie." *Archiv für Begriffsgeschichte* 6 (1960): 7–142.

——. "Pensiveness." Trans. David Adams. *Caliban* 6 (1989): 51–55.

——. *Schiffbruch mit Zuschauer: Paradigma einer Daseinsmetapher*. Frankfurt: Suhrkamp, 1979.

——. "Die Wirklichkeitsbegriff und Möglichkeit des Romans." *Nachahmung und Illusion*. Ed. Hans Robert Jauß. Poetik und Hermeneutik 1. Munich: Fink, 1964. 9–27.

——. *Work on Myth*. Trans. Robert M. Wallace. Cambridge: MIT P, 1985.

Boehmer, Elleke. *Colonial and Postcolonial Literature*. New York: Oxford UP, 1995.

Bongie, Chris. *Exotic Memories: Literature, Colonialism, and the Fin de Siècle*. Stanford: Stanford UP, 1991.

Bonney, William W. *Thorns & Arabesques: Contexts for Conrad's Fiction*. Baltimore: Johns Hopkins UP, 1980.

Boone, Joseph Allen. *Libidinal Currents: Sexuality and the Shaping of Modernism*. Chicago: U of Chicago P, 1998.

Boyle, Ted. *Symbol and Meaning in the Fiction of Joseph Conrad*. Studies in English Literature 6. London: Mouton, 1965.

Brantlinger, Patrick. *Rule of Darkness: British Literature and Imperialism, 1830–1914*. Ithaca: Cornell UP, 1988.

Brewster, Dorothy. *Virginia Woolf*. New York: New York UP, 1962.

Brod, Max. *Franz Kafka: A Biography*. Trans. G. Humphreys Roberts. New York: Schocken, 1947.

Brown, James N., and Patricia M. Sant. "Empire Looks East: Spectatorship and Subjectivity in 'Karain: A Memory.' " *Joseph Conrad: East European, Polish and Worldwide*. Ed. Wiesław Krajka. Conrad: Eastern and Western Perspectives 8. Lublin: Maria Curie-Skłodowska U, 1999. 237–56.

Browne, Sir Thomas. *The Works of Sir Thomas Browne*. Ed. Geoffrey Keynes. 4 vols. Chicago: U of Chicago P, 1964.

Bruss, Paul. *Conrad's Early Sea Fiction: The Novelist as Navigator*. Lewisburg: Bucknell UP, 1979.

Budgen, Frank. *James Joyce and the Making of Ulysses*. Bloomington: Indiana UP, 1960.

Burke, Edmund. *Reflections on the Revolution in France*. London: Everyman's, 1910.

Burroughs, Edgar Rice. *Tarzan of the Apes*. New York: Grosset, 1973.

Bush, Douglas. *Mythology and the Romantic Tradition in English Poetry*. Cambridge: Harvard UP, 1969.

Busza, Andrzej. "Conrad's Polish Literary Background and Some Illustrations of the Influence of Polish Literature on His Work." *Antemurale* 10 (1966): 109–255.

Calinescu, Matei. *Five Faces of Modernity: Modernism, Avant-garde, Decadence, Kitsch, Postmodernism*. Rev. ed. Durham: Duke UP, 1987.

Cannadine, David. "The Context, Performance and Meaning of Ritual: The British Monarchy and the 'Invention of Tradition', c. 1820–1977." *The Invention of Tradition.* Ed. Eric Hobsbawm and Terence Ranger. Cambridge: Cambridge UP, 1983. 101–64.

Cavafy, Constantine. "A Second Odyssey." *Before Time Could Change Them: The Complete Poems of Constantine P. Cavafy.* Trans. Theoharis Constantine Theoharis. New York: Harcourt, 2001. 219–20.

Chapman, Caroline, and Paul Raben, eds. *Debrett's Queen Victoria's Jubilees, 1887 & 1897.* London: Debrett's Peerage, 1977.

Chefdor, Monique, Ricardo Quinones, and Albert Wachtel, eds. *Modernism: Challenges and Perspectives.* Urbana: U of Illinois P, 1986.

Cheng, Vincent J. *Joyce, Race, and Empire.* Cambridge: Cambridge UP, 1995.

Cheyfitz, Eric. *The Poetics of Imperialism: Translation and Colonization From The Tempest to Tarzan.* New York: Oxford UP, 1991.

Cleary, Thomas R., and Terry G. Sherwood. "Women in Conrad's Ironical Epic: Virgil, Dante, and *Heart of Darkness*." *Conradiana* 16 (1984): 183–94.

Conrad, John. *Joseph Conrad: Times Remembered: 'Ojciec jest tutaj'.* Cambridge: Cambridge UP, 1981.

Conrad, Joseph. *Almayer's Folly: A Story of an Eastern River.* Ed. Floyd Eugene Eddleman and David Leon Higdon. The Cambridge Edition of the Works of Joseph Conrad. Cambridge: Cambridge UP, 1994.

——. *The Collected Letters of Joseph Conrad.* Ed. Frederick R. Karl and Laurence Davies. 5 vols. Cambridge: Cambridge UP, 1983–96.

——. "Geography and Some Explorers." *Heart of Darkness.* Ed. Robert Kimbrough. 3rd ed. New York: Norton, 1988. 143–47.

——. *Heart of Darkness.* Ed. Robert Kimbrough. 3rd ed. New York: Norton, 1988.

——. *Lord Jim: A Romance.* Garden City: Doubleday, 1924.

——. *The Mirror of the Sea and A Personal Record.* Ed. Zdzisław Najder. Oxford: Oxford UP, 1988.

——. *The Nigger of the "Narcissus": A Tale of the Forecastle.* Garden City: Doubleday, 1924.

——. *Nostromo: A Tale of the Seaboard.* Garden City: Doubleday, 1921

——. *Notes on Life and Letters.* Garden City: Doubleday, 1923.

——. *The Secret Agent: A Simple Tale.* Ed. Bruce Harkness, S. W. Reid, and Nancy Birk. Cambridge: Cambridge UP, 1990.

——. *Tales of Unrest.* Garden City: Doubleday, 1923.

——. *Under Western Eyes: A Novel.* Garden City: Doubleday, 1923.

——. *Youth and Two Other Stories.* Garden City: Doubleday, 1924.

Conroy, Mark. "Ghostwriting (in) 'Karain.'" *The Conradian* 18.2 (1994): 1–16.

——. *Modernism and Authority: Strategies of Legitimation in Flaubert and Conrad.* Baltimore: Johns Hopkins UP, 1985.

Corner, Martin. "Mysticism and Atheism in *To the Lighthouse*." *Studies in the Novel* 13 (1981): 408–423.

Crews, Frederick C. *E. M. Forster: The Perils of Humanism.* Princeton: Princeton UP, 1962.

Daly, J. P. "Adventures in the Concept of Totality." *Philosophy and Totality: Lectures Delivered under the Auspices of the Department of Scholastic Philosophy.* Ed. J. J. McEvoy. Belfast: Queen's U of Belfast, 1977. 49–62.

Daly, Nicholas. *Modernism, Romance and the Fin de Siècle: Popular Fiction and British Culture, 1880–1914.* Cambridge: Cambridge UP, 1999.

Dante Alighieri. *The Divine Comedy of Dante Alighieri: Inferno.* Trans. Allen Mandelbaum. New York: Bantam, 1980.

——. *The Divine Comedy of Dante Alighieri: Paradiso.* Trans. Allen Mandelbaum. New York: Bantam, 1984.

——. *The Divine Comedy of Dante Alighieri: Purgatorio.* Trans. Allen Mandelbaum. New York: Bantam, 1982.

Deane, Seamus. "Joyce and Nationalism." *James Joyce: New Perspectives.* Ed. Colin MacCabe. Bloomington: Indiana UP, 1982. 168–83.

——. *Strange Country: Modernity and Nationhood in Irish Writing Since 1790.* Oxford: Oxford UP, 1997.

DeKoven, Marianne. "Conrad's Unrest." *Journal of Modern Literature* 21 (1997–98): 241–49.

——. *Rich and Strange: Gender, History, Modernism.* Princeton: Princeton UP, 1991.

DeSalvo, Louise A. *Virginia Woolf's First Voyage: A Novel in the Making.* Totowa: Rowman, 1980.

DiBattista, Maria. *Virginia Woolf's Major Novels: The Fables of Anon.* New Haven: Yale UP, 1980.

Dick, Susan. "The Tunnelling Process: Some Aspects of Virginia Woolf's Use of Memory and the Past." *Virginia Woolf: New Critical Essays.* Ed. Patricia Clements and Isobel Grundy. London: Vision, 1983. 176–99.

Dickinson, G. Lowes. *The Greek View of Life.* Chautauqua: Chautauqua P, 1909.

Dodson, Sandra. "Conrad and the Politics of the Sublime." *The Conradian* 22.1–2 (1997): 6–38.

——. "Conrad's *Lord Jim* and the Inauguration of a Modern Sublime." *The Conradian* 18.2 (1994): 77–101.

Dowden, Wilfred S. *Joseph Conrad: The Imaged Style.* Nashville: Vanderbilt UP, 1970.

Drouart, Michele. " 'Gunrunning,' Theatre, and Cultural Attitude in Conrad's 'Karain.' " *SPAN: Journal of the South Pacific Association for Commonwealth Literature and Language Studies* 33 (1992): 134–49.

Dryden, Linda. *Joseph Conrad and the Imperial Romance.* New York: St. Martin's, 2000.

——. " 'Karain': Constructing the Romantic Subject." *L'Epoque Conradienne* 23 (1997): 29–49.

DuBois, W. E. B. *Dark Princess: A Romance.* Millwood: Kraus-Thomson, 1974.

Eagleton, Terry. *Criticism and Ideology: A Study in Marxist Literary Theory.* London: NLB, 1976.

——. *Exiles and Émigrés: Studies in Modern Literature.* London: Chatto, 1970.

Echeruo, Michael. "Conrad's Nigger." *Joseph Conrad: Third World Perspectives.* Ed. Robert D. Hamner. Washington: Three Continents P, 1990. 131–44.

Eliot, T. S. "*Ulysses*, Order and Myth." *James Joyce: The Critical Heritage.* Vol. 1. Ed. Robert H. Deming. New York: Barnes, 1970. 268–71.

——. *The Waste Land: A Facsimile and Transcript of the Original Drafts Including the Annotations of Ezra Pound.* Ed. Valerie Eliot. New York: Harcourt, 1971.

Erdinast-Vulcan, Daphna. *Joseph Conrad and the Modern Temper.* Oxford: Oxford UP, 1991.

——. *The Strange Short Fiction of Joseph Conrad: Writing, Culture, and Subjectivity.* Oxford: Oxford UP, 1999.

Evans, Robert O. "Conrad's Underworld." *Modern Fiction Studies* 2 (1956): 56–62.

Eysteinsson, Astradur. *The Concept of Modernism.* Ithaca: Cornell UP, 1990.

Faulks, Sebastian. "Cant and Recant: Interview: Salman Rushdie." *The Independent* 30 December 1990: 17.

Feder, Lillian. "Marlow's Descent into Hell." *Nineteenth Century Fiction* 9 (1955): 280–92.

Fleishman, Avrom. *Conrad's Politics: Community and Anarchy in the Fiction of Joseph Conrad*. Baltimore: Johns Hopkins UP, 1967.

——. *Virginia Woolf: A Critical Reading*. Baltimore: Johns Hopkins UP, 1975.

Forster, E. M. *Albergo Empedocle and Other Writings*. Ed. George H. Thomson. New York: Liveright, 1971.

——. *The Eternal Moment and Other Stories*. New York: Harcourt, 1928.

——. *Goldsworthy Lowes Dickinson*. London: Arnold, 1945.

——. *The Hill of Devi and Other Indian Writings*. Ed. Elizabeth Heine. The Abinger Edition of E. M. Forster 14. London: Arnold, 1983.

——. *Howards End*. New York: Vintage, 1921.

——. "Jehovah, Buddha, and the Greeks." *The Athenaeum* 4 June 1920: 730–31.

——. *A Passage to India*. San Diego: Harvest-Harcourt, 1984.

Fothergill, Anthony. "Memory and Experience Lost: Conrad's 'Karain: A Memory' and James's 'The Beast in the Jungle.' " *Conrad, James and Other Relations*. Ed. Keith Carabine, Owen Knowles, and Paul Armstrong. Conrad: Eastern and Western Perspectives 6. Lublin: Maria Curie-Skłodowska U, 1998. 113–21.

Foucault, Michel. *The Order of Things: An Archaeology of the Human Sciences*. New York: Vintage, 1973.

Fowler, Rowena. "Moments and Metamorphoses: Virginia Woolf's Greece." *Comparative Literature* 51 (1999): 217–42.

Fox, Alice. *Virginia Woolf and the Literature of the English Renaissance*. Oxford: Clarendon, 1990.

Fraser, Gail. *Interweaving Patterns in the Work of Joseph Conrad*. Ann Arbor: UMI, 1988.

Freud, Sigmund. *The Standard Edition of the Complete Psychological Works of Sigmund Freud*. 24 vols. London: Hogarth, 1953–74.

Froula, Christine. "Out of the Chrysalis: Female Initiation and Female Authority in Virginia Woolf's *The Voyage Out*." *Tulsa Studies in Women's Literature* 5 (1986): 63–90.

Frye, Northrop. *Anatomy of Criticism*. Princeton: Princeton UP, 1957.

Furbank, P. N. *E. M. Forster: A Life*. 2 vols. New York: Harcourt, 1978.

Geertz, Clifford. *Local Knowledge: Further Essays in Interpretive Anthropology*. New York: Basic, 1983.

Gekoski, R. A. *Conrad: The Moral World of the Novelist*. New York: Barnes, 1978.

George, Rosemary Marangoly. *The Politics of Home: Postcolonial Relocations and Twentieth-Century Fiction*. Cambridge: Cambridge UP, 1996.

Gifford, Don, with Robert J. Seidman. *Ulysses Annotated: Notes for James Joyce's Ulysses*. 2nd ed. Berkeley: U of California P, 1988.

Gillon, Adam. *Conrad and Shakespeare and Other Essays*. New York: Astra, 1976.

——. *Joseph Conrad*. Boston: Twayne, 1982.

Gissing, George. *The Collected Letters of George Gissing*. Ed. Paul F. Mattheisen, Arthur C. Young, and Pierre Coustillas. 9 vols. Athens: Ohio UP, 1990–96.

——. *In the Year of Jubilee: A Novel*. New York: Appleton, 1895.

GoGwilt, Christopher. "Alien Genealogies: Joseph Conrad, Pramoedya Ananta Toer, and Postcolonial American Perspectives." *CON-texts: Journal of the Joseph Conrad Society (Poland)* 2/3 (1999): 67–84.

——. *The Invention of the West: Joseph Conrad and the Double-Mapping of Europe and Empire*. Stanford: Stanford UP, 1995.

Gordan, John Dozier. *Joseph Conrad: The Making of a Novelist*. New York: Russell, 1963.

Gough, Val. "The Mystical Copula: Rewriting the Phallus in *To the Lighthouse.*" *Virginia Woolf: Emerging Perspectives.* Ed. Mark Hussey and Vara Neverow. Selected Papers from the Third Annual Conference on Virginia Woolf, Lincoln University, Jefferson City, MO, June 10–13, 1993. New York: Pace UP, 1994. 216–23.

———. "Teaching Woolf as Feminist Mystic." *Re: Reading, Re: Writing, Re: Teaching Virginia Woolf.* Ed. Eileen Barrett and Patricia Cramer. Selected Papers from the 4th Annual Conference on Virginia Woolf, Bard College, New York, June 9–12, 1994. New York: Pace UP, 1995. 294–98.

———. " 'That Razor Edge of Balance': Virginia Woolf and Mysticism." *Woolf Studies Annual* 5 (1999): 57–77.

———. " 'With Some Irony in Her Interrogation': Woolf's Ironic Mysticism." *Virginia Woolf and the Arts: Selected Papers from the Sixth Annual Conference on Virginia Woolf.* Ed. Diane F. Gillespie and Leslie K. Hankins. 6th Annual Conference, Clemson University, June 13–16, 1996. New York: Pace UP, 1997. 85–90.

Gourgouris, Stathis. *Dream Nation: Enlightenment, Colonization, and the Institution of Modern Greece.* Stanford: Stanford UP, 1996.

Graham, Kenneth. "Conrad and Modernism." *The Cambridge Companion to Joseph Conrad.* Ed. J. H. Stape. Cambridge: Cambridge UP, 1996. 203–22.

Graver, Lawrence. *Conrad's Short Fiction.* Berkeley: U of California P, 1969.

Green, Henry. *Loving; Living; Party Going.* New York: Penguin, 1978.

Guerard, Albert. *Conrad the Novelist.* Cambridge: Harvard UP, 1958.

Haggard, H. Rider. *The Annotated She: A Critical Edition of H. Rider Haggard's Victorian Romance.* Ed. Norman Etherington. Bloomington: Indiana UP, 1991.

Hall, Susan Grove. "Victorian and Edwardian Hellenism and E. M. Forster's Fiction: Idylls and Odes." Diss. U of Louisville, 1980.

Hampson, Robert. *Cross-Cultural Encounters in Joseph Conrad's Malay Fiction.* New York: Palgrave, 2000.

———. " 'Topographical Mysteries': Conrad and London." *Conrad's Cities: Essays for Hans van Marle.* Ed. Gene M. Moore. Amsterdam: Rodopi, 1992. 159–74.

Harper, Howard. *Between Language and Silence: The Novels of Virginia Woolf.* Baton Rouge: Louisiana State UP, 1982.

Harrison, Thomas J. *Essayism: Conrad, Musil, and Pirandello.* Baltimore: Johns Hopkins UP, 1992.

Hay, Eloise Knapp. "A Conrad Quintet." *Modern Philology: A Journal Devoted to Research in Medieval and Modern Literature* 79 (1981): 177–87.

———. "*Lord Jim*: From Sketch to Novel." *Lord Jim: An Authoritative Text, Backgrounds, Sources, Essays in Criticism.* By Joseph Conrad. Ed. Thomas Moser. New York: Norton, 1968. 418–37.

———. *The Political Novels of Joseph Conrad: A Critical Study.* Chicago: U of Chicago P, 1963.

Hayman, David. "Cyclops." *James Joyce's Ulysses: Critical Essays.* Ed. Clive Hart and David Hayman. Berkeley: U of California P, 1974. 243–75.

Heath, Jeffrey. "A Voluntary Surrender: Imperialism and Imagination in *A Passage to India.*" *University of Toronto Quarterly* 59 (1989/90): 287–309.

Heine, Elizabeth. "The Earlier Voyage Out: Virginia Woolf's First Novel." *Bulletin of Research in the Humanities* 82 (1979): 294–316.

Henke, Suzette. "De/Colonizing the Subject in Virginia Woolf's *The Voyage Out*: Rachel Vinrace as La Mysterique." *Virginia Woolf: Emerging Perspectives.* Ed. Mark Hussey, Vara Neverow and Jane Lilienfeld. Selected Papers from the Third Annual

Conference on Virginia Woolf, Lincoln University, Jefferson City, MO, June 10–13, 1993. New York: Pace UP, 1994. 103–8.

Herbert, Wray C. "Conrad's Psychic Landscape: The Mythic Element in 'Karain.'" *Conradiana: A Journal of Joseph Conrad* 8 (1976): 225–32.

Hervouet, Yves. *The French Face of Joseph Conrad*. Cambridge: Cambridge UP, 1990.

Hobbes, Thomas. *Leviathan*. Ed. J. C. A. Gaskin. Oxford: Oxford UP, 1996.

Hobsbawm, Eric. "Mass-Producing Traditions: Europe, 1870–1914." *The Invention of Tradition*. Ed. Eric Hobsbawm and Terence Ranger. Cambridge: Cambridge UP, 1983. 263–307.

Hobson, J. A. *Imperialism: A Study*. Ann Arbor: U of Michigan P, 1965.

Hoff, Molly. "The Pseudo-Homeric World of *Mrs. Dalloway*." *Twentieth Century Literature* 45 (1999): 186–209.

Holtsmark, Erling B. *Tarzan and Tradition: Classical Myth in Popular Literature*. Westport: Greenwood P, 1981.

Homer. *The Odyssey of Homer*. Trans. Allen Mandelbaum. Berkeley: U of California P, 1990.

Horkheimer, Max, and Theodor W. Adorno. *Dialectic of Enlightenment*. Trans. John Cumming. New York: Herder, 1972.

Howe, Irving. *Politics and the Novel*. New York: Horizon P, 1957.

Howkins, Alun. "Rider Haggard and Rural England: An Essay in Literature and History." *The Imagined Past: History and Nostalgia*. Ed. Christopher Shaw and Malcolm Chase. Manchester: Manchester UP, 1989. 81–94.

Humphries, Reynold. " 'Karain: A Memory': How to Spin a Yarn." *L'Epoque Conradienne* [n.v.] (1983): 9–21.

Hussey, Mark. *The Singing of the Real World: The Philosophy of Virginia Woolf's Fiction*. Columbus: Ohio State UP, 1986.

Iser, Wolfgang. *The Fictive and the Imaginary: Charting Literary Anthropology*. Baltimore: Johns Hopkins UP, 1993.

——. *The Implied Reader: Patterns of Communication in Prose Fiction from Bunyan to Beckett*. Baltimore: Johns Hopkins UP, 1974.

——. *Prospecting: From Reader Response to Literary Anthropology*. Baltimore: Johns Hopkins UP, 1989.

Jameson, Fredric. "Absent Totality." *Anybody*. Ed. Cynthia C. Davidson. Cambridge: MIT P, 1997. 122–31.

——. "Beyond the Cave: Demystifying the Ideology of Modernism." *The Syntax of History*. Theory and History of Literature 49. Minneapolis: U of Minnesota P, 1988. Vol. 2 of *The Ideologies of Theory: Essays 1971–1986*. 115–32.

——. "Modernism and Imperialism." *Nationalism, Colonialism, and Literature*. Minneapolis: U of Minnesota P, 1990. 43–66.

——. *The Political Unconscious: Narrative as a Socially Symbolic Act*. Ithaca: Cornell UP, 1981.

——. *Postmodernism, or, The Cultural Logic of Late Capitalism*. Durham: Duke UP, 1991.

——. "*Ulysses* in History." *James Joyce and Modern Literature*. Ed. W. J. McCormack and Alistair Stead. London: Routledge, 1982. 126–41.

Janta, Alexander. "A Conrad Family Heirloom at Harvard." *Joseph Conrad: Centennial Essays*. Ed. Ludwik Krzyżanowski. New York: Polish Institute of Arts and Sciences in America, 1960. 85–109.

Jay, Martin. *Marxism and Totality: The Adventures of a Concept from Lukács to Habermas*. Berkeley: U of California P, 1984.

Johnson, Bruce. *Conrad's Models of Mind*. Minneapolis: U of Minnesota P, 1971.

——. "Conrad's 'Karain' and *Lord Jim*." *Modern Language Quarterly* 24 (1963): 13–20.

Joyce, James. *Letters of James Joyce*. Ed. Stuart Gilbert and Richard Ellmann. 3 vols. London: Faber, 1957–66.

——. *Ulysses*. New York: Random, 1961.

——. *Ulysses: The Corrected Text*. Ed. Hans Walter Gabler with Wolfhard Steppe and Claus Melchior. New York: Random, 1986.

Judd, Denis. *Empire: The British Imperial Experience, from 1765 to the Present*. London: Harper, 1996.

Kafka, Franz. *Hochzeitsvorbereitungen auf dem Lande, und andere Prosa aus dem Nachlaß*. Ed. Max Brod. Frankfurt: Fischer, 1983.

Kane, Julie. "Varieties of Mystical Experience in the Writings of Virginia Woolf." *Twentieth Century Literature* 41 (1995): 328–49.

Kaplan, Carola M., and Anne B. Simpson, eds. *Seeing Double: Revisioning Edwardian and Modernist Literature*. New York: St. Martin's, 1996.

Katz, Wendy R. *Rider Haggard and the Fiction of Empire: A Critical Study of British Imperial Fiction*. Cambridge: Cambridge UP, 1987.

Kenner, Hugh. *The Pound Era*. Berkeley: U of California P, 1971.

Kershner, R. B. "The Culture of *Ulysses*." *Joycean Cultures/Culturing Joyces*. Ed. Vincent J. Cheng, Kimberly J. Devlin and Margot Norris. Newark: U of Delaware P, 1998. 149–62.

Kipling, Rudyard. "The White Man's Burden." *A Choice of Kipling's Verse*. Ed. T. S. Eliot. New York: Scribner's, 1943. 136–37.

Kirschner, Paul. "Conrad, Goethe and Stein: The Romantic Fate in *Lord Jim*." *Ariel: A Review of International English Literature* 10 (1979): 65–81.

Knowles, Sebastian D. G. "Narrative, Death, and Desire: The Three Senses of Humor in *Jacob's Room*." *Woolf Studies Annual* 5 (1999): 97–113.

Koutsoudaki, Mary. "The 'Greek' Jacob: Greece in Virginia Woolf's *Jacob's Room*." *Papers in Romance* 2, supplement 1 (1980): 67–75.

Krajka, Wiesław. "Betrayal, Self-Exile and Language Registers: The Case of 'Karain: A Memory.' " *L'Epoque Conradienne* 19 (1993): 47–69.

——. *Isolation and Ethos: A Study of Joseph Conrad*. Boulder: Eastern European Monographs, 1992.

——. "Making Magic as Cross-cultural Encounter: The Case of Conrad's 'Karain: A Memory.' " *Conrad, James and Other Relations*. Ed. Keith Carabine, Owen Knowles, and Paul Armstrong. Conrad: Eastern and Western Perspectives 6. Lublin: Maria Curie-Skłodowska U, 1998. 245–59.

La Bossière, Camille R. *Joseph Conrad and the Science of Unknowing*. Fredericton, NB: York P, 1979.

——. " 'A Marvellous Thing of Darkness and Glimmers': The Conradian Playhouse of the World." *Kwartalnik Neofilologiczny* 25.2 (1978): 167–77.

Lamberton, Robert. *Homer the Theologian: Neoplatonist Allegorical Reading and the Growth of the Epic Tradition*. Berkeley: U of California P, 1986.

Lang, Andrew. "The Odyssey." *The Oxford Book of English Verse*, 1900. No. 839. 12 July 2000 <http://www.bibliomania.com/Poetry/OxfordEnglishVerse/obev259.html>.

Lant, Jeffrey L. *Insubstantial Pageant: Ceremony and Confusion at Queen Victoria's Court*. New York: Taplinger, 1979.

——. "The Jubilee Coinage of 1887." *The British Numismatic Journal* 43 (1973): 132–41.

Lawrence, Karen. *The Odyssey of Style in Ulysses*. Princeton: Princeton UP, 1981.

——. *Penelope Voyages: Women and Travel in the British Literary Tradition*. Ithaca: Cornell UP, 1994.

Leaska, Mitchell Alexander. *The Novels of Virginia Woolf: From Beginning to End*. New York: John Jay P, 1977.

Lee, Hermione. *The Novels of Virginia Woolf*. London: Methuen, 1977.

Lee, Robert F. *Conrad's Colonialism*. The Hague: Mouton, 1969.

Lenin, V. I. "Imperialism and the Split in Socialism." Trans. M. S. Levin, Joe Fineberg, et al. *Collected Works*. Vol. 23. Ed. M. S. Levin. Moscow: Progress, 1964. 105–20.

——. "Imperialism: The Highest Stage of Capitalism." Trans. Yuri Sdobnikov. *Collected Works*. Vol. 22. Ed. George Hanna. Moscow: Progress, 1964. 185–304.

Leontis, Artemis. *Topographies of Hellenism: Mapping the Homeland*. Ithaca: Cornell UP, 1995.

Lester, John. *Conrad and Religion*. London: Macmillan, 1988.

Levenson, Michael H. *A Genealogy of Modernism: A Study of English Literary Doctrine 1908–1922*. Cambridge: Cambridge UP, 1984.

Levi, Primo. *Survival in Auschwitz: The Nazi Assault on Humanity*. Trans. Stuart Woolf. New York: Collier, 1961.

Lewis, Andrea. "The Visual Politics of Empire and Gender in Virginia Woolf's *The Voyage Out*." *Woolf Studies Annual* 1 (1995): 106–19.

Lewis, Wyndham. *Paleface: The Philosophy of the 'Melting-Pot.'* London: Chatto, 1929.

Lifton, Robert Jay. "The Concept of the Survivor." *Survivors, Victims, and Perpetrators: Essays on the Nazi Holocaust*. Ed. Joel E. Dimsdale. New York: Hemisphere, 1980. 113–26.

——. *Death in Life: Survivors of Hiroshima*. New York: Random, 1967.

Longenbach, James. *Modernist Poetics of History: Pound, Eliot, and the Sense of the Past*. Princeton: Princeton UP, 1987.

Lowell, Robert. "The Voyage." *Imitations*. New York: Farrar, 1961. 66–73.

Löwith, Karl. *Meaning in History*. Chicago: U of Chicago P, 1949.

Lukács, Georg. *History and Class Consciousness: Studies in Marxist Dialectics*. Trans. Rodney Livingstone. Cambridge: MIT P, 1971.

——. *The Theory of the Novel: A Historico-philosophical Essay on the Forms of Great Epic Literature*. Trans. Anna Bostock. Cambridge: MIT P, 1971.

Lyotard, Jean François. *The Postmodern Condition: A Report on Knowledge*. Trans. Geoff Bennington and Brian Massumi. Minneapolis: U of Minnesota P, 1984.

Mandelbaum, Allen. "Dante as Ancient and Modern." *The Divine Comedy of Dante Alighieri: Inferno*. Trans. Allen Mandelbaum. New York: Bantam, 1980. 331–40.

——. "Gates of Horn, Gates of Ivory." Reed College, Portland, Oregon. 3 May 1994.

——. Introduction. *The Divine Comedy of Dante Alighieri: Paradiso*. Trans. Allen Mandelbaum. New York: Bantam, 1984. viii–xxii.

Marder, Herbert. *Feminism and Art: A Study of Virginia Woolf*. Chicago: Chicago UP, 1968.

Marx, Karl. *Selected Writings*. Ed. David McLellan. Oxford: Oxford UP, 1977.

Mazzotta, Giuseppe. "Ulysses: Persuasion versus Prophecy." Trans. Allen Mandelbaum and Anthony Oldcorn. *Lectura Dantis: Inferno*. Ed. Allen Mandelbaum, Anthony Oldcorn, and Charles Ross. Berkeley: U of California P, 1998. 348–56.

McClintock, Anne. *Imperial Leather: Race, Gender and Sexuality in the Colonial Contest*. New York: Routledge, 1995.

McLauchlan, Juliet. "Conrad's 'Decivilized' Cities." *Conrad's Cities: Essays for Hans van Marle*. Ed. Gene M. Moore. Amsterdam: Rodopi, 1992. 57–84.

Meier, Heinrich. *The Lesson of Carl Schmitt: Four Chapters on the Distinction between Political Theology and Political Philosophy*. Trans. Marcus Brainard. Chicago: U of Chicago P, 1998.

Meisel, Perry. *The Myth of the Modern: A Study in British Literature and Criticism After 1850*. New Haven: Yale UP, 1987.

Menand, Louis. *Discovering Modernism: T. S. Eliot and His Context*. New York: Oxford UP, 1987.

Mepham, John. "Mourning and Modernism." *Virginia Woolf: New Critical Essays*. Ed. Patricia Clements and Isobel Grundy. London: Vision, 1983. 137–56.

Miller, J. Hillis. *Fiction and Repetition: Seven English Novels*. Cambridge: Harvard UP, 1982.

———. "Mr. Carmichael and Lily Briscoe: The Rhythm of Creativity in *To the Lighthouse*." *Modernism Reconsidered*. Ed. Robert Kiely and John Hildebidle. Harvard English Studies 11. Cambridge: Harvard UP, 1983. 167–89.

———. *Poets of Reality: Six Twentieth-Century Writers*. New York: Atheneum, 1969.

Minow-Pinkney, Makiko. " 'How Then Does Light Return to the World after the Eclipse of the Sun? Miraculously Frailly': A Psychoanalytic Interpretation of Woolf's Mysticism." *Virginia Woolf and the Arts: Selected Papers from the Sixth Annual Conference on Virginia Woolf*. 6th Annual Conference, Clemson University, June 13–16, 1996. New York: Pace UP, 1997. 90–98.

———. *Virginia Woolf & the Problem of the Subject: Feminine Writing in the Major Novels*. Brighton: Harvester, 1987.

Mongia, Padmini. "Ghosts of the Gothic: Spectral Women and Colonized Spaces in *Lord Jim*." *Conrad and Gender*. Ed. Andrew Michael Roberts. Amsterdam: Rodopi, 1993. 1–16.

Moore, Madeline. *The Short Season Between Two Silences: The Mystical and the Political in the Novels of Virginia Woolf*. Boston: Allen, 1984.

Mouffe, Chantal, ed. *The Challenge of Carl Schmitt*. London: Verso, 1999.

Mufti, Aamir R. "Auerbach in Istanbul: Edward Said, Secular Criticism, and the Question of Minority Culture." *Critical Inquiry* 25 (1998): 95–125.

Naipaul, V. S. "Conrad's Darkness." *Joseph Conrad: Third World Perspectives*. Ed. Robert D. Hamner. Washington: Three Continents P, 1990. 189–200.

Najder, Zdzisław. *Conrad in Perspective: Essays on Art and Fidelity*. Cambridge: Cambridge UP, 1997.

———. *Joseph Conrad: A Chronicle*. Trans. Halina Carroll-Najder. New Brunswick: Rutgers UP, 1983.

———. "Joseph Conrad: A European Writer." Wojewódzka Biblioteka Publiczna w Gdańsku International Joseph Conrad Conference, Gdańsk, Poland. September 1994.

Naremore, James. *The World without a Self: Virginia Woolf and The Novel*. New Haven: Yale UP, 1973.

Neuman, Shirley. "*Heart of Darkness*, Virginia Woolf and the Spectre of Domination." *Virginia Woolf: New Critical Essays*. Ed. Patricia Clements and Isobel Grundy. London: Vision, 1983. 57–76.

Nietzsche, Friedrich. *The Portable Nietzsche*. Ed. and Trans. Walter Kaufmann. New York: Penguin, 1976.

Nolan, Emer. *James Joyce and Nationalism*. London: Routledge, 1995.

North, Michael. *Reading 1922: A Return to the Scene of the Modern*. New York: Oxford UP, 1999.

Novalis [Friedrich von Hardenberg]. *Werke und Briefe*. Ed. Alfred Kelletat. Munich: Winkler, 1962.

Osteen, Mark. *The Economy of Ulysses: Making Both Ends Meet*. Syracuse: Syracuse UP, 1995.

Papazoglou, Dimitra. *"The Fever of Hellenism": The Influence of Ancient Greece on the Work of E. M. Forster*. Diss. U of Athens, 1994. Athens: Parousia, 1995.

Parry, Benita. *Conrad and Imperialism: Ideological Boundaries and Visionary Frontiers*. London: Macmillan, 1983.

Pecora, Vincent P. *Households of the Soul*. Baltimore: Johns Hopkins UP, 1997.

——. *Self and Form in Modern Narrative*. Baltimore: Johns Hopkins UP, 1989.

Perl, Jeffrey M. *The Tradition of Return: The Implicit History of Modern Literature*. Princeton: Princeton UP, 1984.

Perloff, Marjorie. "Modernist Studies." *Redrawing the Boundaries: The Transformation of English and American Literary Studies*. Ed. Stephen Greenblatt and Giles Gunn. New York: MLA, 1992. 154–78.

Phillips, Kathy J. *Virginia Woolf against Empire*. Knoxville: U of Tennessee P, 1994.

Pike, David L. *Passage through Hell: Modernist Descents, Medieval Underworlds*. Ithaca: Cornell UP, 1997.

Pitt, Rosemary. "The Exploration of Self in Conrad's *Heart of Darkness* and Woolf's *The Voyage Out*." *Conradiana: A Journal of Joseph Conrad* 10 (1978): 141–54.

Plato. *Republic*. Trans. G. M. A. Grube, rev. C. D. C. Reeve. Rev. ed. Indianapolis: Hackett, 1992.

Poresky, Louise A. *The Elusive Self: Psyche and Spirit in Virginia Woolf's Novels*. Newark: U of Delaware P, 1981.

Pound, Ezra. *The Cantos of Ezra Pound*. New York: New Directions, 1986.

——. *Literary Essays of Ezra Pound*. Ed. T. S. Eliot. New York: New Directions, 1968.

Pratt, Mary Louise. *Imperial Eyes: Travel Writing and Transculturation*. London: Routledge, 1992.

——. "Postcoloniality, Globality, and the Case of the Stolen Kidney." The Ohio State University, Columbus, Ohio. 3 April 2000.

Prier, Raymond Adolph. "Joyce's Linguistic Imitation of Homer: The 'Cyclops Episode' and the Radical Appearance of the Catalogue Style." *Neohelicon: Acta Comparationis Litterarum Universarum* 14.1 (1987): 39–66.

Rabaté, Jean-Michel. *The Ghosts of Modernity*. Gainesville: UP of Florida, 1996.

Rawlings, Gertrude Burford. *The Story of the British Coinage*. London: Newnes, [1898].

Reilly, Jim. *Shadowtime: History and Representation in Hardy, Conrad, and George Eliot*. London: Routledge, 1993.

Reiss, Timothy J. *The Discourse of Modernism*. Ithaca: Cornell UP, 1982.

Resink, G. J. "The Eastern Archipelago Under Joseph Conrad's Western Eyes." *Indonesia's History Between the Myths: Essays in Legal History and Historical Theory*. Selected Studies on Indonesia 7. The Hague: Van Hoeve, 1968. 305–23.

Richards, Thomas. "The Image of Victoria in the Year of Jubilee." *Victorian Studies* 31 (1987): 7–32.

Richter, Harvena. *Virginia Woolf: The Inward Voyage*. Princeton: Princeton UP, 1970.

Robbins, Bruce. "Modernism in History, Modernism in Power." *Modernism Reconsidered*. Ed. Robert Kiely and John Hildebidle. Harvard English Studies 11. Cambridge: Harvard UP, 1983. 229–45.

——. "Secularism, Elitism, Progress, and Other Transgressions: On Edward Said's 'Voyage In.'" *Social Text* 40 (1994): 25–37.

Roberts, Andrew Michael. *Conrad and Masculinity*. New York: St. Martin's, 2000.

Rosenbaum, S. P. *Edwardian Bloomsbury*. New York: St. Martin's, 1994. Vol. 2 of *The Early Literary History of the Bloomsbury Group*.

Roussel, Roy. *The Metaphysics of Darkness: A Study in the Unity and Development of Conrad's Fiction*. Baltimore: Johns Hopkins, 1971.

Rowlinson, Matthew. "The Ideological Moment of Tennyson's 'Ulysses.'" *Victorian Poetry* 30 (1992): 265–76.

Rushdie, Salman. "Is Nothing Sacred?" *Granta* 31 (1990): 97–111.

Said, Edward W. *Beginnings: Intention and Method*. Baltimore: Johns Hopkins UP, 1975.

——. *Culture and Imperialism*. New York: Vintage, 1994.

——. Introduction. "Philology and *Weltliteratur*." By Erich Auerbach. Trans. Maire and Edward Said. *The Centennial Review* 13 (1969): 1.

——. *Joseph Conrad and the Fiction of Autobiography*. Cambridge: Harvard UP, 1966.

——. *Orientalism*. Harmondsworth: Penguin, 1995.

——. "Travelling Theory Reconsidered." *Critical Reconstructions: The Relationship of Fiction and Life*. Ed. Robert M. Polhemus and Roger B. Henkle. Stanford: Stanford UP, 1994. 251–65.

——. *The World, the Text, and the Critic*. Cambridge: Harvard UP, 1983.

Saintsbury, George. "The Present State of the English Novel." *The Collected Essays and Papers of George Saintsbury: 1875–1920*. Vol. 3. London: Dent, 1923. 120–50.

Schlack, Beverly Ann. *Continuing Presences: Virginia Woolf's Use of Literary Allusion*. University Park: Pennsylvania State UP, 1979.

——. "The Novelist's Voyage from Manuscripts to Text: Revisions of Literary Allusions in *The Voyage Out*." *Bulletin of Research in the Humanities* 82 (1979): 317–27.

Schmitt, Carl. *Political Theology: Four Chapters on the Concept of Sovereignty*. Trans. George Schwab. Cambridge: MIT P, 1985.

——. *Politische Theologie II: Die Legende von der Erledigung jeder Politischen Theologie*. Berlin: Duncker, 1970.

Scholes, Robert. *In Search of James Joyce*. Urbana: U of Illinois P, 1992.

Schwarz, Daniel R. *Conrad:* Almayer's Folly *to* Under Western Eyes. Ithaca: Cornell UP, 1980.

Seaby, Peter. *The Story of English Coinage*. London: Seaby, 1952.

Seidel, Michael. *Exile and the Narrative Imagination*. New Haven: Yale UP, 1986.

Sharpe, Jenny. "The Unspeakable Limits of Rape: Colonial Violence and Counter-Insurgency." *Genders* 10 (1991): 25–46.

Sherry, Norman, ed. *Conrad: The Critical Heritage*. London: Routledge, 1973.

——. *Conrad's Eastern World*. London: Cambridge UP, 1966.

Sherry, Vincent. *James Joyce:* Ulysses. Cambridge: Cambridge UP, 1994.

Silver, Brenda R. "Periphrasis, Power, and Rape in *A Passage to India*." *Novel* 22 (1988): 86–105.

——. *Virginia Woolf's Reading Notebooks*. Princeton: Princeton UP, 1983.

Sinfield, Alan. *Alfred Tennyson*. Oxford: Blackwell, 1986.

Sprinker, Michael, ed. *Edward Said: A Critical Reader*. Oxford: Blackwell, 1992.

Stanford, W. B. *The Ulysses Theme: A Study in the Adaptability of a Traditional Hero*. 2nd ed. New York: Barnes, 1968.

Stark, Bruce R. "Kurtz's Intended: The Heart of *Heart of Darkness*." *Texas Studies in Literature and Language: A Journal of the Humanities* 16 (1974): 535–55.

Stein, William Bysshe. "The Eastern Matrix of Conrad's Art." *Conradiana: A Journal of Joseph Conrad* 1 (1968): 1–14.

Stevens, Carolyn. "The Objections of 'Queer Hardie,' 'Lily Bell' and the Suffragettes' Friend to Queen Victoria's Jubilee, 1897." *Victorian Periodicals Review* 21 (1988): 108–14.

Stevenson, Randall. *Modernist Fiction: An Introduction*. Lexington: UP of Kentucky, 1992.

Stewart, Garrett. *Death Sentences: Styles of Dying in British Fiction*. Cambridge: Harvard UP, 1984.

Stone, Wilfred. *The Cave and the Mountain: A Study of E. M. Forster*. Stanford: Stanford UP, 1966.

Strachey, Lytton. *Queen Victoria*. London: Chatto, 1921.

Sykes, Christopher. *Evelyn Waugh: A Biography*. Boston: Little, 1975.

Tagge, Anne. " 'A Glimpse of Paradise': Feminine Impulse and Ego in Conrad's Malay World." *Conradiana: A Journal of Joseph Conrad Studies* 29 (1997): 101–12.

Tanner, Tony. "Butterflies and Beetles—Conrad's Two Truths." *Lord Jim: An Authoritative Text, Backgrounds, Sources, Essays in Criticism*. Ed. Thomas Moser. New York: Norton, 1968. 447–62.

——. *Conrad: Lord Jim*. Studies in English Literature 12. London: Arnold, 1963.

Tarnawski, Wit M. *Conrad the Man, the Writer, the Pole: An Essay in Psychological Biography*. Trans. Rosamond Batchelor. London: Polish Cultural Foundation, 1984.

Tennyson, Alfred. *The Poems of Tennyson*. Ed. Christopher Ricks. London: Longmans, 1969.

Thorburn, David. *Conrad's Romanticism*. New Haven: Yale UP, 1974.

Tillyard, E. M. W. *The Epic Strain in the English Novel*. London: Chatto, 1958.

Torgovnick, Marianna. *Gone Primitive: Savage Intellects, Modern Lives*. Chicago: U of Chicago P, 1990.

Tratner, Michael. *Modernism and Mass Politics: Joyce, Woolf, Eliot, Yeats*. Stanford: Stanford UP, 1995.

Trilling, Lionel. *E. M. Forster*. 2nd ed. New York: New Directions, 1964.

Turner, Frank M. *The Greek Heritage in Victorian Britain*. New Haven: Yale UP, 1981.

Tvordi, Jessica. "*The Voyage Out*: Virginia Woolf's First Lesbian Novel." *Virginia Woolf: Themes and Variations*. Ed. Vara Neverow-Turk and Mark Hussey. New York: Pace UP, 1993. 226–37.

Twain, Mark. "Queen Victoria's Jubilee." *Europe and Elsewhere*. New York: Harper, 1923. Vol. 20 of *The Complete Works of Mark Twain*. 193–210.

Van Boheemen-Saaf, Christine. *Joyce, Derrida, Lacan, and the Trauma of History: Reading, Narrative, and Postcolonialism*. Cambridge: Cambridge UP, 1999.

Virgil. *The Aeneid of Virgil*. Trans. Allen Mandelbaum. New York: Bantam, 1972.

Visser, Nicholas. "Crowds and Politics in *Nostromo*." *Mosaic* 23.2 (1990): 1–15.

Wallace, Robert M. "Progress, Secularization and Modernity: The Löwith/Blumenberg Debate." *New German Critique* 22 (1981): 63–79.

——. Translator's Introduction. *The Legitimacy of the Modern Age*. By Hans Blumenberg. Cambridge: MIT P, 1983. xi–xxxi.

Warren, Robert Penn. "Introduction." *Nostromo*. By Joseph Conrad. New York: Modern Library, 1951. vii–xxxix.

Watt, Ian. *Conrad in the Nineteenth Century*. Berkeley: U of California P, 1979.

Watts, Cedric. "Conrad and the Myth of the Monstrous Town." *Conrad's Cities: Essays for Hans van Marle*. Ed. Gene M. Moore. Amsterdam: Rodopi, 1992. 17–30.

——, ed. *Heart of Darkness and Other Tales.* By Joseph Conrad. Oxford: Oxford UP, 1990.

——. Introduction. *Lord Jim.* By Joseph Conrad. Peterborough, ON: Broadview, 2001. 7–22.

Waugh, Evelyn. *Black Mischief.* New York: Farrar, 1932.

——. *A Handful of Dust.* Boston: Little, 1999.

——. *Scoop.* Boston: Little, 1999.

Weigand, Hermann J. *Joseph Conrad: Werk und Leben.* Düsseldorf: Bagel, 1979.

White, Andrea. *Joseph Conrad and the Adventure Tradition: Constructing and Deconstructing the Imperial Subject.* Cambridge: Cambridge UP, 1993.

Wicke, Jennifer, and Michael Sprinker. "Interview with Edward Said." *Edward Said: A Critical Reader.* Ed. Michael Sprinker. Oxford: Blackwell, 1992. 221–64.

Williams, Raymond. *The English Novel from Dickens to Lawrence.* New York: Oxford UP, 1970.

Wilson, Robert. *Conrad's Mythology.* Troy: Whitston, 1987.

Winner, Anthony. *Culture and Irony: Studies in Joseph Conrad's Major Novels.* Charlottesville: UP of Virginia, 1988.

Witemeyer, Hugh, ed. *The Future of Modernism.* Ann Arbor: U of Michigan P, 1997.

Wollaeger, Mark A. *Joseph Conrad and the Fictions of Skepticism.* Stanford: Stanford UP, 1990.

Woolf, Virginia. *The Common Reader: First Series.* Ed. Andrew McNeillie. San Diego: Harvest-Harcourt, 1984.

——. *The Complete Shorter Fiction of Virginia Woolf.* Ed. Susan Dick. 2nd ed. San Diego: Harvest-Harcourt, 1989.

——. "The Death of the Moth." *Collected Essays.* Vol. 1. New York: Harcourt, 1967. 359–61.

——. *The Diary of Virginia Woolf.* Ed. Anne Olivier Bell. 5 vols. San Diego: Harcourt, 1977–84.

——. *Jacob's Room.* San Diego: Harvest-Harcourt, 1978.

——. *The Letters of Virginia Woolf.* Ed. Nigel Nicolson and Joanne Trautmann. 6 vols. New York: Harcourt, 1975–80.

——. *Melymbrosia: An Early Version of* The Voyage Out. Ed. Louise A. DeSalvo. New York: New York Public Library, 1982.

——. *Moments of Being.* Ed. Jeanne Schulkind. 2nd ed. San Diego: Harvest-Harcourt, 1985.

——. "Mr. Conrad's Crisis." *Times Literary Supplement* 14 March 1918: 126.

——. *Mrs. Dalloway.* San Diego: Harvest-Harcourt, 1990.

——. *Orlando: A Biography.* San Diego: Harvest-Harcourt, 1956.

——. *A Passionate Apprentice: The Early Journals 1897–1909.* Ed. Mitchell A. Leaska. San Diego: Harcourt, 1990.

——. *A Room of One's Own.* San Diego: Harvest-Harcourt, 1989.

——. *Three Guineas.* San Diego: Harvest-Harcourt, 1966.

——. *To the Lighthouse.* San Diego: Harvest-Harcourt, 1989.

——. *To the Lighthouse: The Original Holograph Draft.* Ed. Susan Dick. Toronto: U of Toronto P, 1982.

——. *The Virginia Woolf Manuscripts: From the Henry W. and Albert A. Berg Collection at the New York Public Library.* Woodbridge: Research Publications International, 1993.

——. *The Voyage Out.* San Diego: Harvest-Harcourt, 1948.

——. *The Waves.* San Diego: Harvest-Harcourt, 1978.

Wordsworth, William. *The Thirteen-book Prelude*. Ed. Mark L. Reed. 2 vols. Ithaca: Cornell UP, 1991.

Wright, Christopher J. H. "Jubilee, Year of." *The Anchor Bible Dictionary*. Ed. David Noel Freedman, et al. Vol. 3. New York: Doubleday, 1992. 1025–30.

Wright, Walter F. *Romance and Tragedy in Joseph Conrad*. Lincoln: U of Nebraska P, 1949.

Yarrison, Betsy C. "The Symbolism of Literary Allusion in *Heart of Darkness*." *Conradiana* 7 (1975): 155–64.

Žižek, Slavoj. "Carl Schmitt in the Age of Post-Politics." *The Challenge of Carl Schmitt*. Ed. Chantal Mouffe. London: Verso, 1999. 18–37.

Zwerdling, Alex. *Virginia Woolf and the Real World*. Berkeley: U of California P, 1986.

Index

184–89; "The Elizabethan Lumber Room,"
202–3; *Jacob's Room*, 14, 15, 180, 182,
190–91, 213 n23; "The Mark on the Wall,"
201–2, 210; "Moments of Being," 183 n6,
204; *Mrs. Dalloway*, 177–79, 205, 210,
217–18, 220; "On Not Knowing Greek,"
184, 190–92; *Orlando*, 207; *A Room of One's
Own*, 179–80; "A Sketch of the Past,"
213–16; *Three Guineas*, 174; *To the Lighthouse*, 204–8, 210–11, 214, 216, 218; "An
Unwritten Novel," 210; *The Waves*, 203;
The Years, 183 n6. *See also The Voyage Out*
World War I, 82, 85, 192
World War II, 82

Yorke, Henry. *See* Green, Henry

Žižek, Slavoj, 169–70